The World's Thought Leaders

Kristy Guo

Disclaimer

Copyright Disclaimer © 2025 Cuilan Guo. All rights reserved. This book, including all intellectual property rights therein, is solely owned by Cuilan Guo. No part of this book may be reproduced, distributed, or transmitted in any form or by any means, including photocopying, recording, or other electronic or mechanical methods, without the prior written permission of the copyright owner, except in the case of brief quotations for review, commentary, or other non-commercial purposes as allowed by law. Unauthorized use is strictly prohibited.

Publisher Disclaimer This book is published by Signature Global Network PTY LTD. While the publisher facilitates the production, printing, and distribution of this book, all rights, ownership, and control over the content remain solely with Cuilan Guo. The publisher does not claim any ownership over the intellectual property contained within this book.

Accuracy Disclaimer While every effort has been made to ensure the accuracy and completeness of the information in this book, the authors and publisher make no representations or warranties, express or implied, about the accuracy, completeness, suitability, or availability of the content. Readers are advised to independently verify any information and consult with professionals where appropriate. The authors and publisher disclaim any responsibility for errors, omissions, or any losses, damages, or disruptions arising from reliance on this book.

Similarity Disclaimer This book is a non-fiction work and includes real-life experiences. However, names and details may have been altered to respect privacy and confidentiality, and any resemblance to persons, businesses, or incidents is coincidental unless otherwise noted with explicit consent.

Opinion Disclaimer The views, thoughts, and opinions expressed in this book belong solely to the authors and are not necessarily reflective of any affiliated organizations or entities. These opinions are based on personal experience and interpretation, and readers are encouraged to form their own views.

Explicit Content Disclaimer This book may contain explicit language, sensitive content, or themes of a mature nature. Reader discretion is advised. The content is intended for an adult audience.

Expertise Disclaimer While the authors have extensive expertise and experience in the fields discussed, this book is not intended to provide professional advice. It is meant for informational and educational purposes only. Readers should seek professional counsel for advice specific to their situation.

Ownership & Acknowledgment While the co-authors have contributed to the creation of this book through their life stories and insights, all rights, ownership, and control over this work remain solely with Cuilan Guo. Co-authors have no claim to ownership or control of the content or intellectual property, beyond what is acknowledged here.

Publisher: Signature Global Network PTY LTD
Authors: Kristy Guo, Peter Sundara, Cassie Gruber, Justus Kluver-Schlotfeldt, Victor Hermosa, Simon De Raadt, Douglas Gozmao, Leslie Swamy.
Cover Design: Kristy Guo & Signature Global Network Creative Team
ISBN: 978-1-7638198-3-2 (paperback)
ISBN: 978-1-7638198-4-9 (E-book)

Authors of The World's Thought Leaders

- **Kristy Guo** – Chinese-born Australian
- **Peter Sundara** – Singaporean, with Indian heritage
- **Cassie Gruber** – American, with Filipino heritage
- **Justus Kluver-Schlotfeldt** – German
- **Victor Hermosa** – Filipino
- **Simon de Raadt** – Dutch, with extensive experience living in China
- **Douglas Gozmao** – Indian-born, based in the UAE
- **Leslie Swamy** – Indian

All authors have got global connections and networking travelling experiences across the world.

"A voice of GLOBAL thought leaders! Mission impossible—completed!"

Content

Acknowledgements vi
Foreword vii

Chapter 1   The World's Thought Leadership 1
             Kristy Guo

Chapter 2   D.A.D 38
             Peter Sundara Swamickannu

Chapter 3   Little but Fierce 77
             Cassie Gruber

Chapter 4   Never be afraid of being confident 117
             Justus Klüver-Schlotfeldt

Chapter 5   A Learner for Life 138
             Victor Hermosa

Chapter 6   Life Lessons to become a
             Thought Leader 157
             Simon De Raadt

Chapter 7   The Journey to Entrepreneurship:
             Lessons, Challenges & Growth 195
             Douglas Gozmao

Chapter 8   Thought Leadership: A Journey of Discipline,
             Influence, and Transformation 209
             Leslie Swamy

Let's Connect 223

"If there are many types of explanations about what thought leadership is, and no explanation will be better than reflecting from the authentic stories from these real world thought leaders!"

Kristy Guo

Acknowledgements

Writing and getting all co-authors to write this book has been a journey of passion, perseverance, and purpose. It would not have been possible without the unwavering support of those who stood by me.

To my **wonderful husband, Luke**, your love and belief in me are the foundation of everything I do. Thank you for holding our family together, for managing the beautiful chaos of life with **Sze Sze and Selena**, and for giving me the space to create. Your patience, encouragement, and endless support mean the world to me.

To my **two incredible children**, Sze Sze and Selena—your laughter, hugs, and boundless energy have been my greatest source of strength. You remind me why I chase dreams and create with purpose.

To my **remarkable co-authors**, thank you for sharing this vision and bringing your voices to life in these pages. This book is a testament to our collective wisdom, passion, and belief in the power of thought leadership.

To my **dedicated SGN team**, your hard work and commitment fuel the mission behind everything we do. You are more than colleagues—you are the heartbeat of this journey, and I am grateful for each of you.

To my **C-Suite coaching clients**, your trust challenges me to evolve and reach new heights. I am honored to walk alongside you in your journeys of leadership, growth, and transformation.

To my **church community**, your prayers and unwavering faith have been my compass, keeping me grounded and reminding me of the greater purpose behind this work.

To my **friends, mentors, and supporters**—those who have lifted me up, encouraged me, and believed in me even when the path was uncertain—thank you. Your words, your kindness, and your presence have been a gift beyond measure.

This book is not just mine **or these co-authors**—it belongs to all of us who believe in the power of ideas, action, and impact.

With immense gratitude,
Kristy Guo

Foreword

Hey there, my friend!

Thank you for stepping into the world of **thought leadership**. You're not alone on this journey—I, too, am constantly exploring what it truly means to be a thought leader, just like so many others today.

I'm **Kristy**, my given name is Cuilan, and I live in the beautiful city of **Melbourne**, which has been named the **world's most liveable city** multiple times. Moving here was a dream come true for me!

I have two wonderful daughters, **Sze Sze** and **Selena**. Sze Sze, who is 10, became a **published author** last year—with **two books** under her belt already! She seems to be following in my footsteps, but truth be told, she inspires me even more than I inspire her. **Leadership knows no age limits, right?**

Selena, my youngest, 5 years-old little sweetie. She's a funny, loving, and incredibly witty little girl who absolutely adores her sister, believing she is the **best in the world**.

I met my husband, **Luke**, in China while he was living in **Hong Kong**. After getting married and welcoming our first daughter, Sze Sze, we made a bold decision—one that changed our lives forever. Because of a **dream of mine**, and out of **his love for me**, Luke **quit his job** so we could start fresh in Melbourne, Australia—the place we now proudly call **home**.

A Humble Beginning

My journey didn't start from privilege. I was born in a **small town**, and like many, I experienced **childhood trauma**. If you've never faced such challenges—**congratulations**! But if you are **struggling right now**, I feel your pain. If you have deep wounds that still need healing, **don't give up**. You're on your way!

Foreword

Life is ironic in many ways—it's often **easier to build from scratch** than to **repair what's been broken**. I've shared my story and journey in previous **books, podcasts, webinars, and speeches**, and if you'd like to explore more, here are some of the books I've co-authored or written:

- *Changemakers Volume 6*
- *The Joyful Leader in You*
- *The Joyful Balance Code*
- *The Logistics Legends*
- *The World Thought Leaders* *(the book you're holding right now!)*

Why This Book?

So, why am I sharing my thought leadership journey? **Not because I believe I am the best leader in the world**—but quite the opposite.

The **mistakes I've made** have shaped me into the **recognized Thought Leader** I am today. They've allowed me to lead people toward success, manage great teams, and achieve my dreams.

After publishing **The Logistics Legends** in October 2024, we received **amazing feedback and testimonials** from readers who found inspiration in it. That book was written for those looking for **motivation, empowerment, and the courage to chase their dreams**.

The World Thought Leaders takes a different approach. This book is about **leadership**, bringing together **leaders from different countries, cultures, and backgrounds**. What's truly fascinating? Despite their diverse journeys, they share **common leadership lessons**. I won't spoil it for you—I'll let you draw your own conclusions. But here's something interesting: **none of these leaders communicated with each other while writing their chapters**. And yet, their messages resonate in unexpected ways.

Obsessed with Leadership

Generations Y, Z, and Alpha are eager to **become leaders** the moment they step out of school. We see young CEOs, entrepreneurs,

and **self-made millionaires under 30** everywhere. The world is filled with **millions—perhaps even billions—of leaders.**
The problem? **Not all of them are equipped to lead.**
Whether it's **Baby Boomers, Millennials, or Gen Z**, everyone is chasing leadership. Even children display **a natural desire for power and control.** But **leadership isn't just about holding a title**—it requires **guidance, experience, and clarity.**

Unfortunately, many young people today fall into the trap of **idolizing the wrong role models,** losing their own **identity and confidence** in the process. Others try to **imitate successful figures** but end up **lost along the way.**

And if you're from an **older generation,** you might be nodding along, thinking, *Yes! They're wrong, and I'm right!* But let's be honest—**past generations weren't immune to mistakes either.** Baby Boomers and Millennials worked their way up the corporate ladder—starting as employees, climbing to **manager,** then **director,** and finally achieving a **leadership** position.

But here's the catch: **Leadership was never formally taught.** Most of them learned **through experience, books, seminars, and trial and error.** Some became **performance-driven** leaders, focusing only on **results,** while others became **people-driven, obsessed with excellence,** and committed to lifelong learning.

Where Does Your Leadership Begin?

I've worked with **global C-Suites, CEOs, and entrepreneurs** since I started my career. By the time I was 18, I had **CEO friends around the world.**

Some call it **luck**—coincidence, even—that the CEOs and directors I worked for always **recognized my potential.** I was fortunate to be involved in **billion-dollar business journeys,** and I was constantly surrounded by **successful entrepreneurs, millionaires, and billionaires.**

But it wasn't until **recent years** that I started to **value my own expertise,** stepping into the role of a **global CEO coach** and achieving remarkable success.

At the same time, I run my own business—**Signature Global Network**—a global community for **entrepreneurs and logistics companies**. We also provide **marketing, publishing, and business solutions**.

Why? Because our goal is simple: to **deliver value to global CEOs** and help their businesses thrive. **They are the leaders—we are their supportive force.**

Starting a business alone was manageable at first, but within **three months**, I began hiring a team. I quickly realized two key things:

1. *No business succeeds without a team.*
2. *A successful business requires a strong leader.*

Leadership isn't just about **making decisions**—it's about **guiding people through challenges, creating a vision, and building a powerful team**. A leader must be **a visionary**, one who can **inspire people toward their dreams**.

What Makes a Leader?

Some people hesitate to step into leadership because they **fear they're not good enough**. When we think of **Winston Churchill, Nelson Mandela, Julius Caesar, Mahatma Gandhi, Martin Luther King Jr., Abraham Lincoln, or Mother Teresa**, we feel **intimidated**.

But here's the truth: **No leader is perfect.**

Leadership is **not a destination—it's a journey**. The best leaders are not flawless, but they are:

- ✓ Willing to listen
- ✓ Committed to learning
- ✓ Always striving to grow

My leadership experience comes from **mentors, global entrepreneurs, personal mistakes, and decades of working with successful leaders**.

So, you might be wondering—**what does this mean for YOU?**

Why Mentorship Matters

The Power of Mentorship: A Lifelong Impact

There is overwhelming evidence proving that a lack of mentorship negatively impacts young people, contributing to challenges such as mental health issues and even higher suicide rates. Mentorship provides essential guidance, emotional support, and life skills that help young people navigate difficult times, preventing feelings of isolation and hopelessness.

Research and Findings:

- According to The Mentoring Effect Report, young people with mentors are more likely to engage in positive behaviours, set higher educational goals, and contribute meaningfully to their communities.
- The **American Psychological Association (2023 Trends Report)** highlights that youth mental health is in crisis, urging further research into how mentorship can be a solution.
- The **Youth Nominated Support Team Program**, designed to support suicidal youth, has shown that participants had lower suicide rates and overall mortality even 11 to 14 years later, proving the long-term protective effects of mentorship.

Personal Reflection: The Mentor Who Changed My Life

Everyone needs guidance at some point in life. Reflecting on my own journey, I lacked mentorship during my early years and had to navigate challenges alone. However, a single conversation with a mentor later in life changed my perspective entirely, opening doors I never knew existed.

That experience taught me that mentorship isn't just about advice—it's about transformation.

I have been blessed to have mentors who shaped my journey:

- **Miss Zhang**, my first English teacher, whose belief in me gave me hope during my hardest childhood moments.
- **Ms. Guang**, my university teacher, who entrusted me with responsibilities that built my confidence and leadership skills.
- **Anthony**, my first manager, who believed in me so much that I turned down a higher-paying job for his offer—a decision that changed my career forever.
- **The President, VP, and MD** I worked under for a decade, each of whom shaped different aspects of my leadership, discipline, resilience, and ability to connect with people. Vincent taught me his charisma and great leadership skills in dealing with overseas partners; Wicky taught me unbelievable discipline; Victor taught me perseverance and resilience.
- **Pastor Richard**, my first senior pastor in Melbourne, who influenced me and his sermons taught me that it's okay to be myself—humorous, confident, and humble.
- **CEOs/Entrepreneur friends I met along my journey –** This list will be too long to count.

Without these mentors, I cannot imagine how my life would have turned out. Their impact was not just guidance—it was empowerment, confidence, and unlocking my true potential.

The Hidden Crisis: Mentorship Gaps and Mental Health

Despite its benefits, mentorship remains inaccessible to many. The absence of a supportive role model leaves young people vulnerable to depression, anxiety, and self-doubt. This mentorship gap extends beyond youth and into professional spaces, where many aspiring entrepreneurs and leaders struggle due to a lack of guidance.

Imagine a 15-year-old battling self-doubt. Now, imagine that same teenager with a mentor—someone who believes in them, encourages their dreams, and provides direction. The difference is life-changing.

How Mentorship Transforms Lives

One of the most powerful mentorship stories I've ever heard is from **Jim Rohn's seminar recordings**, where he talks about his mentor, **John Earl Shoaff**.

- Jim Rohn was born into poverty.
- He became a millionaire by 30.
- He lost it all at 33.
- He rebuilt his wealth and later was worth over $500 million.
- Without Shoaff, his life would have been entirely different.
- Tony Robbins, one of Rohn's students, would not be who he is today without his mentorship.

Finding the right mentor transforms your life to an unpredictable level—it's a shift that can redefine your entire future.

Bridging the Gap: Becoming a Mentor and Finding One

So how do we ensure more people, young and old, have access to mentorship?

1. **Becoming a Mentor:** If you're reading this, you have wisdom and experience to share. Whether you're a leader, entrepreneur, or parent, your guidance can change lives. Mentorship isn't about being perfect—it's about being present. And remember, mentorship should never be driven by

money; genuine passion for helping others will always be more rewarding.
2. **Finding a Mentor:** Seeking mentorship isn't about asking for favors; it's about building relationships. Join professional networks, attend industry events, and approach potential mentors with authenticity and respect.
3. **Creating Mentorship Programs:** Businesses and organizations can play a crucial role by implementing mentorship initiatives that foster growth and development.

The Ripple Effect of Mentorship

Mentorship isn't just about individual success—it creates a ripple effect. One mentor can shape a life, and that person, in turn, will uplift others. Whether in business, education, or personal growth, mentorship has the power to transform lives and communities.

I challenge you today:

- Will you be a mentor?
- Will you seek mentorship?

The world needs more thought leaders, mentors, and role models. If you have a child, grandchild, or younger generation in your family, wouldn't you want them to learn life's hardest lessons through wisdom rather than struggle?

The Purpose Behind Mentorship

After countless conversations with global leaders, I've realized one profound truth: **every successful leader has an intense passion to mentor, inspire, and empower the next generation.** Not because they get paid for it, but because they've suffered before and don't want others to experience the same struggles.

This is not an accident. **We are meant to build each other up.**

At the core, mentorship is not about **you** or **me**—it's about **purpose**. When you find your purpose and move toward your dreams each day, you experience genuine fulfillment.

Why does mentorship matter? Just like love, it's something we can't fully explain, yet we instinctively know it's essential. We all want to make a difference in someone's life. We want to leave the world a better place.

The question is: **Will you take action?**

The World's Thought Leaders

In this book, you'll discover the incredible stories of **eight thought leaders** from around the world. Each of us comes from different **countries, cultures, backgrounds, and experiences**, yet we share one common trait—**the courage to lead and the boldness to share our journeys.**

What makes this book truly special is its **diversity of perspectives**. No matter where you are in your journey, you will find a story that resonates with you. The lessons within these pages are golden nuggets of wisdom, shaped by real-life experiences and leadership breakthroughs.

This book is more than just a collection of stories; it's another **"mission impossible" completed**—a testimony to **resilience, transformation, and impact.**

Meet the Thought Leaders
- **Peter (India → Global → Singapore)**

Born in Singapore, Peter's journey has taken him across the world before settling in **Singapore**. He has always been a thought leader—though he never imagined himself as an author. His voice is **powerful**, his story is **compelling**, and his insights are **unforgettable**. You will be amazed by his words. This is **his moment, and he is more than ready to share his story with the world.**

- **Cassie (USA + Multinational Background)**

Foreword

The **only female leader** who dared to take on this challenge, Cassie represents the **USA with a global mindset**. Her pursuit of **excellence and diligence** is inspiring, but what truly sets her apart is **her boldness in sharing her truth**. Her story is one that both **women and men** will find powerful—**a journey of courage, leadership, and breaking barriers.**

◆ **Justus (Germany + Global Networking Influencer)**
A true **global connector**, Justus has built a **strong presence in the logistics industry**. If he hadn't participated in this book, his **remarkable journey might have never been told**—and that would have been a huge loss. His story is a testament to the power of **daring to live the life you truly desire**. If you're ready to step outside your comfort zone, **this is the chapter you can't afford to miss.**

◆ **Victor (The Relentless Learner & Marathon Leader)**
Victor never imagined himself as a writer—perhaps because he **reads an unbelievable number of books** every day, week, and year! His passion for **learning, leadership, and marathons** reflects his **unwavering consistency**. His story isn't just about success; it's about **dedication, endurance, and the mindset of a true leader**. You will love the insights he shares.

◆ **Simon (China → Netherlands + Corporate Powerhouse)**
Simon's story is **nothing short of dramatic**. I won't spoil the surprise, but—you'll want to read it yourself! His journey from **China to the Netherlands**, along with his extensive experience in the **corporate world**, will resonate deeply. His unique perspective will challenge you to think differently, proving that **not everyone needs to follow the same path to success.**

◆ **Douglas (India + UAE, Leading a 100+ Team)**
Running a company of **over 100 people** is no small feat, and Douglas has earned the **respect of every single one of them**. Like many of us, he has faced **setbacks and challenges**, but what truly matters is **how he**

overcame them. His story provides **a roadmap for anyone navigating difficulties in leadership and business.** If you come from **India or the UAE,** you'll see parts of yourself in his journey.

* **Leslie (The Humble & Quiet Leader)**
Leslie is, without a doubt, one of the **humblest** people I have ever met. If there was **anyone least likely to write a book or share their story**, it was him. And yet, here he is—a miracle participant in this project. He doesn't use many words, but his **deep humility and empathy** speak volumes. His story may not be flashy, but it holds **profound lessons** that will stay with you long after you turn the last page.

Your Turn

I can't wait to hear your thoughts after reading these incredible stories. **Which one resonated with you the most?** What insights did you take away?

One thing is for sure: **these stories will change the way you see leadership, courage, and success.**

Enjoy the journey!

Chapter 1
The World's Thought Leadership

Kristy Guo

Background

Thank you once again for choosing to read this book.

If you've read my previous books, you already know who I am and where I come from. But for those who are new to my story, here's a brief introduction.

From a Small Town in China to a Global Journey

I was born in a small town in China and set off on my first big adventure at around 13, moving to a more developed city for further studies. I skipped high school, went straight into university preparation, and was soon navigating an entirely new world.

My childhood was filled with struggles—not just physically, in terms of my appearance – due to my chubby shape and health -constant struggled illness due to my weak immunise system, but also emotionally, due to the domestic violence my father inflicted on my mother. Many times, I wanted to give up or run away, but I never truly had the chance. Instead, I worked relentlessly to escape the life I was born into and create a future I could be proud of.

Despite the darkest moments, I never wanted to complain or accept my reality as unchangeable. Instead, I committed to breaking through my circumstances and making the world a better place.

A Career Move to Hong Kong – And a Wake-Up Call

In 2009, the company I worked for, headquartered in Hong Kong, sponsored my work visa. I thought this was my big break, the beginning of the life I had worked so hard for. But reality hit me fast.

Life in Hong Kong was far from what I envisioned. I was stuck in the 9-to-5 grind, only getting home around 7 PM every night, feeling like a robot enslaved to a job many would dream of. The city was fast-paced, expensive, and overwhelming. My personality—friendly, expressive, and unique—felt stifled. The only moments I felt like myself were when I travelled with overseas friends.

One of the most shocking experiences in Hong Kong was the response to simple greetings. Saying "Good morning, how are you?" often earned me strange looks, as if I were insane. People were always in a rush, too busy even to acknowledge each other. A professor from a prestigious university once described it as feeling like he was "walking through a graveyard—seriousness, silence, like death." It wasn't that people were unkind; they were simply trained to be efficient, effective, and emotionless. As my husband humorously put it, "No time to talk about it!"

One day, while pregnant with my first daughter, I received shocking news: I was already too late to register her for kindergarten. She wasn't even born yet! That was the final push I needed to make a change.

A New Life in Melbourne, Australia

In 2014, after exploring various options, I received an interview request from an employer in Melbourne. A man (The Director of an Australian Company) flew from Australia to Hong Kong just to meet me for my interview. Long story short, I secured a work sponsorship, and my dream of living in Melbourne came true. At the time, Melbourne was considered one of the safest and most liveable cities in the world. What a privilege! It might sound easy, but looking back, it took me huge time, energy and efforts to get this opportunity and to make my dream come true!

Moving to Melbourne was both thrilling and terrifying. After more than a decade of hard work, I had climbed to one of the highest positions in my company, advising top executives. But in Melbourne, I had to start from scratch. I found myself at the bottom of the corporate hierarchy, with layers of management above me. My voice, once influential, suddenly carried little weight.

This humbling experience reshaped me. It tested my confidence and forced me to rebuild, but it also strengthened me. The struggles I faced added resilience to my character and deepened my understanding of true leadership.

The Early Years: Where My Leadership Journey Began

Primary School & Family Struggles

In the early years of primary school, before my family turmoil began, I was a bright, adventurous child, eager to try new things. However, as domestic violence, my father's accident, and my struggles with weight took a toll on my self-esteem, I withdrew. My mother's constant comparisons to my peers only deepened my insecurities. By the time I finished primary school, my confidence was shattered.

Despite this, I knew one thing for certain: ***the only way to overcome fear is to face it.***

Two of My Biggest Fears Before:

1. **What Others Thought of Me** – Deep down, I always knew I wanted to lead, but my family's chaos and my declining academic performance made me question whether I was still capable. The fire inside me never died, but I was terrified of judgment.
2. **Avoid & Scared of My Weakness** – One **biggest mistake and challenge** was the fear I had for anything I don't believe I could do and then I would avoid to even try. **For example,** I

convinced myself that I was only good at Chinese and literature-related subjects. Math was my Achilles' heel—until one moment changed everything.

My First Leadership Breakthrough

It was my first math class in Year 7. As we sat waiting for our teacher, in walked a woman with short hair and a strikingly large light brown mole on her right cheek. I had never seen anything like it before. At first, I stared out of shock, then out of guilt, not wanting to seem rude. To distract myself, I focused on listening intently to her lesson.

Then came the moment that changed my life.

At the end of class, she asked for volunteers to be the math captain. My heart raced—I wanted to raise my hand but hesitated. Before I could decide, she looked straight at me and said, *"You. You've been listening the most carefully. You will be the math captain."*

Just like that, I got my first official leadership role. Until today, when I was talking about this story, I could still laugh. It is dramatic, isn't it?

This moment taught me a powerful lesson: leadership isn't just about being the loudest in the room—it's about being present, paying attention, and stepping up when the opportunity arises.

And this was just the beginning.

The World's Thought Leader: Leadership Shapes and Matures You

Why am I sharing this with you? Because leadership was a transformative force in my journey—it shaped me, challenged me, and ultimately changed my perspective on life.

Think about it: When you step into a leadership role, something inside you shifts. The moment I was nominated as a math captain, I felt an unexplainable surge of determination. I pushed myself harder, not because anyone told me to, but because I had a responsibility to uphold.

And that responsibility made me stronger, more capable, and more resilient than I had ever imagined.

At first, I wondered—was it just ego? Maybe I didn't want to look bad, so I worked tirelessly to prove myself. But looking back, the reason doesn't really matter. What *matters is what I learned:*

1. **Nothing is impossible when your will is strong enough.** *Failure can be the stepping stone to success if you refuse to give up.*
2. **Everything is temporary.** *No situation is permanent, and you always have the power to turn things around if you truly believe in it.*
3. **Leadership is one of the fastest ways to grow into a better version of yourself.**
4. **The more you go after something, the more likely you are to achieve it.** *And with each success, your confidence multiplies.*
5. **Listening is a superpower.** *The more you listen; the more opportunities will come your way.*

With this foundation, I embraced leadership fearlessly. From being the Captain of English, leading classroom singing sessions, to skipping three years of high school and thriving in university, I found myself in leadership roles everywhere—performing arts, community projects, creative initiatives, podcasting, and even becoming school captain.

It was through these experiences that a powerful instinct developed within me—I call it my **"mother version."** I started seeing my peers as people I needed to nurture, support, and uplift. I told myself:

"I need to take care of the people around me. I need to bring value to them. I need to help them solve their problems. I need to be the kind of leader who brings joy, like a mother who takes pride in seeing her children thrive."

Some of my most cherished leadership moments were about transforming lives:

> ➢ **Moon's Story:** A **girl who lost her mother to suicide**, leaving

her with **deep emotional scars**. In **less than a month**, through our **conversations** and **shared experiences**, she **rediscovered her inner child** and **found joy again**.

I still remember the time when **Moon** was as **silent and miserable as a bitter melon** (No disrespect intended—I hope this comparison helps you understand the situation better). She was **bitter**. She **never even smiled**.

After knowing her story, I could not sleep well and I was determined to do something to bring light to her life again.

I tried a few times to connect with her and break her wall, and it didn't succeed at the beginning. Until … after many **failed attempts** to **speak to her**, get her to **share things**, and make her **laugh**. One day, I finally found her **ticklish spot**—I said something really **funny**, and she **cracked**. She trusted me because she also saw what I had built with other classmates and my sense of **humour** and ability to **influence** and **empower**. Once the **connection** was built, she started to **trust me deeply**, and from then on, she began **sharing deeper thoughts** and what had happened to her **family** with me. She came to **chat with me every day**, and every time after chatting, she felt **light and joyful**!

I was filled with a **sense of superpower** when I saw that my **influence** and **leadership** could transform her into a **completely different person**. In **less than a month**, she started **chatting with more people**.

Six months later, one day, her **behaviour shocked me**! She told jokes and **laughed as loudly as I did**, and most of the days!

"Oh man, I think I have awakened her inner child! In fact, a wild one!"

My heart was filled with **joy, fulfillment, and satisfaction**.

After school, I still received Moon's messages to thank me for what I did. She got married and had beautiful kids.

A sad story and a tragedy from the last generation can still be possibly rewritten to the next generations when there's enough **empowerment** and efforts from a leader in life. I am retelling this story many times, because it is **powerful**!

> **Lydia's Story:**

Lydia was a **quiet, shy** girl who struggled to **connect** with others. By breaking through her **icy exterior**, making her **laugh**, and genuinely **understanding her story**, I watched her **blossom**—from an **introvert** to a **lively, talkative person** who no longer hid behind **silence**.

Lydia was someone who **didn't want to make any effort** to connect with others. With my **motherly nature** and role as a **captain and leader**, I felt **responsible** for **helping every child**. When I **noticed her personality**, she seemed to **hate the environment**, so I decided to **observe her daily**. I tried to **start conversations** with her and later I **became her trustful friend**.

As usual as the other cases, at first, it was **challenging**, but my **consistency** touched her **soul** after **one to two months**. The result? **Lydia's inner child awakened—as wild as Moon's**.

There were **countless others**. And with each **connection**, I built **trust, respect**, and a **reputation** that **opened doors** I never expected. One of my **classroom teachers** even **invited me to her home** to **teach her daughter**—years later, she still follows my journey, **sending me messages filled with pride and encouragement**.

Whenever I look back on these **stories**, my **strong belief** that I have the **superpower** to **awaken everyone's inner child, influence**, and **empower** grows stronger each time.

I became **addicted to encouragement and empowerment**.

But leadership didn't just help others—it saved me, too.

During one of the hardest times in my life, when I struggled with my self-image, when my family was going through constant turmoil, when financial struggles made even the basics difficult, **leadership was my anchor**.

I was directing shows, making people laugh, bringing joy to others—all while silently navigating my own challenges. Ironically, my biggest dream at the time was **to make everyone happy**. I even considered becoming a stand-up comedian! (I don't recommend this now—because, let's be honest, you can never make *everyone* happy. And trying to will only drain you.)

But back then, my intentions were pure and simple. I just wanted to spread joy. And while I later learned that universal happiness is impossible, I also discovered something even more valuable:

You are not meant to serve everyone. You are meant to serve the people who are aligned with you.

Not everyone will resonate with you, and that's okay. True leaders don't try to please the masses—they find their people, the ones who are waiting for them, and they give their all to serve them.

That, my friend, is one of the greatest lessons leadership will teach you.

Leadership: A Rewarding Journey

After graduating from university, my peers scattered across China, and some even went abroad. But in 2015, when I secured my sponsorship job in Australia, my lifelong dream became reality. Overwhelmed with excitement, I messaged a few classmates to share the news. To my surprise, within two days, nearly 30 former classmates—including some from neighbouring classes—gathered to bid me farewell.

At that moment, I realized something profound: leadership isn't just about titles or roles. It's about the impact we create the lives we touch, and the invisible bonds we build along the way. I call it the "Leadership Butterfly Effect."

Fast forward to 2024, ten years later. I returned to China for a business trip, keeping it low-key. I sent just one message to a classmate a few days before arriving. Yet, when I landed, 20 people showed up—fellow business owners, parents, individuals juggling immense responsibilities. Some even drove two to three hours just to see me.

I was speechless. Grateful beyond words. I asked myself: *What on earth did I do to deserve this?*

The same thing happened when I left my previous company, HLS, before embarking on my Australian journey. The Managing Director gathered the entire top management team and over 20 of my team members for a farewell karaoke night. I never expected it, but I recognized it for what it was—a silent yet powerful acknowledgment. It moved me deeply.

I still vividly remember my last conversation with the Managing Director. Before I stepped out of the car, he looked at me and said sincerely:

"Kristy, I have to say that I respect you as a leader. Today, watching you guide your team, seeing how effortlessly you brought them together—it was unity like I've never seen before. Well done."

I hadn't expected such words, but they filled me with an immense sense of fulfillment. I grinned, feeling a whirlwind of emotions—grateful for the recognition, heartbroken to leave an amazing team behind, yet excited for the new journey ahead.

Why am I sharing this with you? Because leadership is a rewarding journey. My early leadership experiences shaped me into the best version of myself.

None of this happened simply because I held a leadership position. Wearing a crown doesn't make you a king, just as holding a title doesn't make you a true leader. Leadership is about influence, impact, and the lasting connections we create.

Leadership Confessions: Knowing That We Are Humans

As an **optimist**, I must also acknowledge the **less glamorous sides of leadership**—the **struggles, realities, and truths** we often **overlook**. **Awareness** is the first step toward **transformation**. If we fail to **recognize these realities**, we'll never take action to **improve**.

These insights are **crucial** for **younger leaders**—they can either **learn from their own mistakes** or from the **experiences of others**. They are **equally vital** for **seasoned leaders**, serving as **reminders** to mentor and guide the **next generation effectively**.

The more we **understand** these **hidden truths**, the **fewer pitfalls** we encounter. **Knowledge is power**, and **self-awareness** is the **foundation** of **true leadership**.

I recently formulated what I call the **9×90% Laws**—a **reflection of human nature**, not based on **scientific research**, but on **real-life experiences** and **observations**:

1. **90%+ of people won't change unless the pain of staying the same outweighs the pain of change.** Tragedy or crisis often forces transformation.
2. **90%+ pretend to listen to advice but rarely act on it.**
3. **90%+ are more inclined to take advantage of others rather than genuinely help them succeed.**
4. **90% procrastinate, especially when making decisions.**
5. **90% look for excuses rather than solutions when facing challenges.** They resist taking full responsibility.
6. **100% of people break promises. 90% do so habitually without accountability, while 10% fail unintentionally but take ownership of their commitments.**
7. **100% of people operate on autopilot at times. 90% live most of their lives passively, lacking purpose or passion.** Only **10% wake up each day driven by dreams and goals.**
8. **100% of people have lied before. 90% lie out of fear—fear of judgment, failure, or consequences.** The remaining **10% lie occasionally, but with kind intentions.**
9. **90% are controlled by money and time rather than mastering them.** Like the proverbial **frog in boiling water**, they **adapt to circumstances rather than taking charge of their lives.**

Oh, and when I say **90%**, I'm being **generous**. I know **YOU** are always the **exception**, right? **Me too…** I always thought I was the **ONLY one** who was **different and wiser**. That's what I used to tell myself when I read about **human flaws**. After all, it's always good to have **self-defence** to make ourselves **feel better**. But the question is: **is it true?**

It is **NOT EASY** to admit that we are **not humble enough**, that we have **egos**, and that we **love to defend ourselves**. Because **ego** means **"I am."** And **"I am"** is a **powerful phrase**—in fact, according to **scientific research**, it is the most **powerful two-word phrase in the world**.

Confidence is **good**, but in **leadership**, to remain **confident ALL THE TIME**, we tend to be **blindfolded and half-deaf** when we need to be **firm and fearless** in making decisions **day and night**.

Our **identity matters**. Our **beliefs shape our destiny**. That's why one of the **best-selling books of all time** is called *Think and Grow Rich*—not *Talk and Grow Rich* or *Act and Grow Rich*.

However, our **thoughts** can be our **best friends** or our **worst enemies**. If we are not willing to **reflect on our journey**, to **admit the imperfect elements** or **mistakes** we have made along the way, our **growth** will be **slow**.

I don't know about you, but today, **I'm confessing.**

It's up to you whether **you want to or not**. But I do know this: **only when we admit our flaws can we open the door to breakthroughs and transformation.**

I could list countless **other truths**, but my point is this: **we are all human. We are imperfect.** But **self-awareness** is the **first step** to **real change.**

You might ask, **"Why should I change? I'm happy where I am."** *Well, here's what I believe:*

Change is a choice—when you choose it. But when you don't, eventually, you'll have no choice left.

My life has always been a journey of transformation, and one commitment I have always upheld is to **embrace change.** I believe that change is inevitable, and if we resist it, we will ultimately be left with no choices. **The only way to lead a life with choices is to embrace change.**

Change for the better. Change to become stronger. Change to grow wiser.

Now, here's my **brutally honest** question for you: **As a leader, how much are you truly willing to embrace change?**

Lead Like a Parent

What happens when conflict arises in your community or team?

The truth is, there's no single answer to what makes the perfect leader or the best leadership skill. Every situation, background, and challenge is different. That's why understanding your role and identity as a leader is essential.

Looking back, leadership often mirrors parenthood. A strong team's unity is much like sibling love—built on trust, care, and support.

My daughters have their disagreements, just like all siblings do. At times, it can be heartbreaking to witness. But the most rewarding moments are when they hug, care for, and love each other. In those moments, I am reminded of the power of unity.

In life and business, conflicts and challenges are inevitable. But the true strength of any team, family, or organization lies in how they come together after conflict. Just like my daughters, a strong team knows when to lean on each other, lift one another up, and move forward with care and respect.

True leadership is about fostering an environment where disagreements don't break bonds but strengthen them.

A leader is like a parent because every parent carries the responsibility of guiding their children to grow and thrive—even when those children give them the worst attitude in the world. You can't send them back to school for an overnight stay or return them to your tummy when you're frustrated!

As a parent myself, I fully understand the struggles. It's painful, but it's also rewarding—just like leadership. Sometimes your team will test your patience, but you still have to lead with wisdom, composure, and integrity—not just authority.

My friend, the **good old days** are gone!

Why? Because in the past, leaders were simply "the boss." Today, leadership and "being a boss" are two different things. I don't know exactly when the shift happened, but one thing is clear—people now have more rights, freedom, and expectations. You can't just **be the boss**; you have to **lead while taking care of your people.**

The same goes for raising children. In Australia, you can't discipline kids physically because, in a way, they are considered children of the government. But growing up in China, I witnessed a different reality—harsh discipline was common, sometimes extreme, like the punishments you see in ancient dynasty films.

Different cultures, different times, different results.

So, where do I stand?

I believe in **leading wisely.** Balanced leadership matters.

I don't support violent discipline, but I want you to understand that we are living in a **new era**—one where everything around us, from global events to cultural shifts, shapes people's perspectives on leadership and authority.

And this brings me back to my main point: **being a leader is just like being a parent.**

We have to take full responsibility for our teams—even when things don't go as planned. There's always a way to improve outcomes. Of course, finding the right team members is crucial, but if you already have a strong team, the challenge becomes **uniting them** and **placing them in the right roles.**

Because let's be honest—if you try to **write with your feet and run with your hands, things will get messy!**

(Don't laugh—I can sense your smile now! But seriously, this is an important topic.)

Great leadership isn't about controlling people—it's about guiding them. Just like parenting, it's a journey of patience, learning, and finding the balance between discipline and care.

Are you leading like a boss, or leading like a parent?

Leadership Success Story: Rewarding My Team

Throughout my leadership journey, I've dedicated time, energy, and meaningful rewards to my team. Recognizing their efforts isn't just a nice gesture—it's an essential part of building a strong, motivated, and committed team.

Here are some of the ways I show appreciation:

1. **Weekly Team Bonding** – We engage in team bonding activities, from games to sharing personal milestones and celebrating wins together.
2. **Birthday Celebrations** – Every team member gets a special birthday surprise, a paid day off, and a thoughtful gift from the company.
3. **Bi-Weekly & Monthly 1-on-1 Conversations** – I take the time to connect individually with each team member, understanding their visions, challenges, and personal goals, ensuring alignment with the company's growth.
4. **Regular Monthly Recognition** – While I uphold high standards and push for excellence, I also make sure to acknowledge and reward great work through monthly recognition awards.

There are many more ways to support and uplift a team, but I want to highlight a recent moment that truly stood out.

A Special Celebration After SLCC

The Thursday after our **SLCC event**, I took my team on a cruise to soak in the breathtaking views of **Xiamen**.

We booked **first-class seats** to enjoy the best experience, and it was an unforgettable day filled with laughter, joy, and deep appreciation.

Honestly, they **deserve the best.** I am beyond grateful for each and every one of them.

During the cruise, I took a moment to **recognize three outstanding team members**—those who have stood by my side, selflessly committed to our vision and mission.

The Power of Appreciation in Leadership

One of the greatest lessons in leadership is the power of appreciation.

When you **recognize your team's efforts** and show **genuine generosity**, you create a culture of **loyalty, passion, and excellence**.

Cherishing these moments makes all the hard work **worthwhile.**

How do you reward and appreciate your team? I'd love to hear your leadership success stories!

Leading with empathy

The Two Types of Leaders: The Good and the Bad

Leadership is a fascinating topic—one that my 10-year-old daughter, Sze Sze, and I often discuss. She's an avid reader, constantly absorbing new knowledge, and recently, she was selected as her school's **Community Captain**. Naturally, our dinner conversations frequently revolve around leadership.

One evening, as we sat at the dinner table, I shared a thought with her:

"One of the most important qualities of a true and good leader is empathy."

Without missing a beat, she nodded and said, **"You're right, Mum! There are also bad leaders, like Hitler. He was a leader, but a bad one."**

WOW. That moment hit me. **Powerful and true.**

The Two Types of Leaders in History

Throughout history, leadership has shaped nations, movements, and even entire civilizations. But not all leaders have led with integrity and compassion. Some have built empires through wisdom, while others have destroyed them through cruelty.

The Good Leader: Inspiring Through Empathy and Vision

A great leader leads with **purpose, integrity, and the ability to connect with people on a human level**. They don't rule with fear—they inspire with vision. They make tough decisions, but always with **empathy and the greater good in mind**.

Take **Mahatma Gandhi** as an example. He led India's independence movement through **nonviolence and perseverance**. He believed in unity and equality, and even in the face of oppression, he never abandoned his principles. His leadership didn't just change a nation—it changed the world.

Or consider **Nelson Mandela**. After spending **27 years in prison**, he didn't seek revenge. Instead, he chose **forgiveness and reconciliation**, uniting a divided South Africa. His leadership was rooted in **understanding and hope**, proving that true strength comes from lifting others, not tearing them down.

The Bad Leader: Ruling Through Fear and Oppression

On the other hand, history has also seen leaders who have taken the path of **tyranny, selfishness, and destruction**. These leaders had power, but they **abused it**, causing suffering rather than progress.

Adolf Hitler is one of the most infamous examples. He was a leader, but his rule was driven by **hatred, dictatorship, and cruelty**. He manipulated people with propaganda, ruled through fear, and led one of the darkest chapters in human history. Instead of uniting people, he divided them—leading to war, genocide, and devastation.

Similarly, **Joseph Stalin** ruled with an iron fist, eliminating anyone who opposed him. Millions suffered under his oppressive regime, proving that leadership without **morality and empathy** leads to disaster.

The Leadership Choice: Who Do We Want to Be?

That conversation with Sze Sze reminded me of an important truth:

Leadership is **not** just about being in charge. It's about **how you lead**.

A **good leader uplifts** people, making them better. A **bad leader destroys**, leaving behind pain and chaos.

As parents, business owners, and individuals shaping our communities, we all have a choice—**do we lead with empathy, vision, and courage? Or do we let power consume us?**

The world has seen both kinds of leaders. The question is, **which one will we choose to be?**

A Letter to the World's Most Special Thought Leader: YOU

Hey you,

We haven't met in person yet, or maybe we have, but not much chance to have a deeper conversation. I want to write you this letter, and **through this letter, I am sure you will get to know more about me and you.** I guarantee you the time you spend reading my letter is worth it. **I don't just say what I write to you; I live what I say.**

Maybe you didn't grow up in privilege. Maybe you didn't have **a financial safety net or a prestigious background.** But deep inside, **you always knew you were meant for something bigger, didn't you?**

Here's the truth—**are you ready to face it?**

I've spent years studying successful people, **investing significant** time, energy, and resources to learn from the best. **In less than three years, I built a company that expanded to 80 countries, all while wearing multiple hats—author, publisher, high-performance coach, and leader in various fields.**

I've met **thousands of CEOs, listened to their stories, and witnessed firsthand what it takes to thrive.** And yet, let me be clear—**I am not perfect. No one is.**

I have struggled. **I have felt disappointment, heartbreak, and setbacks.** There were times when **I poured my energy, resources, and trust into people, only to have them break their promises.**

What have I learned?

True leadership isn't about perfection; it's about humility, resilience, and continuous growth. Only when you **put aside your ego, open your mind, and embrace the wisdom of others** can you elevate yourself to new heights.

The Most Common Entrepreneurial Traps—Are You Stuck in One?

1. **Comfort Zone Syndrome:** You've built stability and now fear taking bigger risks.

    The truth? Playing safe limits your potential. The most successful entrepreneurs treat every day as a new beginning, embracing change with hunger and drive.

2. **Thinking You Don't Need a Mentor:**

    The best leaders have mentors—sometimes younger than themselves. A fresh perspective can keep you accountable and propel you forward.

3. **Believing Past Success Means You Can Do It Alone:**

    The greater your responsibility, the more crucial it is to surround yourself with people who complement your strengths. Success is never a solo journey.

4. **Staying in the Same Role for Too Long:**
Status should never replace hunger for learning. If a leader stops evolving, so does their team. Growth requires constant reinvention.

5. **Being Enslaved by Money or Fame:**
If fear of losing status or financial security keeps you trapped in a repetitive cycle, you're not truly free. The courage to pursue passion over profit leads to a more fulfilling life.

6. **Hoarding Money Instead of Investing:**
The wealthiest people understand that the best way to build more is to invest wisely. Systems, skills, and opportunities multiply when you put money into the right places.

7. **Indecisiveness Leading to Procrastination:**
The most successful people make decisions quickly and confidently. Delayed decisions stem from a lack of confidence. The faster you act, the more you train yourself to lead with clarity.

Knowledge, experience, and skills can turn nothing into something—when you take action. The right mentors and strategies can save you years of struggle and unlock immense growth.

Your wealth isn't just in money—it's in the value you create, the impact you leave, and the lives you change.

Dare to lead. Dare to grow. Dare to step into your full potential!

8. **Want Things Without Sacrificing**
In the past, if you wanted something, you had to give something in return. It was an exchange, and if not done properly, both parties would feel uncomfortable. That was the beauty of sacrifice.

Even in the Bible, people sacrificed lambs when asking for miracles. Today, people fast when they seek something big. Everything has a cost.

But in modern life, instant gratification has taken over. People want things quickly and effortlessly. Are you familiar with that moment when you want to buy something, but because of free samples, you hesitate, wanting to try before committing?

I experience this constantly in my business. Running a network, people see the value and want to try—but when it comes to joining and making a financial commitment, they hesitate or change their minds. The same happens in my coaching career. Clients are eager to work with me, but the moment I present the fee, almost 90% step back.

I get it—investing a large amount can be scary. But that's exactly why you need to do it!

I invested over AUD 10K in self-publishing and writing, and what I gained was worth far more. I invested over USD 10K for my first business coach, and within a week, I won my first client, who paid me double —followed by more clients!

Invest in yourself. Invest in your future. Instead of working harder in your job, work harder on yourself. Personal development is the key to growth in all areas—health, wealth, and happiness.

Why Haven't You Broken Through Financially?

1. **Not Willing to Invest or Spend**

You want to feel safe with your cash, so you play small. But a billionaire once told me: *Start from zero every day, and you'll grow faster.* Grant Cardone says, *Cash is trash; cash flow is king.* Money itself has no value unless it's used.

Think about those new clothes you bought for your kids. They sit in the wardrobe, your kids outgrow them, and fashion changes—making them worthless. The same happens when you hoard money without investing it.

2. **Not Willing to Sacrifice Time or Energy**

If you want to build a strong business, you **CANNOT** spend excessive time with family. Family is important, but priorities must shift in different seasons of life.

The key is **quality over quantity**. My kids used to complain about me not spending enough time with them. But the issue wasn't the length of time—it was my presence. If I was with them but still answering calls and messages, it hurt our relationship. The result? Screaming, rebellion, bad parenting moments.

Once I started **scheduling** time for them—intentionally playing, being fully present—their complaints stopped, and my days became more productive.

Sacrifice is necessary, but choose wisely. If you want your business to thrive, it needs more of your time. If you want to nurture your family, that requires time and energy too.

Key Lessons on Financial & Time Freedom

Be Content With "Enough"?

If "enough" means just covering basic needs, sure, you have it. But life isn't just about eating and sleeping. What separates us from animals? Beyond language, we thrive on connection and contribution.

In other words, what makes us different from pigs—besides our ability to speak—is the fact that we have purpose, meaning, and the ability to shape our own destiny.

Financial & Time Freedom Take Time

Financial freedom means having a system that continuously generates wealth. Time freedom means having the ability to do what you WANT, not just what you NEED.

Even my daughter's primary school teaches the difference between "WANT" and "NEED." So why do so many grown-ups still mix them up?

I believe we are born to be abundant. When God created Adam and Eve, He didn't hand them a budget spreadsheet or tell them to hustle for their daily bread—He gave them gold in the garden. And guess what? There wasn't even an economy back then! No trade, no business deals—just pure abundance.

But here's the thing—most of us weren't raised with that mindset.

Many of our parents grew up in times of war or financial instability, where survival was the priority, and scarcity was the norm. So, we inherited the belief that we were born poor.

Let's be real—**that's a total lie.**

It took me years to shake off that limiting belief, but here's what I know for sure:

👉 You always get what you believe.

👉 If you believe you were born to be free and abundant, you will be.

👉 If you believe it's impossible, it will be.

So why do so many people struggle to achieve it?

Because success takes time. But let me be clear—it doesn't take your whole life.

Think about it. More and more self-made millionaires are emerging these days. Why?

💡 They found great mentors.

🔥 They wanted it badly enough.

💪 They put in the work—no matter what.

It's exactly like getting six-pack abs.

You see someone with Greek-god-level muscles, and you have two choices:

1, **Convince yourself it's impossible and go back to eating chips on the couch.**
2, **Accept that it's achievable—but only if you put in the right effort.**

Real Stories of Rapid Transformations

A lot of people think getting in shape takes forever, but let me introduce you to some legends who proved otherwise:

🚀 Arnold Schwarzenegger went from a scrawny Austrian kid to a bodybuilding champion in just five years—because he trained like a maniac and believed it was possible.

🐊 Sylvester Stallone wasn't born looking like Rocky. Before filming the first Rocky movie, he trained like a beast for six months—boxing, lifting, running—to transform his body.

👍 Dwayne "The Rock" Johnson was once a struggling football player with just $7 in his pocket. Fast-forward a few years, and he was headlining WWE, building an empire, and sporting those famous muscles.

⧗ Chris Pratt went from the lovable, chubby Andy in Parks and Recreation to a ripped action star in less than a year—because he committed to the process.

These guys didn't spend their whole lives wishing for results. They put in the work, stayed consistent, and got there faster than most people think is possible.

And the same applies to financial freedom.

🌱 If you plant the right seeds today—through learning, strategy, and consistency—you can grow wealth and time freedom sooner than you think.

But here's the catch:

Just like getting six-pack abs, financial and time freedom won't happen overnight.

It's not about finding a shortcut—it's about finding the right process and sticking to it.

So… are you ready to train?

Let's go!

Two Lies I've Discovered

1. " Overnight success-> You can build a million-dollar business in 90 days."

Maybe. But at what cost? Family time? Health? A massive financial risk? Be aware of the sacrifices required.

Sure, you can do it. But why?

I get it—you can't wait to get there. I've been there too. The moment

I saw success within reach, I became obsessed. I joined a high-level mentorship program, and as soon as I realized I was this close, everything else faded into the background.

- ✘ *My creative work? Forgotten.*
- ✘ *My family time? Neglected.*
- ✘ *My health? Not a priority.*
- ✘ *My quality of life? What quality?*

I knew building success required sacrifices, and I was willing to make them. But at what point do sacrifices turn into self-sabotage?

I became so focused on my target that I started losing myself. My passion dimmed. My purpose blurred. Money became the priority again.

Until one day, I stopped and asked myself: Is this really the life I want?

That's when I changed my approach. Instead of chasing just the goal, I started designing a life I actually wanted—and then reverse-engineered the path to get there.

And guess what? I still built my million, but I did it on my own terms, at the right time, without losing what matters.

What I Learned:

- ✅ *Always ask yourself what you truly want.*
- ✅ *Understand why you want it.*
- ✅ *Be specific—clarity is power.*
- ✅ *Break big dreams into actionable steps.*
- ✅ *Set realistic timelines.*
- ✅ *Wherever your focus goes, success and money will follow.*
- ✅ *Never be enslaved by money and goals—be empowered by them to serve and lead.*
- 💡 Being a thought leader is about having a clear vision, practical plans, and rallying people who believe in your mission. Lead them to where you all want to go—without losing yourself in the process.

2. "It takes years to build something -> Don't you ever want to be successful unless you work LONG enough."
No, **it doesn't!**

- 🎯 *I built a company in* **one week**.
- 🌐 *I built a global network of 10 members in a month and up to* **80 countries** *in less than 3 years*
- 📱 *I launched an app in* **three** *months.*
- 📖 *I co-authored and published a book* **in 90 days**.
- 📖 *I* **authored 2 books**, **co-authored 3 books**, *and altogether published* **7 books** *in* **less than 3 years**.

The truth? You can achieve big goals fast—if you commit fully.

So stop saying, "It takes time" while sitting around waiting for magic to happen. Set a deadline. Honor it.

The question isn't whether you can hit a million—it's how long you're willing to take to get there.

So many people accept the idea that it's okay to take 10 or 20 years to become a millionaire.

Sorry, but I'm heading into my 40s, and I've realized something important:

- 💡 Becoming a millionaire in one year is not a dream. But making money shouldn't be the ultimate goal.

It's not about how much we make—it's about how fast we create wealth and how we use it. What impact do we want to make?

Because let's be honest—once you reach a point where you no longer stress about:

- ✓ The price of things.
- ✓ Where to live.
- ✓ What car to drive.
- ✓ What food or clothes to buy.

…you realize there's so much more to life.

And this is where thought leadership comes into play.

Being a thought leader means turning ideas into realities and dreams into tangible results—not over a lifetime, but within a reasonable timeframe.

I'm not saying you'll do it in three days. Not even five. But 100 days? 365 days? Absolutely possible.

With modern technology and tools, these aren't dreams anymore—they're opportunities.

Think about it:

🔍 If you take 50 years to save your first million, but someone else earns it in one month, one week, or even one day—who has more time freedom to actually enjoy life?

This took me years to understand.

🚀 In my business, our third-year revenue was 400% higher than the second.
💰 One month's revenue matched an entire previous year's income.

So what changed? Belief.

Most millionaires and billionaires didn't struggle because they weren't smart enough—they struggled because they didn't believe it was possible.

So my question to you is:
DO YOU THINK IT'S POSSIBLE?

😏 "Wait a minute, Kristy… why are you talking about money so much?"

Because for years, I avoided the money conversation. I felt ashamed of wanting more to achieve a better life. But the more we avoid it, the more we struggle with it. The moment we face it, we master it. The truth is the more you have, the more difference you can make to invest in others. Just like what I do with what I earn. Except for investment to people, what I earned was always giving back to the community.

Mastering your money mindset is essential. If we want to be thought leaders, we have a responsibility to:

- ✅ Keep the right mindset.
- ✅ Stay in the right environment.
- ✅ Use the right strategies.
- ✅ Guide others to do the same.

This is exactly what happened with my co-authoring books.

At first, none of my authors believed they could write and publish their chapters in 90 days. But we did it—again and again. Once, twice, and more…

My Advice?

My friend, you don't need decades to achieve your dreams.

💡 If you are:

- ✔ Focused enough.
- ✔ Faithful enough.
- ✔ Fearless enough.
- ✔ Consistent enough.
- ✔ Committed enough.
- 🚀 You will make it happen.

Believe in yourself—so your followers can be inspired and empowered by you!

"I'm Rich Enough—Why Bother?"

Even if you have money and time freedom, life isn't just about you. The more capable you are, the more demand you'll have—from your family, employees, church, and community.

Money alone won't fulfill you if you lack purpose. After our global conference in Xiamen, I was invited to run a masterclass for local logistics companies. I was exhausted and finally had time to breathe, yet I still said yes. Within 2 days, 80 people registered and more want to get in but too full due to the limited room.

Did I get paid? No. But the countless testimonials I received made it worthwhile.

The Game of Prioritization

This isn't easy, my friend. But here's what I do:

1. **Plan intentionally—include family in your agenda.**
2. **Prioritize quality time—be fully present.**
3. **Sacrifice wisely—know what's worth giving up.**
4. **Never regret—just move forward.**
5. **Be present & work for the future.**

Nothing comes for free. Everything has a cost. What are you willing to sacrifice for the life you truly want?

Disbelief

You get what you believe.

So many CEOs don't believe in themselves, in others, or in new ideas. And that's exactly why they fail to reach their biggest goals.

"Believe" is a simple word, but it carries magic.

Don't be skeptical—try it. Trust with your whole heart. When you find the right people and the right services, the return will be far greater than what you invest.

I may not be the most famous, but I am deeply honoured to have helped entrepreneurs win, grow, and succeed. As a leader, as a consultant trusted by world leaders, I know one thing for certain—anything is possible.

- § Seven figures? No problem.
- § Eight figures? No problem.
- § Nine figures? No problem.

💡 Leadership? No problem.
⚖️ A balanced life? No problem.

The real key?
Success in business should never come at the cost of your authenticity. You should be able to enjoy the journey—filled with joy, passion, and purpose—while continuously learning and sharpening your skills.

The Lessons That Held Me Back

For a long time, I played small.
I played small because I cared too much about what others thought.
I played small because when I tried to step up:

- The people who loved me wanted to "protect" me from failure.
- The people who didn't love me didn't want me to rise above them.
- I believed my potential was limited by my background, culture, gender, and age.
- I prioritized making others feel comfortable over stepping into my true power.

So I hid.
I made myself invisible.
I downplayed my strengths—even when, deep down, I knew I was capable of so much more.
And then... everything changed.
My Transformation
My life transformed the moment I chose to lead my own life—to take control and become the director of my own story.
The moment I fully embraced my authentic self.
The moment I began pursuing what truly mattered to me—my real dreams.

▶ I stopped listening to the doubts and the noise.
▶ I became fearless and unstoppable.

- ▶ I realized that my identity wasn't defined by others—it was defined by me.
- ▶ I understood that leading others starts with leading by example.
- ▶ I stopped fearing judgment.
- ▶ I stopped apologizing for being great.

And something incredible happened:

- ▶ I didn't just achieve greatness for myself—I empowered others to do the same.
- ▶ I've influenced thousands.
- ▶ I've helped countless individuals awaken their dreams.
- ▶ I've broken boundaries, constantly challenging myself.
- ▶ I've committed to lifelong learning.
- ▶ I've found true freedom—self-discipline and self-mastery.

Ego, Confidence, Arrogance?

How can a KING not look good? Have you ever considered this question in your mind? Have you ever felt you are like a king because you are the leader?

I want to bring Jesus's story into this picture for a moment. If you're familiar with the Bible, you'll understand. If not, I highly recommend reading it—after all, the **HOLY BIBLE** is the best-selling book in history.

Jesus is a KING, yet he washes his disciples' feet. Jesus is wise, the Son of God, yet he walks humbly among men.

His story teaches us 1, A true thought leader is the humblest one and the one who serves his people; 2, We no longer live in a world that worships people at the top. True leadership today is about influence and empowerment.

So, my challenge to you is this: Every time you make a decision, ask yourself:

- Am I doing this because I want to look good?
- Am I trying to be a boss who rules above all?
- Am I doing this because I think I'm better than everyone else?
- Am I respecting people in my life, or do I just want authority?
- Am I doing this because I want to help more people or just want fame and validation?
- Am I focused on creating real leaders, or just followers?
- Am I leading to make a difference, or for my own sense of importance?

Throughout my leadership journey, I was challenged many times. But I am grateful that I am no longer the **old** version of me. I have learned that **true thought leadership is never about me**—it's about making an impact and transforming lives.

The Danger of Ego in Leadership

Ego is one of the greatest enemies of leadership. It blinds us, isolates us, and stops us from growing. It makes us think we know it all, that we don't need help, and that we are above others. And that's the exact moment when opportunities slip through our fingers.

Have you ever met a leader who refuses to listen, who believes they have all the answers?

Perhaps you've worked for a boss who never admits mistakes, who surrounds themselves only with "yes-men." These types of leaders create environments where people are afraid to speak up, where innovation dies, and where teams fall apart.

The best leaders are those who put their egos aside. They know that real power isn't about control—it's about trust. They aren't afraid to ask for help, to admit when they are wrong, or to learn from others.

Think about the opportunities you may have missed because of ego. Maybe you rejected feedback that could have helped you improve. Maybe you didn't reach out to a mentor because you didn't want to appear weak.

Maybe you let pride stop you from collaborating with someone who could have accelerated your success.

True greatness comes when we silence our egos and open our hearts to growth.

Confidence vs. Arrogance

There is a fine line between confidence and arrogance. Confidence is knowing your worth. Arrogance is thinking you're worth more than everyone else.

Confidence is a magnet—it attracts people. Arrogance, on the other hand, pushes people away.

A confident leader lifts others up, celebrates their wins, and empowers them to grow. An arrogant leader belittles others, takes credit for everything, and needs to be the smartest person in the room.

Confidence says, "I can do this."

Arrogance says, "Only I can do this."

Confidence says, "I am good."

Arrogance says, "I am better than you."

Confidence says, "I am smart."

Arrogance says, "I am too smart and smarter than you."

This list can go on and on.

Which kind of leader do you want to be?

A Personal Story

Leadership Lessons Since Primary School

I have been leading for more than 20 years, but my leadership journey started much earlier than most. Even in primary school, I found myself stepping up, organizing, and influencing. I wasn't the loudest, I wasn't the biggest, but something about my presence made others look to me for direction. If calculating that, it's been more than 30 years leadership experience.

I remember one particular incident when I was about 10 years old. Our school had an event where students had to work together in teams. While most kids were arguing about who should be the leader, I was already thinking about the goal.

Instead of fighting for the spotlight, I asked, "What are each of you best at?"

At first, the group was confused. They were used to leadership being about power, not about contribution. But as we started assigning roles based on strengths, something magical happened. The quiet ones who were usually overlooked found their voices. The ones who weren't academically strong discovered they had talents in creativity or organization.

We worked as a team, and we won that competition—not because I was the best, but because I understood that leadership is about bringing out the best in others.

That experience shaped me. It taught me that leadership is not about proving yourself. It's about serving others. It's about guiding people to find their own strengths, to step into their own power.

Even at 10 years old, I learned that the greatest leaders don't lead with their egos. They lead with their heart, their power of strengthening the team.

I used this strategy along my leadership journey, and it worked well.

Can I assume bravely that you are reading this because you, too, want to be remembered as a **GREAT THOUGHT LEADER**? You want to experience the joy of seeing others succeed. You want to create more leaders, not just followers. Because one day, we will all leave this world—but the legacy we leave behind, the impact we make, **that's what truly matters**. Because that can bring you deep sense of achievement and happiness, right? If you haven't experienced this yet, I challenge you to start today to find someone in your life, to lift him/her up. Seeing him/her becoming the king and queen by expecting NOTHING in RETURN! Then share with me how you feel.

High-five, my friend!

My Mission

At **SGN – Signature Global Network**, the global network I founded, our mission is to **lift 1 million world leaders**—and these leaders, in turn, will create **another million leaders and beyond.**

I am still on a mission—to **empower, inspire, and uplift** more leaders so that together, we can make the world a better place.

Because the truth is—it was **never about me**. (*So important that I have to keep mentioning this!*)It's about **the people I serve.**

But here's a reality check: **If we don't strive to become the best versions of ourselves, we risk bringing bad influence into the lives of others.**

So, what do I choose to do?

Just like I shared in my very first book, The Joyful Leader in You, I firmly believe that ***YOU ARE YOUR OWN JOYFUL LEADER.***

You lead your life. You are the director and main character of your own movie.

Here's what I commit to every single day:

- ✓ Be the best version of myself.
- ✓ Lead my own life first—before leading others.
- ✓ Take full responsibility for every decision I make.
- ✓ Influence, impact, encourage, and empower others.

Now, I ask you: What will you do?

Think about it—without other characters, how boring would a movie be? Even in the classic film Cast Away (Yes! That's the name I almost forgot!), Tom Hanks gave an incredible solo performance, but even then, the story needed interactions with other characters—like Wilson the volleyball!

We are meant to live together as a community. No one succeeds in isolation.

It is impossible to live a fulfilled life without interacting, affecting, and growing alongside others.

The Key Takeaway

If you take just one lesson from this chapter, let it be this:

- Being a thought leader starts with being a wise leader.
- First, lead your own life in the right direction.
- Then, guide others toward success, freedom, and a life with no regrets.

A true thought leader knows where they are headed—and ensures their team thrives alongside them.

But here's the reality:

This cannot happen without personal development, self-investment, and an open, teachable mindset.

Someone once said:

"The best leader was once the best follower."

So, I ask you:
Are you willing?
Are you ready?
I look forward to hearing your story in our next book!
Now, it's time to enjoy the inspiring journeys of other World Thought Leaders in this book.

Would love to hear your thoughts after reading them!

The Circle of Leadership

Your **impact** will always be measured by **the leaders you create**. **Great leaders don't just succeed—they empower others to rise.**

Your mission, should you choose to accept it, is not just to **achieve personal success**—but to **lift others along the way**.

That is the mark of a true, unforgettable thought leader.

💡 **Let's rise together!**

✉ **Connect with me—I'd love to hear your story!**

Kristy Guo – The C-Suite Whisperer, Award-winning High-performance Coach, Global Speaker, and Best-Selling Author

Kristy Guo is a **global award-winning leader, publisher, and visionary strategist** who has transformed the way C-suite executives lead, connect, and thrive. Known as *The C-Suite Whisperer*, she has been recognized by **Forbes** as a multicultural networking expert and hailed by **The New York Times** as *"The Fearless Force Behind World-Class Success & Global Leaders."*

As the **founder of Signature Global Network PTY, Signature Growth Academy, and The Joyful Leader in You brand,** Kristy has built a powerhouse of leadership transformation, helping executives scale their businesses while maintaining a life of balance and fulfillment. Her expertise in global logistics, leadership development, and high-performance coaching has made her a sought-after speaker on international stages.

A **best-selling author and publisher**, Kristy has penned multiple books, including *The Joyful Leader in You* and *The Joyful Balance Code*, both of which have received global acclaim for their impact on leadership and personal development. She has also pioneered groundbreaking co-authored programs that bring together some of the world's most influential thought leaders.

Kristy's career spans more than two decades of empowering C-suite leaders, facilitating **billions of dollars in international business partnerships**, and building a thriving global community of high-achieving executives. She is a firm believer in **transformational leadership**—guiding leaders to amplify their **income, influence, and impact** without compromising their well-being.

Beyond the boardroom, Kristy is a dedicated philanthropist, a passionate advocate for **breaking biases of age, gender, and culture**, and a mentor to world-class leaders. She is also a devoted wife to her husband Luke and a loving mother to her daughters, Sze Sze and Selena. Deeply connected to her faith and values, she actively contributes to her church and various charitable causes, living by her motto: *"In lifting others, we rise."*

Join Kristy in the mission to redefine leadership and connect with her at:
✉ **cuilanguo@outlook.com**
🔗 **linkedin.com/in/cuilan-kristy-guo-1776b5182**

Chapter 2
D.A.D

Peter Sundara Swamickannu

Everyone needs a role model. It could be an inspiring political leader, a close friend, immediate manager, a successful entrepreneur or even an intellectually stimulating educator. My role model and mentor has always been my late dad. His qualities greatly inspire me. Relocating from India to Singapore, helping his 2 brothers to settle in Singapore and Johore and raising a family of five as a sole bread winner, he epitomises energy, determination, focus, empathy and discipline.

Not only he provided the basic needs for his immediate family but also helped his brothers in Singapore/Johore and his sister and other brothers in India. He created a bright future for my mum, who he relocated her to Singapore after marrying her in India. When me and siblings were born in Singapore, he created a solid foundation for us by allocating his limited resources into education. His life philosophy is Education will open up windows of opportunity. This is one tenant in life that has a deep impression in me as it has been helped me to succeed in my personal and working life.

How can one man, uprooting himself from his village in South India in the early 60s, settling in Singapore, working in various jobs and finally securing a civil servant post in Ministry of Environment, able to single handedly raise a family of five children; and at the same time, established a cleaning company under his brother and wife's names and with a community spirit, initiated the founding of a Tamil community association to rally and help fellow Indian families in his neighbourhood ?

There is so much I picked from his sheer goal to establish a solid future for his family, relatives, friends and community. Turn back time, you will also be able to identify someone in your life who has made this deep impression and laid the foundation for cultivating that leadership skills you possess now.

Early childhood experiences have a profound impact on us and leadership skills, in my views, are both innate and instilled through experiences and influences from people from all walks of life. My solid pillar in laying the initial tenets of leadership qualities was my dad.

My perspective of leadership can be abbreviated in 1 word – **D. A. D – Discipline, Adaptability and Determination**. This chapter is my dedication to the man who laid the foundation.

Discipline

From Dreams to Destiny: Where Discipline Shapes Success

My two and half years of national service in the Singapore Armed forces at the age of 18 laid the foundation for my leadership skills. Among the many skills I picked up, Discipline stands out as the utmost importance.

Even before we being enlisted in the army, I love long distance running. It gives me great satisfaction in setting a running course – be it 5km or 10 km – and successfully completing it, regardless of the time I take to complete the course. I came in long distance running by accident as I was always a 100m or 200m sprinter during my primary school days. When I got myself, a muscle pull during on the heats in my secondary school sport meet that I decided short sprints is no longer for me. The other motivation was the sport sneakers that seniors in the school cross country team used to wear – Nike Cortez, Adidas Samba, and Puma Suede to name a few. If you are a school country runner and represent the school in national competition, you will be entitled to a pair. As I cannot afford a running sneaker on my own, this was a quick way to get shinning pair. That was my first learn in motivation. I picked up cross country as one of my Extra Curricular Activities (ECA) and trained hard in all practise sessions. Once a week, a group of boys and girls from ages 13-14 would embark on a gruelling up and down hill 5km road run. As a pint-sized underweight boy, I generally get beaten by the older boys, who were well built and envious horsepower. The "adidas sneaker" was the carrot daggling in front whenever I was practising. The shoes I donned during these practises were BATA, which was famously abbreviated as "Buy And Throw Away". Durable but heavy and it slows your pace. The second lesson I learnt is determination and discipline. Running every week on a humid morning and putting extra personal training over the weekend, finally borne fruits for me. When I turned 14 years old, I was selected to be one of the school national country runners ! My fitness and timing has improved, and I has better timing than some of seniors in my team (who had become complacent due to other distractions associated with growing up as teenager in a rough neighbourhood in the early 1980s). This is the third lesson I learnt. If you want to achieve your goal, not only you need to have determination and undivided focus but also iron discipline not to be easily distracted. Short lived enjoyments are transitory and always aim for the BIG Dream and look at the BIG Picture. Goal, focus, determination and more importantly having the iron discipline to complete a self-set goal brings in sheer accomplishment. These are "small wins" in my personal life and little I realise will lay a solid foundation to achieve the bigger goals in my career and family lives. Though my primary school instilled in my interests in reading, oratory, drama and sports, it was my formidable secondary school life that had a lasting impact on my journey towards becoming a leader in my own right. My pre-university days were equally memorable. Excelling in education and balancing sports and keen interest in reading and debating provided the maturity in thoughts and allowed me to strike a fine balance between education and leisure, which is never easy in an examination focused, unforgiving and grade-based education system in Singapore, especially in the 1970s and 1980s. During this period of rapid transformation, Singapore was undergoing a remarkable journey from a small, resource-poor island to a thriving global city-state. The only asset it had and even now is its People.

The lessons I picked up from secondary and pre-university days were necessary but not sufficient to prepare me for one of my toughest periods in my early adulthood – Life as a Solider and an Officer in the Singapore Armed Forces (SAF). We all know fitness is one of the main criteria if we want to survive life in the army, especially the 3 months Basic Military Training (BMT) in the remote island off Singapore – Pulau Tekong. Together with fellow Pre-University classmates, I embarked on the journey to getting myself mentally prepared for the enlistment. As soon as our pre-university examinations were over, we did out ritual morning and evening runs. First day reporting to National Service is a milestone in every "army boys' in Singapore. Nervous and palpitating with uncertainty, we waved goodbye to our loved one during the sendoff ceremony at Dempsey Camp. The camp during the 1960s till 1990s was primarily a site for housing soldiers, as well as training facilities but it now thriving as a cultural and leisure hub. Another example of an evolving Singapore, not in any way resemblance of my transformation at that time from a rugged, spirited schoolboy to a nervous, clueless army boy !

Not all is ever ready for life as a solider in SAF. No matter how mentally and physically you are prepared, army life is a "box of chocolate". The army crew cut, need to run from one point to another in humanly impossible timeframe, with corporals and sergeants sarcastically shouting "Take Your Time, Recruits… Take Your Time… and "My Grandmother can run faster than you lot…." are the rituals showered on minted recruits. Whether you are the "Patricks" (boys who speak good English and generally from well renowned schools but struggled with physical fitness, discipline, or adjusting to the army regimentation) or "Ah Bengs" (boys who may not have a good command of the English Language but with brash, and street-smart personality), army training and expectation are standard. Luckily for me, I was neither the "Patricks" not the "Ah Bengs" but someone who falls between these two categories. I had one trait that many of my cohort had. The natural ability to have a smiling countenance, in good times and bad times ! A nature I inherited from my mum and a high sense of humour, a give from my dad. Only later in life I understood what is IQ vs EQ but little did I realise the first lessons on these traits were unknowingly seeded during the army days as a (a) Recruit in BMT, (b) Officer Cadet in Officers' Cadet School (OCS) and as a (c) Commissioned Officer in the company line and as a (d) Reservist with unit (after your ROD, Run-Out-Date, which is a date when a full-time National Serviceman (NSF) completes his 2.5 years compulsory National Service and is officially discharged from active service. This ROD is now replaced by ORD, Operationally Ready Date**)**.

The first task every recruit does when he wakes at 4am for his morning ritual "BMX exercise" is to make up his bed. You don't have your mum or maid do it this for you. To me, this is the first seed of discipline and a simple act that motivates us to successfully complete the remaining of strenuous tasks ahead in a day. Whether you are training for a marathon or competition or heading to school or to the office, the mundane task of folding and keeping one's bed prom and proper instil the iron discipline to complete our tasks ahead. We also get "married" during the BMT – our personal M16 (and it is now SAR-21) is to be wife for the next 3 months. The true meaning of responsibility was instilled in us during the weapon presenting ceremony. We had to guard and keep our "wife" functional and safe at all times. There were seriously hilarious moment of we losing our "wife' during night field camps, especially during dug out exercise. Through exhaustion and sleep depravity, we sometimes are found to be holding parts of M16, and the remaining parts mysteriously disappeared ! Though punishments are the norm when this happens, the key lesson is this: Total responsibility and ownership over our personal items, especially the M16. Such impressionable lessons in the SAF had a profound impact on my personal when I got married and set up a family and professional life when I am tasked to manage a team or project, More on this on later party of my leadership journey.

This has always been ingrained to me ever since I joined the SAF. As often said, life in the army make boys into men, and without discipline it is insurmountable task to complete the BMT, OCS and graduating as a fully-fledged commissioned officer.

My innate nature of having a beaming smile in good times and hard times in the BMT is a bonus. My corporals and sergeant admired me for having this positive mindset and allowed me to take leadership tasks during my 3 months strenuous BMT. Leading a section of recruits instil in me a purpose driven leadership. However, to earn the respect of your team members, you need to first have that positive attitude that tasks can be completed and equally we need to have the basic know how and be hands on. Every 2.4KM run was a moment me to excel. My cross country running in schools came in handy. I always aim to finish the top 3 and was always encouraged by my section commander and platoon mates to excel in this areas and taking up leadership tasks. I had first-hand experience of team management and how to gain the respect of your platoon mates during this formidable years in BMT. To share an anecdote – I am slightly acrophobia, fear of heights but there are training in the BMT that involves height elements. You cannot display such fear in front of your teammates or corporals. In the Asian culture especially, we do not want to "lose face". In one of the confidence building course that involves a high element of at least 3 meters, all of us have to jump into a trampoline, held by your teammates. When it was my turn, I was shivering and literally peeing in my pants. Thankfully no one saw my wet army pants as it was a hot day, and we were all profusely sweating.

The mantra to overcome this fear that frightening moment is to look forward, swallow your fear and display your guts feeling and tell yourself you Can Do It ! This is the mental discipline that I cultivated in the army. Though I overcame the obstacle successfully, even now I do carry that acrophobic feeling, but I tell myself nothing is going to stay in my way so long I have the iron discipline to accomplish the tasks. Jumping from a high element and running long distance involves individual effort. No one is there to do these tasks with you. You are all alone. And that is what we need to build a 'monster' attitude. We have to train ourselves to complete such tasks as in life sometimes we have to embark on a journey alone or take a path that no one has ever attempted.

I further honed myself the 3 basic tenants of BMT – Discipline, Focus and Positive Mindset. After successfully completing the 3 months BMT, I was selected and posted to the Support Office Cadet School (SOCC) in OCS for 3 months and to the Engineer Officer Cadet School (EOCC) for 6 months and after completing both these strenuous and mentally and physically exhausting courses, graduated as a commissioned officer and posted to an operational unit. If the 3 months BMT was "hell", can you imagine the 6 months officer cadet courses in OCS and EOCC ?

The first shock I had in SOCC was the unexpected "turned out" on the 1st day by my senior cadets at 4am, without any form of alerts ! My platoon mates and me were just given 5 mins to get into our military physical training (PT) outfit and assembled in the open field. We literally went through a plethora of rigorous exercise in the name of "cadet officer initiation". Just imagine if you do not have the right attitude, discipline and sheer stamina to complete this unexpected called out at 4am; and more importantly, all this 1 hour of strenuous initiation was done without a proper breakfast or shower and the usual morning routine we embark in our daily lives before heading to work or school ! What was memorable and inspirational for me was the aftermath of this initiation when we were given 20 minutes to shower and get into our No.4 military attire. Never did I imagine what does an Officer Cadet means in the SAF !

Our company comprising of 3 platoons of officer cadets were marched to an auditorium at 6am. It was still pitch dark with the morning sun peeking through the horizons of the hills surrounding the Office Cadets School. We were ushered into a dimly light auditorium, which was pin silent. Trepidation and anticipation were the order of the day. At precisely 6:30am, some senior cadets marched into the auditorium with candles, lighting up the majestic auditorium. With the SAF and Singapore Flags proudly placed in the centre of the auditorium and OCS motto – "To Lead, To Excel To Overcome" ubiquitously displayed, we took the OCS oath and wore the 1 "white bar" insignia on our epaulettes to indicate our cadet status until we achieved the two "white bars" to become senior cadets. This motto, which till now continue to have a profound impact on me personally and professionally, reflects the core values and mission of OCS, emphasising the development of leadership qualities, the pursuit of excellence, and the resilience needed to overcome challenges. It embodies the spirit expected of all officer cadets as they undergo rigorous training to become future leaders of the SAF. A sense of pride and purpose radiated among all of us. It was a moment to be treasured and to me, it was key lessons on mission and leadership and to lead. Excel and overcome, not only I need to have the stamina and attitude but more importantly the discipline to meet my ultimate goal – becoming a SAF Officer during my 2.5 years servicing national service in Singapore. Even till now, I always make it a point to understand and appreciate the vision and mission of organisations I work for and how these form the cornerstone of a purpose driven organisation.

The 9 months in OCS was one of the best free lessons and training I received on leadership, discipline, stamina, focus and teamwork. Few institution would ever provide free education, accommodation and meals and on top of that a monthly salary !

What key lessons I learnt in that 9 strenuous but exhilarating and fulfilling months ? Stay focus on all times no matter how mentally and physically exhausted you become. The early morning physical training, afternoon lectures and evening military missions demanded a superhero ability of stamina and iron discipline to stay alert at all times. Organising missions involved strategic and resource planning and leading the team to successfully complete the objectives. Art of motivating a mentally and physically exhausted section of team is not an easy task. However, it has to be done.

One of the most memorable moments was my first ever overseas military training to Brunei. At the age of nineteen, I have never travelled beyond north of Singapore – Malaysia; and have flown an airplane. Here I was, together with my cohort, embarked on training mission, taking a 2-hour flight from Singapore to Bandar Seri Begawan, capital of Brunei. From the airport, we have to take another 3 hours barge ride to reach base camp, which was located in the deep jungles of Brunei.

One of the first mission is a group topography, where group of 6 cadets, without any training officers (or mentors as we called them) to guide, has to navigate and complete 6 checkpoints before returning back to base camp. It has been done within 2 days. Armed with ratios and first aid kits and camping equipment, we ventured into the deep jungles, which is so thick that you will not be able to locate the ravines till your reach the top of the hill. Under the scorching hot weather, we were always reminded to drink plenty of water and was also given water purification tablets to kill germs, bacteria, viruses, and parasites in untreated water from sources like rivers, streams, or lakes, making it safe to drink. I, having a dark complexion, will ask to take temperature at every check point and report to base camp as dark complexion absorbs heat. I learnt about stamina, discipline and teamwork from this 2 days group topography. We took turn to lead and take care of each other. We built tents when dark falls and ensure no snake or wild boar attacks us by taking turn to guard our self-protected premises. We were clear with our mission – to complete all the checkpoints and return to base camp safely. Blessed with a focused and discipline team, we were one of the first sections to return to base camp.

At the end the two weeks military training, we returned home and got ready to receive our two "white bars" insignia on our epaulettes to be promoted to senior cadets. Most of us made it, even though they were some dropouts due to medical conditions. The ceremony to receive the two "white bars" was much more grandeur and symbolic than receiving the one "white bar" at the auditorium. We had to embark on 10km full battle order long march at 4pm and reach the top the hill in OCS before the sun arises. I had the privilege of leading my platoon as Platoon I/C (In charge for short). When the sun rose, our officers replaced the one "white bar" with the two "white bar" insignia on our epaulettes. Holding back tears and emotions, it was symbolic of an officer in making. With the rays of the morning sun brilliantly showering on us, we make a giant step towards becoming a fully commissioned officer.

It will be another 6 months of challenging yet electrifying "monster" task ahead of us. However, we lived for the moment and enjoyed the success of our hard work and sacrifice. The power of discipline is the key to turning dreams into reality. Dream Boldly, Achieve Relentlessly is my mantra till now. Transiting from OCS to EOCC is never an easy journey. We were senior cadets specialising in a specific field within the SAF, undergoing six months of specialised training to be fully commissioned as officers. This time around, discipline, along with knowledge and practical skills, is crucial to successfully completing the intensive six-month course.

At the end of the 6 months course, we finally graduated as 2nd Lieutenant Officer in an illustrious and plomb passing out parade at OCS. My parents and my brother attended this memorable occasion. It was a proud for my parents, especially my dad. I had 3 brothers and 1 sister. I am the first one to be commissioned as an officer. When my hero and role model – My Dad – replaced the two "white bars" insignia with 1 black to commissioned me as a full-fledged officer was an emotional and touching moment for me. With tears pouring day my face, it was the proudest and memorable moments in my adult life. Whenever I missed my late dad, I browsed through the photos on the Officer Cadet Graduating Ceremony and embark on a mental journey of his presence during those touching moments. I dedicated my successful journey from a raw recruit to a distinguished officer to my hero – My Dad.

Adaptability

Adaptability as an Executive Globetrotter

Adaptability empowers leaders to navigate change, overcome challenges, and thrive on the global stage.

Becoming a lawyer has always been my dream. The seed for this aspiration was first planted during my primary, secondary, and pre-university years, when I actively participated in oratorical and debate competitions. I was also the most talkative and mischievous among all my four siblings. Naturally, I was confident that I will become a well-known lawyer due to my keen interest for reading and augmentative conversations. However, God has other plans for me.

After completing my pre-university and in the midst of military training, I received our GCA "A" level results. With this results, we apply for the local universities. My first choice was always to do a law degree. Though my grades allowed me to apply, I did not qualify after going through a written examination and an interview. The whole world collapsed. I was given a place in the Arts and Social Sciences faculty, which was my second choice as I also had a keen interest in economics and political science. I did not want to take up this offer. Upon my dad and my second elder brother's persuasion, I reluctantly took up the course after completing my military training. Their argument was I can always do law as a second degree on a part time basis in one of the local private schools offering Bachelor of Law Degree. However, it did not materialise till now.

Getting deep into economics and political science, my interest gradually gravitated towards majoring in political science, with a keen focus on economics and public policy. I did well in my sophomore years of my varsity and was offered a place in the honours class, a privilege only for about 20 students in my cohort. My dad was beaming with proudness during my graduation ceremony as I was the first to become a graduate in my family and in his extended family. Once you have an inspiring role model in your life, especially during those formidable years, you can create wonders. My dad was a role model for me then and even now as an executive and a father of two teenagers. More on this in the next section.

After completing my honours degree in political science, I still had an unquenchable thirst for knowledge in public policy and economics. I applied and was successfully enlisted into the master's degree program in public policy at my university, which was later rebranded as the Lee Kuan Yew School of Public Policy, named in honour of the late first Prime Minister of modern Singapore.

Armed with an honours and master's degree in political science/public policy, naturally my dad encouraged me to join the Singapore Civil Service. After all he and my siblings were in one way, or another were working for the Singapore government. My dad used to work for the Ministry of Environment, whilst my siblings are in the banking (indirectly affiliated with government), public education, public health care and home affairs sectors. To the disappointment of my dad, I took a different path. My dad's philosophy in life is simple – Government jobs provide an iron rice bowl and comes with peaks, which are critical when we get married and set up a family of our own. This was how he single handedly raised us.

I had a different plan. I wanted to see the world. My dad is a firm believer in astrology. Each of his children has horoscope or natal chart ("Jathagam" in Tamil), carefully crafted by a renowned Tamil astrologer located at Ceylon Road in the eastern part of Singapore. This natal chart maps the positions of the planets, stars, and other celestial bodies at the exact time of birth. It is created based on the principles of Vedic astrology and is widely used in Tamil culture for naming ceremonies (based on the child's birth star and planetary positions), predicting life events such as education, career, health, and relationships, matching horoscopes for marriage compatibility and determining auspicious times for important life events. In my natal chart, it was predicated that I will study well and my work will bring me around the world. We, Indians, also strongly believe in the significance of black mole in our body. I have distinctive black moles or birthmarks in my forehead and legs. This symbolises an intellectually curious mind who is blessed with an impeccable memory and a person who will indefatigably travel overseas. To a large extent, this is true !

Upon graduation, I was eager to secure a management trainee position in a multinational corporation (MNC). But careers rarely follow a script—they evolve through a mix of intent and serendipity. I never envisioned starting mine in a container shipping company. Yet, at a recruitment fair in my final year, I stumbled upon an opportunity that promised global exposure and a deep dive into the industry through job rotations in Customer Service, Trade Management, Marketing, Operations, and Finance. The prospect was too compelling to ignore.

Out of 200 applicants, only 10 were shortlisted after two rigorous interview rounds. One question from the one of regional managers stood out: "What's one memorable thing you did during your university vacation?" I instinctively shared my experience of a 10-hour bus ride from Singapore to Kedah, Malaysia, where I spent two weeks in a rural village. The vast paddy fields, swaying palm trees, and starlit nights were a stark contrast to Singapore's cityscape. Unknowingly, I had highlighted traits that would define my career—adaptability, curiosity, and a willingness to embrace the unfamiliar. That story left an impression, reinforcing my first leadership lesson: technical skills open doors, but soft skills define how far you go.

The final stage was a lunch interview with senior management—an unspoken test of social intelligence and composure. Thanks to my military training, I had a foundation in fine dining etiquette, which proved invaluable. Beyond formalities, I prepared extensively, immersing myself in container shipping and international trade. In the pre-Google era, knowledge came from newspapers and industry reports, but that diligence paid off. I was the only Indian candidate among predominantly Chinese applicants, and I had to stand out. Two weeks later, the General Manager of Operations called with the news—I had secured a spot. My first role was in Operations, and the reason I was one of the selected few was the General Manager, like me, had served as a military officer. That was another key insight: shared experiences forge professional connections and open unexpected doors.

The learning curve was steep. My colleagues had decades of experience, while I was still decoding industry jargon. It was overwhelming at times, but I learned that adaptability is about mindset—absorbing knowledge, asking questions, and carrying a notebook (now replaced by smartphones and tablets) to capture every lesson. A year and a half into my traineeship, I faced my first major test of resilience: a corporate merger. Six months before completing the programme, my company merged with a major shipping line. Uncertainty loomed—job security was at stake, and the fate of the management trainee programme was unknown. The process was brutal. If human resource department called your direct line, it meant your position was being eliminated. When the dust settled, the programme was scrapped, and all trainees were assigned full-time roles in their last department. I was placed in container control operations and unexpectedly promoted to lead a team of 10. My predecessor, who had mentored me, was laid off. Overnight, I was responsible for managing a team with decades of combined experience—people who knew the business inside out. How do you lead when you are the least experienced person in the room?

Leadership is rarely about having all the answers. It is about building trust, fostering a shared vision, and adapting to change. I had to unite a team divided by two corporate cultures, align them under a common identity, and create a purpose-driven environment. Open communication and fairness became my guiding principles. I leaned heavily on my mentor, the General Manager of Operations of the newly merged company, using every available moment—especially lunch breaks—to absorb his wisdom on managing people and navigating change.

That period shaped my leadership philosophy. Team management is not just about authority; it is about inspiring, empowering, and bringing out the best in others. The next two years in the newly merged company became one of the most rewarding phases of my career. The lessons in dedication, adaptability, and determination formed the bedrock of my professional journey, proving that the ability to evolve and lead through uncertainty is what truly sets leaders apart.

Leadership demands tough decisions, especially when leading senior team members. Adaptability must be coupled with strong leadership. In a merger, employees bring ingrained cultures and biases from their previous organizations. The challenge? Uniting them under a new identity. One common phrase echoed through the office: "This is how we used to do it." Memorabilia from former companies adorned desks, reinforcing division. The first step? A symbolic change—replacing old identities with the new company's branding. However, culture is not just about symbols; it is about communication. The two team leaders, coming from different companies, refused to speak directly, relying on me as a bridge. One afternoon, I gathered them all, took a firm stance, and made it clear—this inefficiency had to stop. Leaders must own their roles, make decisions, and communicate directly, not just during team-building events or casual lunches. After my blunt confrontation, I walked out. When I returned, an eerie silence filled the room. But from that moment on, communication improved.

Leadership is not something you are taught—it is about stepping up, making difficult calls, and standing firm. I often recall Standard Chartered Bank's old motto: "Firm, Fair & Friendly." This philosophy has shaped my leadership approach: firm in setting performance expectations, fair in decision-making, and friendly in customer relations. While companies chase ambitious growth, success starts with fundamentals—open communication and people management. Without a solid foundation, no strategy will hold. This reminds me of a childhood memory. In the 1970s and 1980s, before modern steam irons and ironing boards, my mother and cousin sisters used dry irons on thick blankets to smooth out clothes. If the blanket layers were not laid properly, the clothes would have "iron marks" or "press marks" despite the effort. This simple task taught me a lifelong lesson: a strong foundation determines the quality of the outcome. Likewise, in leadership, structure, clarity, adaptability and culture form the bedrock of success.

After two years in Singapore, I found myself yearning for a new challenge in a different operating environment. My immediate manager and country manager recognised my ambition to venture abroad. Hard work, adaptability, and execution open doors to new opportunities—but sometimes, luck plays a role too. The merged company was launching a new Finance, Operations, and Customer Service (FOCUS) business system. To drive this initiative, it required talented and experienced employees to part of the global project team based in London, UK. Each region was tasked with forming its own business implementation team. Sydney, Australia, was selected as the first pilot site, followed by Taiwan. I was one of three employees selected to represent Asia Pacific in this global project—a prelude to my executive globetrotter journey.

The first stop: Sydney, Australia

It was March 1999. My wife and I landed in Sydney, Australia, early in the morning after a seven-and-a-half-hour red-eye flight from Singapore. This marked my first overseas secondment—a six-month assignment to help my Australian colleagues test and implement a global business system.

On our way from the airport to the hotel, I experienced my first cultural shock as a sheltered Singaporean. Sydney was in the midst of celebrating the Sydney Gay and Lesbian Mardi Gras, one of the world's largest and most iconic LGBTQ+ pride events. The city was alive with dazzling outfits, bold makeup, and an electrifying atmosphere filled with music and dance. Coming from Singapore, where such events were not permitted or were frowned upon, this was a striking contrast. At that time, Singapore had no equivalent event—Pink Dot SG, the country's first LGBTQ+ advocacy gathering, would only be established a decade later in 2009.

That first day in Sydney was a culture shock for my wife and me. We had visited the Gold Coast for our honeymoon in 1996, but this was the first time we would be living and working in such a vibrant yet unfamiliar environment. What leadership lessons did I take from this short stint in Sydney?

First, adaptability is key. In a diverse and globalized world, cultural differences in expression and lifestyle are inevitable. Learning to adapt and accept these differences is essential for personal and professional growth. Second, work-life balance. In Sydney, it was normal for employees to leave the office at 5 PM—or even 4 PM if they started at 8 AM. Shops closed early, and work-related calls outside office hours were rare. Coming from a work culture that emphasized long hours and relentless dedication, this was a new concept for me. Today, work-life balance is a major expectation, particularly among millennials and Gen Alpha, especially with the normalization of remote work post-COVID-19. Third, immerse yourself in the local culture. Weekends should be spent exploring, trying new foods, and engaging with locals. In multinational corporations, we work with colleagues from various nationalities and backgrounds. Exposure to different cultures builds adaptability and prepares us for leadership in a globalised world.

The next stop: Taipei, Taiwan.

After six months in Sydney, my next destination was Taipei, Taiwan—my second site for implementation. During my army days, I had visited Kaohsiung for a two-week military exercise, where I was struck by the warmth and hospitality of the Taiwanese people. The local generosity, offering us fruits and water during long marches, left a lasting impression. So, when I moved to Taipei, I was mentally prepared, though my wife's challenge was packing, unpacking, and adjusting to new cultures with every move.

In Taipei, the working style and food were similar to Singapore's, but English was less commonly spoken. Thankfully, a colleague became not just a mentor but a close family friend, helping us settle in. Taiwanese hospitality was unparalleled, and their hardworking, determined attitude mirrored the Singaporean spirit. With their support, the project was a success, and I took away two crucial leadership lessons.

First, *empathic leadership*. Working with a team of mostly working mothers, I had to embrace empathy. Deadlines were tight, but some colleagues could not stay late due to family responsibilities. Rather than insist on more hours, I adjusted my approach, recognising the complex balance they had to maintain between career and home. It reminded me of the book *Men Are from Mars, Women Are from Venus*—how men and women handle tasks differently, with women mastering multitasking, an ability I deeply admired in my colleagues and wife. Second, *embracing change*. Living in Taipei, we experienced our first major natural disaster—the 1999 Chi-Chi earthquake. The tremor shook our apartment, throwing us from bed. Yet, the locals showed remarkable resilience, staying calm and continuing their lives amidst the chaos. I learned the importance of being prepared—physically, mentally, and emotionally—to navigate life's unpredictabilities. Resilience, adaptability, and preparedness became essential pillars of my leadership journey—traits every leader must cultivate to thrive in a VUCA world: Volatile, Uncertain, Complex, and Ambiguous. As a supply chain and logistics practitioner, the training I received in Taipei has enabled me to navigate today's global supply chain disruptions with calm and clarity, especially in the aftermath of COVID-19. The challenges I faced then have shaped my ability to tackle the complexities of our industry now. My time in Taipei taught me these timeless values—empathy, adaptability, and resilience. For that, I am forever grateful to my Taiwanese colleagues and friends.

The next stop: Busan, South Korea

The next stop was Busan, South Korea—initially planned for six months but wrapped up in just one. As my Taipei stint ended, my regional CFO in Hong Kong, a key sponsor of our global business system, needed to provide a resource for the global project team in London. TCS (Tata Consultancy Services) required regional business representatives to collaborate on developing and testing system modules. Given my expertise in Full Container Load (FCL) and Less Container Load (LCL) operations, I was nominated for a two-year secondment at our corporate headquarters in London. While my Asia project and Korean teams were sad to see me go, I embraced the opportunity to expand my network beyond Asia—an invaluable asset in the MNC world, especially with many major players headquartered in Europe.

One key lesson from Busan left a lasting impression: the discipline and deep reverence for authority in Korean corporate culture. On my first day, I witnessed a striking morning ritual—employees lined up in two lanes, bowing to each other in mutual respect. The synchronized uniformity, structure, and decorum spoke volumes about their corporate values. Today, thanks to my children's love for BTS (Bangtan Sonyeondan, a globally renowned South Korean boy band known for its powerful performances, meaningful lyrics, and diverse music styles and a dedicated fanbase called ARMY) and K-dramas, I have become a fan myself. Watching corporate-themed dramas always brings me back to Busan, reminding me that respect for colleagues—expressed in any form—is a fundamental trait of a great leader.

The next stop: London, United Kingdom

London was my next stop—a dream come true for a lifelong English Premier League fan. While my siblings supported Manchester United,

Arsenal, and Tottenham, for me, it was always *The Kops—Liverpool Football Club*. Living and working in the UK felt like a privilege, but my introduction to British culture came with an unexpected jolt. The moment my wife and I stepped off our 14-hour Singapore Airlines flight, a stern-faced British officer pulled me aside, gripping my collar. It was a cultural shock. He demanded my passport—one I have always carried with pride, knowing the strength of the Singaporean passport—and questioned my reason for traveling to London. After presenting my company letter, we were allowed to proceed. Only later did I realise the heightened security stemmed from the 1999 London nail bomb attacks, which had targeted Black, Bangladeshi, and LGBT communities. The second attack, on April 24, had occurred in Brick Lane—coincidentally where our corporate office was located. I brushed off the incident, understanding their vigilance in preventing potential retaliation. Yet, I could not shake the thought that the questioning could have been handled with more dignity. That moment reinforced a crucial leadership trait: *calmness under adversity*. In challenging situations, especially in an unfamiliar environments, a leader must control emotions and maintain composure—traits essential for navigating adversity with grace and effectiveness.

Living and working in London, the heart of the UK, marked a defining moment in my career. I was fortunate to have an exceptional British manager and mentor, a man who had worked in Hong Kong and understood Asian culture. Despite being a fan of West Ham United and Southend Football Club, we quickly bonded like old friends. Our core team was a blend of local Brits, a Dutch colleague, and a Singaporean, but as our team expanded, we welcomed colleagues from Germany, Italy, Hong Kong, Spain, Brazil, India, and the USA. This exposure to such a diverse group offered me invaluable insight into different cultures, helping me refine one of the most essential leadership traits—adaptability. The differences in our cultural approaches were striking: British, American, and Indian colleagues were more outspoken in their work style, whilst the Germans were meticulous, the Dutch bluntly frank, Spaniards passionate, and Brazilians expressive, often using body language and gestures to emphasise their points and forge strong personal connections. It was like working in a "mini–United Nations." As a Singaporean, I have always emphasised clearly articulating my views, listening to all perspectives, and then making a firm decision while taking responsibility for the outcome. Singaporeans value planning and execution over lengthy brainstorming sessions, and this approach has consistently helped me drive results efficiently—an approach that continues to serve me well.

In my free time, weekends and bank holidays were opportunities to explore the rich cultural tapestry of London. Living in Limehouse Docklands, just a stone's throw from Brick Lane and Canary Wharf, offered us a vibrant urban lifestyle. Fish and chips and Chicken Tikka Masala became our go-to meals, and Camden Town quickly became our favourite hangout spot. My wife and I often took long train rides to the pastoral and seaside landscapes of Cranbury Town, Bath, Brighton, the Yorkshire Dales, Cambridge, and Oxford. Even short weekend trips to Glasgow and Edinburgh in Scotland provided us with fresh perspectives on life beyond the city. The way the British spoke, their mannerisms and wit, left a lasting impression on me, and even now, I enjoy watching British sitcoms and movies, having grown up in Singapore watching the high-adrenaline James Bond films and the hilarious "Billy Hill Show" and "Mind Your Language." As a former colony of the British Raj, British culture has had a profound impact on Singaporeans, especially in education. With English as both the language of business and the primary language of instruction in schools, Singaporeans have gained a competitive advantage in the global arena. This foundation in English has paid dividends to me when travelling or working in the Western world, where English is predominantly spoken.

During my time in London, I occasionally took business trips to Rotterdam, the other corporate office for my company, as well as to New Delhi, India, where the TCS development team was located. This was my first opportunity to work closely with India's highly skilled IT professionals and coding experts. As someone without an IT background, coding was initially foreign to me. However, before getting involved in this global project, I took a project management course at the Singapore Institute of Management and a basic coding course on weekends in London. My goal wasn't to become an expert in either field but to familiarize myself with the terminology and best practices. My TCS team in New Delhi were impressed when I used project management and coding terms during our brainstorming sessions. The experience with TCS developers in India opened my eyes to the world of IT, and it sparked a lasting interest in digitalisation and AI. I truly believe the roots of this passion were planted during my time in London and India, working closely with the TCS software developers and project managers.

What were some of the key leadership learning from 2 years in London ? The two years I spent in London were transformative, both professionally and personally. Some key leadership lessons I learned during that time shaped my approach to work and life. Firstly, stepping out of our comfort zone. Asia had always been my home ground, and moving to a Western environment opened up new knowledge, networks, and connections. The ability to adapt and adjust to different working cultures helped me become a more globally aware and culturally diverse leader. Secondly, having a clear and candid communication style. Singaporeans, myself included, tend to speak quickly, almost like a machine gun. However, when interacting with colleagues from the UK, USA, Germany, Netherlands, Spain, and Brazil, I had to adjust my speaking speed and tone. Cultural sensitivity became key in establishing rapport and connections, and slowing down helped ensure clarity and effective communication. Thirdly, never look down on yourself. Many times, we may feel inferior just because we are from a different background, especially in a Western context. I have learned not to fall into that trap. Regardless of where we come from, we each have something valuable to contribute. No one knows everything, and the key is to focus on continually enhancing our expertise and becoming exceptional in our field. Finally, continuous Learning. Leadership is about constantly learning. I embraced the challenge of picking up new skills to stay relevant in the changing business landscape, especially with the rise of generative AI. A true leader is a lifelong student. By listening more than talking, we open ourselves to new knowledge and perspectives. When you talk too much, you are simply sharing what you already know. However, by listening, you gain fresh insights and ideas that can drive growth and innovation. These lessons, learned through real-world experience, continue to guide me as I navigate the evolving dynamics of leadership and professional development.

The Next Stop: Ho Chi Minh City, Vietnam
As my London secondment came to an end, I faced one of the most emotional farewells of my career. My mentor and colleagues surprised me with a farewell party, gifting me Liverpool and England football jerseys—symbols of the bonds we had built beyond work.

Departing alone from Heathrow, a profound emptiness set in. London had become more than just an assignment; it was a defining chapter filled with friendships, growth, and unforgettable experiences. When I landed in Singapore, my wife was waiting at Changi Airport. As I hugged her, the weight of leaving behind my colleagues and mentor overwhelmed me.

Even today, we remain connected through LinkedIn and WhatsApp, but digital ties can never replace the human connections that shape us. Leadership is not just about strategy and execution—it is about people. True leaders embrace emotion, not as a weakness, but as a reflection of empathy, respect, and the deep relationships that define their journey. In supply chain and logistics, relationships are the bedrock of success.

Now, a new adventure awaited me in Ho Chi Minh City (HCMC). In November 2000, U.S. President Bill Clinton made history as the first sitting American leader to visit Vietnam since the war's end in 1975. His trip was a turning point, laying the foundation for stronger U.S.-Vietnam economic and diplomatic ties. In January 2002, my wife and I landed in HCMC, stepping into a nation on the brink of an economic revolution. Vietnam was emerging as Southeast Asia's next economic powerhouse, mirroring the rapid industrialisation and trade-driven growth that had once propelled the "Four Asian Tigers"—Singapore, Hong Kong, Taiwan, and South Korea—to global prominence. With a booming economy, rising foreign investment, and an ambitious vision for the future, Vietnam was poised to follow in their footsteps. Once again, fortune had placed me at the heart of transformation—this time, in a city buzzing with opportunity.

My country manager in Singapore, a visionary Dutch leader, also oversaw Vietnam—a market that, at the time, operated through an agency agreement rather than a full-fledged office. Recognising Vietnam's immense growth potential, his strategy was clear: transition from an agency setup to a fully integrated corporate presence, bringing the agent's staff into our organisation.

To make this transformation seamless, he needed someone to implement corporate processes and business systems alongside our owner's representative. As luck would have it, just as my London secondment was concluding, my country manager entrusted me with a two-year assignment in HCMC. It was an opportunity that many could only dream of, and to this day, I remain deeply grateful to him for placing his trust in me at such a pivotal moment.

HCMC holds a special place in my heart—not just professionally, but personally. Our first child, my daughter, was "made in Vietnam," as my wife discovered she was pregnant on Christmas Eve. She called it our early Christmas present. Even today, as a family—including my son, who, by the way, was "made" in Thailand during a quick getaway—we maintain a ritual of returning to HCMC, drawn by its incredible food, warm hospitality, and the industrious spirit of the Vietnamese people.

My time in Ho Chi Minh City was not just a career milestone—it was a leadership masterclass. The dynamic business landscape, cultural nuances, and interactions with local colleagues reshaped my leadership approach in ways I carry with me to this day. First, the relentless pursuit of knowledge. Emerging from a closed socialist economy, the Vietnamese were eager to absorb new business and IT knowledge. Though English proficiency was still developing, my colleagues took night classes to sharpen their language and technical skills, fully aware that these competencies were essential to securing jobs in the rapidly expanding MNC sector. This experience gave me a front-row seat to Vietnam's transformation into an emerging economic powerhouse, shaping my later thought leadership in global logistics. Second, the art of consensus building. Vietnamese decision-making is not immediate; it is deliberate. When discussing corporate processes and KPIs, my colleagues would request time to confer in Vietnamese before reaching a conclusion. While it seemed slow at first, it reinforced a key leadership lesson: imposing a top-down approach without buy-in rarely works. Effective leadership requires situational adaptability—balancing directive leadership with collaborative decision-making. Finally, never assume, always observe. During a presentation to port officials—who arrived in full military uniform—I was told they needed translation as they spoke little English. My agency director interpreted every word. Later, I discovered they actually understood English but preferred the translation process to buy time for analysis—an ingenious negotiation tactic. That day, I learned a valuable lesson: in high-stakes discussions, silence and strategic delays can be just as powerful as words.

Vietnam was more than an assignment—for me, it was a masterclass in adaptability, cultural intelligence, and leadership in emerging markets.

The Next Stop: Hong Kong

The pivotal moments in my career reinforced a key leadership lesson: growth comes from stepping into the unknown. As my secondment in Ho Chi Minh City neared its end, a leadership transition took place. The new Chief Representative—young, sharp, and fresh from a stint in Latin America—brought a different perspective to the role. From him, I absorbed critical management lessons, from crafting precise executive emails to mastering stakeholder engagement. However, the most profound impact he had on me was shaping my next career move. During my evaluation, he astutely pointed out that while I had extensive experience in operations and business systems, I lacked direct exposure to the commercial side of the business—pricing, trade management, and Profit and Loss (P&L) responsibility.

Opportunity came knocking when he travelled to our regional office in Hong Kong and discovered that the General Manager for Asia-based trades was seeking a Senior Trade Manager to lead the Asia–East Africa and Indian Ocean Islands market. Recognising my potential, my Chief Representative strongly recommended me for the role.

With that, I was thrust into the high-stakes world of trade management in container shipping—an arena where strategy, market dynamics, and commercial acumen dictated success. It was a defining career shift, proving once again that growth is not about staying in your comfort zone—it is about taking the leap into new, uncharted territory.

Living and working in Hong Kong marked another pivotal phase in my career. The challenges were many, particularly during my wife's pregnancy, when I had to balance my professional development with being physically absent during such a significant life event. While my focus was on career progression that time away from my pregnant wife is a painful regret that I reflect on deeply. More on that in the next chapter.

In the world of trade management in container shipping, I quickly learned that the role is defined by power and influence. As a trade manager, you control pricing and space allocation on vessels, which directly impacts the profitability of a trade lane. The ability to make quick decisions and respond promptly to emails became critical. Speed in responding to pricing requests was non-negotiable; any delay could cost valuable business opportunities. This ability to act decisively remains a core skill I continue to value and stress to the teams I manage, both in container shipping and freight forwarding. Living in Hong Kong reminded me of the similarities between it and Singapore, often referred to as twin cities. Both are bustling financial hubs with impressive skyscrapers, but Hong Kong had an undeniable buzz. The energy in Hong Kong's work culture was palpable. Unlike Singapore, where work often ends at the office, Hong Kongers would frequently continue networking after work hours, frequenting bars and eateries to connect with others in the industry. This after-hours networking culture was instrumental during the 1997-1998 Asian Financial Crisis. The financial markets in Hong Kong, fuelled by close-knit networking and timely information sharing, were far more agile and able to anticipate the crisis earlier than their counterparts in other Asian markets. The value of personal connections and the exchange of market intelligence—before the advent of the internet and modern communication tools—proved to be an X-factor that shaped Hong Kong's financial landscape during that critical period.

The key leadership lesson I learned is that timely decision-making, effective networking, and staying in tune with market trends are essential for achieving success, both personally and professionally.

Back to Singapore

During one of my regular quarterly business trips to Middle East and East Africa—mainly Dubai, Kenya, Uganda, and Tanzania—I received the announcement that a larger company was acquiring my current employer. I had experienced a merger early in my career, but this was a buyout. Naturally, I found myself wondering: What are my chances of securing a position in the new organisation? With a family now, I was filled with a mix of worry and excitement, uncertain about the future, yet intrigued by the potential of working for a larger, financially stronger company.

Lady luck was on my side, but more importantly, it was my positive growth mindset, adaptability, and hard work that helped me overcome the challenge. Thanks to my dad, these soft skills were deeply ingrained in me. When my new employer reviewed the trade teams in Hong Kong, they saw my potential, much of which was due to my general manager's strong recommendation. As a result, I was shortlisted for a General Manager position in the South East Asia Route Management Team in Singapore, where I would lead a team of 10, overseeing Intra-Asia, Asia to Africa, the Middle East, and Asia to Oceania trades. With three direct trade managers reporting to me, along with managers and management trainees, I was humbled to see my promotion as the talk of the town. This achievement would not have been possible without the support of my superiors and, most importantly, the soft skills I had developed over the years.

Though it was a relief to reunite with my family in Singapore, adapting to the new culture and DNA of the organization proved more difficult than I had anticipated. Despite my adaptability, I realised this time it wasn't working for me. After nearly 10 years in container shipping, I felt the need for a change. My focus shifted toward exploring the broader scope of end-to-end supply chain and logistics, eager to step away from being immersed solely in the container shipping sector. It was time for a new challenge, one that aligned more closely with my evolving interests and aspirations.

Thanks to connections from the past, I secured a senior trade manager position with a promising third-party logistics company, overseeing its Asia-Europe trade. Although the company's regional headquarters were in Hong Kong, I had the flexibility to work from a sub-regional office in Singapore, while my immediate manager and the rest of the trade management team operated out of Hong Kong. This opportunity allowed me to leverage my experience in a fresh, dynamic environment while maintaining strong ties with the broader team. I stayed with the company for the next 10 years, steadily progressing from a senior trade manager to ultimately becoming the Vice President of Ocean Freight for the Asia Pacific region. This journey not only refined my leadership and industry expertise but also solidified my commitment to growth and excellence within the logistics and supply chain space.

The key leadership lessons I gained from transitioning from container shipping to third-party logistics (freight forwarding) were profound. Firstly, my experience in the larger container shipping firm offered an invaluable opportunity to lead diverse teams, from experienced senior trade managers to eager management trainees. This sharpened my team management skills, especially in guiding young talents who were often impatient for promotion. I recognised that beyond technical expertise, mastering soft skills—especially stakeholder management and communication —is crucial for long-term success. Secondly, the transition required not only a new skill set but a shift in mindset. In container shipping, I was a "price maker," negotiating freight rates with container lines. In third-party logistics, I became a "price taker," focusing on cost-effectiveness and delivering optimal solutions. Thankfully, with the support of a patient and approachable manager, I learned to think like a freight forwarder, which required adaptability and a willingness to learn. Thirdly, building strong relationships with overseas offices was paramount. Unlike trade management, which was typically a cost centre, these offices were P&L-driven. We had to provide tailored solutions rather than just negotiate rates—selling solutions became my key mantra.

This shift broadened my approach to creating value for both clients and the company. Lastly, pursuing my passion for new challenges was a driving force. I thrive on new experiences and enjoy the process of overcoming challenges. Moving from a general manager position in a well-established company to starting anew in a different sector tested my adaptability and resilience. With the right mentors, network, and a win-win mindset, I gradually advanced from senior trade manager to vice president of regional ocean freight. Ultimately, this journey reinforced the importance of adaptability, passion for growth, and the ability to pivot when faced with new challenges.

Return to Hong Kong

The advent and application of technology and digitalisation in supply chain and logistics deeply fascinated me. While I was briefly involved in the rollout of a digitalised quotation module at my current company, I knew I needed to dive deeper. My curiosity grew, driving me to explore the broader world of technology and its transformative potential in freight forwarding.

This thirst for knowledge led to a breakthrough when a recruiter from a digital freight forwarder reached out to me on LinkedIn. After several rounds of interviews with senior managers in Hong Kong and the corporate office in the USA, I was offered the opportunity to lead the ocean freight procurement and operations teams as Senior Director, based in Hong Kong, with teams in both Hong Kong and Shenzhen. This role allowed me to fully immerse myself in the intersection of logistics and technology, further fuelling my passion for the digital transformation of the industry.

I decided to bring my family with me to Hong Kong, eager for my daughter and son to experience life and education in a foreign country. Their time there exposed them to a world beyond the structured and sheltered environment of Singapore. More importantly, they had the chance to connect with students from Hong Kong, China, and Singapore in an international school setting. Unlike me, they began building a global network early on and continue to stay connected through social media.

Working for a start-up digital freight forwarder that evolved into a more established company taught me valuable leadership lessons. First, I learned the importance of agility and adaptability—being able to pivot quickly in response to new technologies and market changes. Switching from a ThinkPad with Windows to a MacBook with macOS marked a significant personal and professional shift. After using Windows for nearly two decades, adapting to macOS reflected the broader transition I was undergoing as a digital freight forwarder. It required me to rethink my approach to technology, learn new workflows, and embrace a digital-first mindset, symbolising my evolution in adapting to the rapidly changing tech-driven logistics landscape. One of my mentors in the digital company introduced me to the phrase "Unlearn and Relearn," which profoundly impacted me. It emphasised that learning is not just about acquiring knowledge but also about adapting and evolving as circumstances change. Going through a digitalisation process means shedding outdated knowledge, processes, and ways of thinking, replacing them with new, relevant, and more effective approaches. It requires adaptability, a willingness to embrace change, and continuous learning to stay ahead in an evolving digital landscape. As the company matured, I balanced innovation with structure. Leading diverse teams and fostering cross-functional collaboration became crucial for growth, especially when managing millennials who sought purpose-driven roles. "Huddle" was a term I first encountered in this digital tech company, and it resonated with me so much that I continue to use it for my team-building events to this day. Pioneering change was a key focus, requiring a willingness to experiment and challenge the status quo. A customer-centric mindset became essential, ensuring that solutions met evolving needs. Scaling the company's culture while maintaining its start-up energy was a significant challenge. Visionary thinking helped anticipate market shifts, while data-driven decision-making informed strategic moves. Lastly, resilience was critical—navigating setbacks and staying focused on long-term goals. This experience taught me flexibility, adaptability, mentoring millennials, collaboration, and forward-thinking leadership essential in navigating a rapidly evolving industry.

Back to Singapore

After living and working in Hong Kong for about 1.5 years, I had to make the difficult decision to return to Singapore due to the city's severe political crisis. The 2019 Hong Kong student revolt, part of the broader Anti-Extradition Law Amendment Bill Movement, led to widespread protests and disruptions. With schools closed frequently and concerns for my family's safety, I felt it was best to relocate. It was a tough choice, especially since my children had grown attached to their school life and friendships in Hong Kong.

After a 6-month sabbatical, where I helped a close friend build his social commerce startup, I returned to the workforce, this time leading the regional ocean freight division of a traditional freight forwarding MNC. Though my tenure lasted only 9 months, one key lesson was the importance of having a single direct manager. Reporting to two managers with conflicting priorities was both physically and mentally draining. This experience has stayed with me, influencing my approach in future roles, where I ensured I had one clear manager responsible for setting KPIs and priorities, with others serving functional roles.

Global Role in Hong Kong

It had always been my dream to take on global roles, a goal heavily influenced by one of my mentors in the 3rd Party Logistics MNC. His astute leadership, strategic planning, and team management left a lasting impact on me. This opportunity materialised when another mentor in the digital freight forwarding sector shared my CV with a large sourcing and logistics MNC in Hong Kong. After completing the initial due diligence interviews with HR, I underwent three rounds of interviews: with the Senior Vice President (SVP) of Freight Forwarding, the Group CEO, and the Country Head of the China Freight Forwarding unit. After successfully completing the interviews and an aptitude test, I was offered the position of Vice President (VP) of global ocean freight and tender management, leading a team of five and reporting to the Senior Vice President (SVP). Given the ongoing COVID-19 pandemic, I chose to relocate to Hong Kong alone, as I did not want to disrupt my family's stability in Singapore, especially for my young children. This marked the second time in my career that I had to live and work in another country, separated from my family.

What are the key leadership lessons from this global role? First, adapting to a female boss. Throughout my career, I had never reported to a female boss, and initially, I was apprehensive about how to navigate this new dynamic. Seeking advice from my network, including HR professionals, I learned key differences in leadership styles. Female leaders tend to be more meticulous, excel at multitasking, and balance both EQ and IQ in decision-making—whereas male leaders often lean more heavily on IQ. Any hesitation I had was unfounded; in fact, I gained valuable insights from her leadership.

- The Power of Small Wins – While a big-picture vision is crucial, focusing on small, achievable goals builds momentum and sets the stage for greater success.
- The 3H Approach: Head, Heart, and Hand – Rational thinking (Head), people-centric decision-making (Heart), and hands-on leadership (Hand) create a balanced and effective management style. These principles resonated so deeply with me that I now keep them as a reminder at my workstation.

Secondly, making tough decisions. Letting go of underperforming employees does not come naturally to leaders. Firing an employee for the first time in my career was one of the most challenging leadership moments I faced. Despite guidance from my boss and HR, the final responsibility lay with me. The experience reinforced a critical lesson: leadership is not just about driving success—it is also about making tough calls to protect team morale and performance. An underperforming employee who disrupts team dynamics can hold everyone back, and as a leader, decisive action is sometimes necessary. Finally, communicating at the C-suite level. Interacting directly with Group CEO, CFO, and senior executives, particularly during the supply chain disruptions caused by COVID-19, sharpened my ability to distil complex information into concise, strategic insights. These leaders required precise, real-time updates to inform board of directors and global clients. Navigating these high-stakes conversations strengthened my confidence in engaging with C-suite executives and reinforced the importance of clarity, brevity, and strategic thinking.

Returning to Singapore – A Decision Beyond Career

After nearly a year in my global role in Hong Kong, family needs took precedence, prompting my return to Singapore. My children were at a formative stage where parental presence mattered deeply. While my daughter, mature and closely bonded with my wife, adapted well, my son struggled. As his confidant and closest ally, my absence weighed heavily on him. His once jovial and outgoing nature gave way to quiet reserve, and my wife noticed the shift. Virtual celebrations and video calls, no matter how advanced, could never replace the warmth of physical presence. The decision was clear—I had to be home.

Fortunately, my company recognised the situation and allowed me to work from Singapore, given its strong presence there. However, leading my team remotely presented new challenges. While COVID-19 normalised virtual management, I have always believed in the power of direct, face-to-face leadership. Digital tools like Zoom and MS Teams facilitate communication, but they cannot replace the deeper bonds formed through in-person interactions.

Just as I was navigating this transition, an opportunity arose—another MNC was seeking a global head for ocean freight, based in Singapore. The timing was perfect, making my move back home seamless. More than just reuniting with my family, I was fortunate to step into a role that completed my career's full-circle journey through the supply chain and logistics industry—a trilogy spanning container shipping, global 3PLs, and direct shippers. Key lesson: while luck plays a role, solid experience in globally renowned companies paves the way for new opportunities. When the right role opens, having both expertise and credibility puts you at the top of the list.

Determination

To balance life as a Husband, Dad, & Corporate Executive

True leadership is defined by the determination to excel professionally while staying grounded in the roles that matter most—at home and in life.

"You need to return to Singapore. Your son misses you deeply—he has become unusually quiet, reserved, and is not openly communicating with me or his sister." That one sentence hit me harder than any business challenge I had ever faced when I was still working and living alone in Hong Kong in 2021. My wife's calm voice over the phone carried a weight that no corporate crisis could match. My son—once lively and expressive—had withdrawn into silence. At that moment, I realised that no professional success could ever compensate for the time lost with family. Leadership is not just about driving results in the boardroom; it's about knowing when to pivot in life's bigger picture. A close friend in the supply chain and logistics industry once told me, *"In our senior years, success is not measured by our own achievements, but by how successful our children become. Their success is the true testament to our success as parents."*

A father is a son's first hero, just as my own dad was mine. When my wife told me our son had grown quiet and withdrawn, I knew I had to act. The teenage years are critical, and no career milestone could outweigh my role as a father. I arranged to transfer back to Singapore, but leading a young team remotely did not sit well with me. Even after the COVID-19 era proved that virtual management was possible, I firmly believed in the power of face-to-face leadership—mentorship that goes beyond the screen. Then, fate intervened. A headhunting firm reached out, seeking recommendations for a global ocean freight role in Singapore. Though I was not actively job-hunting, I seized the moment. Several rounds of interviews later, I landed the role and returned home. To this day, I remain grateful to the senior leaders who made that transition possible. They did not just give me a career move—they gave me back my family.

Back in Singapore, I made a conscious decision—to balance the trilogy of being a husband, a dad, and an executive. It was never going to be easy. Each role demanded time, effort, and commitment, often pulling me in different directions. Something always has to give. The challenge was not just in managing time but in making deliberate choices—when to lean into work, when to prioritise family, and when to carve out moments for myself with my better half. True balance is not about perfection; it's about knowing what matters most at any given moment and having the courage to act on it.

As they say, "Happy Wife, Happy Life." I am a firm believer in this mantra, a lesson ingrained in me by my first mentor upon entering the workforce. Every time I relocated for work—from Australia to Taiwan, the UK, Vietnam, and Hong Kong—my first priority was ensuring my wife felt happy, comfortable, and secure. More importantly, she needed something meaningful to do, having sacrificed her own career, family, and friendships to move across borders with me, practically living out of a suitcase. Thankfully, in each country, she built her own network, adapted seamlessly, and even picked up new languages—Vietnamese being one of them, thanks to her remarkable ability to learn foreign tongues. She even worked in London, taking on roles at the Bank of Egypt International and the London Borough of Newham Social Services. Her adaptability and sacrifice for my career cannot be measured in dollars and cents. Her calm disposition, sharp decision-making, and street smarts allowed me to focus on my work while she navigated new social landscapes with ease. She has been my confidante, my partner in every challenge, and the anchor of our family.

Even now, we joke about our roles—she remains the "Finance and Home Affairs Minister," keeping everything in order, while I proudly take on the "Education and Foreign Minister" portfolio. Together, we make it work. I recently consulted an astrologer, who, without hesitation, said, "Your dad is no longer with you. Your wife is now your dad, your guiding force. Listen to her, and the future of you and your children will shine brightly." Powerful wisdom indeed!

My daughter is mature, focused, and financially savvy, always planning her future meticulously. With a high IQ and a strong-willed personality, she is determined to succeed and competitive by nature. Like my wife, she can be stoic and does not make friends easily, and while her EQ could use some fine-tuning, her independent mindset shines through, especially as a teenager. Her favourite phrases to us are "You don't understand" and "Don't tell me what to do." When she started her internship during her university break, I jokingly asked, "So, did you tell your boss, 'Don't tell me what to do'?" She smiled coyly in response. My relationship with my daughter is similar to that in the series *Young Sheldon*, the father-daughter relationship between George Cooper Sr. and his daughter, Missy. Our relationship, though not as emotionally intricate as my wife's relationship with her, is filled with love, mutual respect, and moments of understanding that highlight the typical father-daughter dynamic, with my daughter occasionally testing my patience with her independent spirit. Our shared love for K-Drama (e.g. Vincenzo, The Glory, Extraordinary Attorney Woo and Hierarchy), British dramas and inspirational films—especially The Crown (2016-2023 series in shown in Netflix), The Blind Side (2009), and The Boys in the Boat (2023)—has sparked many meaningful conversations. My daughter, with a shy smile, admitted that part of her love for The Boys in the Boat came from the rugged charm of the rowers. Beyond entertainment, these moments of bonding have unexpectedly refined my leadership approach. Navigating fatherhood, especially with a daughter, has deepened my ability to lead with empathy—an essential skill when working with female colleagues and team members. I have come to realise that the emotional intelligence I apply in leadership is a direct reflection of the personal connections I cherish with my wife and daughter.

One Sunday afternoon, my teenage son watched as I carefully glued my worn-out running sneakers—the front gaping open like an alligator ready to strike. They were battered but reliable, a pair I had worn since moving to Singapore in 2021. "Dad, why don't you just buy a new pair?" he asked, his tone casual but confident. I paused, met his eyes, and said, "Your dad can afford it. But my dad couldn't." He did not argue. Instead, he quietly walked away, deep in thought. Teenagers rarely respond well to lectures. I have learned that subtle moments like these are far more powerful than words. Unlike my daughter, who is naturally frugal, my son is an extrovert like me—full of energy but not always mindful of finances. My wife and I often seize these everyday moments to instil in him the value of money, planning, and the wisdom of living simply today to secure tomorrow. Whilst my wife is a 'tiger mum' when it comes to managing our son, I tend to be more of a confidante. I have a soft spot for him, as I see a lot of my mischievous, playful side in him. He carries more of my genes than my wife's, which makes balancing discipline and approachability a challenge. It is a daily learning process, but it reflects what leadership is all about—guiding with patience and understanding. In leadership, we often face challenges with difficult colleagues—those who lack motivation, are lazy, or are not team players. I have learned the hard way that it is impossible to make everyone happy. Instead, our focus should be on creating a collaborative, and supportive environment while mentoring those who struggle. If efforts do not bear fruit, we must have the courage to make tough decisions and bring in fresh talent. The patience I have developed with my son has shaped the way I lead my team. Patience is a virtue, but true leadership sometimes requires tough choices. It is all part of the journey.

In my current corporate role, I have consciously shifted from being an active leader to adopting a mentoring approach, both within my organisation and beyond. While I no longer oversee every detail, I still make critical strategic decisions, hire talent, and step in front of senior executives to present solutions and suggestions. This transition allows me to focus on empowering others, sharing knowledge, and guiding the next generation of leaders, while ensuring the broader vision and goals of the organisation are met through collaboration and strong decision-making. Mentoring has become a key element in shaping a sustainable leadership culture, where success is shared and multiplied. As we transition into senior roles, the focus shifts from personal achievement to fostering the success of those around us. True leadership is not about individual accolades or the work we accomplish alone, but about empowering our teams to thrive. A leader's role is to inspire, support, and guide, providing the tools, vision, and motivation necessary for others to excel. Effective leadership involves cultivating trust, encouraging open communication, and recognising each team member's strengths. It requires adaptability, the ability to navigate challenges, and a commitment to developing others' potential. When your team performs at its best, their success becomes a direct reflection of your leadership—demonstrating that the ability to nurture talent and foster collaboration is what truly defines a leader's impact.

As a leader, lifelong learning is essential. It empowers us to stay relevant, adapt to change, and continuously improve—qualities that are crucial in driving success and inspiring growth in others. I am constantly upgrading my skills, especially in Artificial Intelligence, Digital Transformation, and Corporate Finance—areas where I have limited exposure but see great potential. At the time of writing this, I am also pursuing a six-month course in 'Digital Marketing & E-commerce Accelerator.' While seemingly unrelated to supply chain and logistics, digital marketing and e-commerce are crucial for personal branding. In today's career landscape, no one will advocate for us unless we take the initiative to showcase our own value. I recently came across an infographic on TikTok titled '7 Things Not to Say to Your Boss (and what to say instead).' It highlighted common questions like 'Can I have a raise?' or 'When's my promotion?'. I have learned not to ask these but instead focus on delivering impactful results. By driving success in key areas and making these achievements known—with humility—we naturally elevate our visibility and recognition. Personal branding is not just about self-promotion; it is about making your hard work and talent known, both within your organisation and beyond. Never underestimate your potential or the talent within your team.

In my 'Digital Marketing & E-commerce Accelerator' course, I learned about a crucial concept in marketing—CTA, or Call to Action. It is about prompting immediate, meaningful action, a tool that drives engagement and results. As I close this chapter, dedicated to my D.A.D., my CTA to readers is clear: Discipline is the cornerstone of success and the tool to achieve your dreams. Never compromise it. Invest in yourself.

Embrace lifelong learning, adapt to change, and lead with determination. Your journey, fuelled by dedication and growth, will not only shape your success but also inspire those around you to reach their potential.

For those who are married or planning to get married, strive to find balance in the multiple roles we play in life—husband, dad, and executive. It is not easy, but by prioritising what truly matters, staying present in each moment, and maintaining a sense of purpose across all areas, we can lead fulfilling lives. The key is not perfection, but intention—dedicating time and energy where it is most needed, and being flexible enough to adapt when life demands it

For all current and future dads, take a moment to reflect on your journey. What changes will you make to be a D.A.D – Disciplined, Adaptable, and Determined? What stories will you share with present and future generations? How do you want to be remembered by them?

As I transition to my next role as a mentor and thought leader in supply chain and logistics, I want to be remembered, not just for my career, but in the future as a doting granddad, sharing stories of my journey to my grandkids —from 'Army Boy' to 'Corporate Executive Globetrotter' to Mentor, Thought Leader, Parent, and Supportive Husband. Your legacy begins with the actions you take today.

Peter Sundara Swamickannu is a distinguished professional serving as the Head of Global Ocean Freight Product within the esteemed Global Logistics division at Visy Industries, a renowned global leader in the packaging, paper, and resource recovery sectors. Focused on delivering high-quality, innovative automation services and sustainable packaging solutions, Visy excels in manufacturing corrugated cardboard boxes, creating specialized printed and non-printed packaging, facilitating wastepaper collection, and operating paper recycling mills. Visy, a global leader in packaging, recycling, and logistics, is dedicated to creating a better world by manufacturing a diverse range of products—including cardboard boxes, water bottles, jam jars, and food and beverage cans—utilising recycled content in all of their operations.

Boasting an impressive 27-year tenure in the container business and logistics realm, Peter Sundara has honed his expertise through roles at prominent global container liners such as P&O Nedlloyd and Maersk Line, as well as leading 3rd Party Logistics companies and Digital Freight Forwarders including Agility Logistics, Flexport, Scan Global Logistics, and LF Logistics. His multifaceted background spans Operations, Commercial, Global Business System Project Management, and Trade Management, with professional engagements in diverse locales such as Australia, Taiwan, Hong Kong, the UK, and Vietnam.

Beyond his profound involvement in the intricacies of the ocean freight supply chain, Peter Sundara also maintains a fervent enthusiasm for technology and digitalization, underscoring his versatile skill set and forward-looking approach to industry trends.

https://www.linkedin.com/in/sundara-sundara-a632502

Chapter 3
Little but Fierce

Cassie Gruber

Fire and Flour: A Feast of Presence

It was below zero Fahrenheit, a hard-core Buffalo winter day in December 2024.

I was happy to be inside and remember my lungs filling with clean air filtered by my bounteous plants, a comforting reminder of life thriving against the cold, as I shifted from a long day in my office to my kitchen heated to 80 degrees by my roaring 700-degree pizza oven. My hands were already like sandpaper from kneading five batches of my 24-hour Neapolitan pizza dough, a delicate process I had mastered over the past few years.

My children and dad joined the "chopping party," as I like to have an array of pizza toppings to arouse and satiate anyone's cravings. As my mother arrived, my son rushed outside with the crunch of snow beneath his boots to help her navigate the icy terrain with her walker. Our three-year-old Siberian husky, Suka, hardly contained himself as he excitedly greeted both my parents.

The air became smoky as my indoor grill range burned off residue and the rhythm of grilling various vegetables and meats took over. I opened the window to cool down as the room temperature neared 90. My kitchen resolved into a chaotic yet soothing environment as I shifted people around on their wheeled ergonomic chairs while tossing hickory wood chips inside the oven, where the magic came to life.

Art was served as a bubbly, airy, crispy crust that encased a delicious chew in the center, all compliments of Italian 00 flour and the combined art and science of an 18-hour bulk fermentation and a 6-hour proof, all at room temperature. The cheese and toppings were charred a bit while masterfully melted together. I switched gears to my gluten-free dedicated space as I continued to hone the shaping of non-gluten dough for my son, who developed celiac a few years ago in his early twenties. Creating a safe and fulfilling food experience for him was and is a heartfelt priority of mine.

The scene unfolded with joy and selflessness. I had recently opened my doors to my ex-husband and the father of my children, openly embracing change and fostering a space where everyone felt welcome in a home filled with good company, dogs, and thriving plants. The evening brimmed with quenched thirst, nurtured taste buds, and full bellies, surrounded by conversation, music, and laughter.

As the night wore on with the soothing sounds of Jack Johnson, my children and I faced the daunting task of cleanup, a lively yet exhausting dance of scrubbing, echoing our day of culinary creation, a celebration of presence and unity. Things weren't always so joyful or harmonious.

The Unscripted Arrival

Some say time is the most precious gift, while others believe the only time that truly matters is now. I entered the world on March 12, 1978, as Cassie Marie Doneza on an Air Force base in Adelanto, California, a desert town poised between the bustling energy of Los Angeles and the vibrant allure of Las Vegas.

My mother, Betsy Brylinski, a first-class airman of Norwegian and Polish descent, served at George Air Force Base in San Bernardino County, a place that has since converted to a prison. My biological father, Byron Doneza, was a proud Filipino, a police officer, and a 10th-degree black belt in Taekwondo. Their story began when Byron and his father, Donald Doneza Sr., a retired Army veteran, taught Taekwondo classes on the base, and from there, the genesis of my journey began.

When I was just two years old, my parents separated, and my mother moved us to Buffalo, New York, where we settled among family. My godmother, Alice, my mother's oldest sister, cared for me while my mother was working. I have distant and fuzzy memories of jumping in puddles with her, and I remember her as joyful in what was my first experience with loss; she was murdered when I was two and a half years old. I cannot imagine the depth of pain, suffering, and loss everyone in my family experienced and lived with, especially my grandparents. Until I was about five, my world was steeped in the warmth of my Filipino relatives and heritage. My grandmother, Mae Doneza, who passed away when I was 11, bragged that I was "flawless," a sentiment she attributed to the "perfectly round" shape of my head.

As I grew, my childhood became eminently shaped by my Buffalo-born and raised grandparents' steadfast faith and values. Their influence left an indelible mark, grounding me in traditions and the strength of community.

The Tender Blueprint: Sketches of a Fearless Heart

I took an interest in astrology as a child, likely around the time my mother converted to paganism, and later, I connected my explorations with metaphysical philosophy.

I've always felt a deep connection to the free-spirited energy of being a Pisces. My slender, limber body moved with ease as I climbed onto the counter at just four years old, learning to prepare meals for myself in a world that often required me to be self-sufficient. My mother, a wild child in her own right, worked long hours, and until I was almost 10, my mornings and evenings were spent in daycare or with babysitters. Yet, even in her absence, the love she gave me was unwavering. My mother and I shared a profound bond; her nurturing affection was immense, as magnetic as she was, and she became both my hero and my most significant influence.

Being an only child, I craved connection with others. When I went to daycare, every day before the children left, I made sure all my classmates had something to remember me by a drawing, no matter how simple, to show my gratitude for just being there and to ensure they left with something special. Even the mischievous ones received a piece of my heart in the form of art. At that age, we were all pure, open-hearted sponges, absorbing love and connection with ease. I never lost the ability to feel and give without barriers; in many ways, I'm still that child. So many people get stuck in their unconscious bias and judgment state of mind; I think I am fortunate that I bridged that pollution gap.

We didn't have much and were often considered part of the lower class, but that never stopped my mom from bringing home something special for me. I spent much of my free time immersed in drawing and creating art, so one of my favorite gifts was an extra-large crayon box with a sharpener built into the back. Even now, I smile, thinking about how magical it felt to have so many vibrant shades cascading down, all paired with the convenience of an embedded sharpener. It was a small luxury, but to me, it was everything.

When I was in first grade, my mother was involved in a tragic motorcycle accident, and we were told she would never walk again. She was thrown 30 feet in the air and shattered part of her spine. I was so scared. I lived with my grandparents for nearly a year, who welcomed me again with open arms. They were adventurers, always ready to hit the road in their creeper van and hitched camper, exploring parks and hidden gems across the United States. I experienced the country's beauty with them, and those memories are forever with me. Having lived through the depression, their meals were often simple but memorable. My grandmother, Betty, cherished her simple yet flavorful American cheese sandwich with banana peppers and Weber's horseradish mustard—a Buffalo staple condiment created in 1922 by Joseph C. Weber and John Heintz. At the same time, my grandfather, Richard, delighted in his classic combination of sliced tomato, Miracle Whip, and cracked black pepper—both lovingly encased by soft, squishy white bread.

As loved as I felt by my grandparents, I was terrified of my grandfather, having seen him lash out at one of my relentlessly misbehaved cousins. All my fear was bundled up in being the best and most polite child for them. I don't think I ever said 'no' to anything and pretended to like and eat everything they put before me. My grandmother occasionally offered to buy me a toy to remind me of how well-behaved I was. Still, I preferred a new pair of shoes.

During that time, my grandparents lured me to church a couple of times a week, which felt strange but comforting at the same time. It's probably why, to this day, I feel a sense of peace whenever I walk into any Catholic church, no matter where it is in the world. They all seem to smell the same; that familiarity brings me back home and makes me feel closer to my grandparents. After months of pain, physical therapy, and weight loss, my mother defied the odds. With a metal rod placed along her spine, she walked again, and she's still walking as I write this—though not without her health challenges.

We didn't have a car for the first couple of years, so my Godfather, John, my mother's youngest brother, one of the most selfless and humble human beings I am lucky to call family, picked us up every day on his way to work so we could use his car. John worked for AM&A's, a retail staple in Buffalo, for over a century until it was phased out in 1994 by the York, Pennsylvania, Bon-Ton stores. My mother and I often perused the basement clearance sections at AM&A's.

Some of my most incredible memories with my mother were in the middle of Buffalo winter at the break of dawn. We would sit bundled up in zero-degree weather inside our beat-up Chevy and sing songs, hoping the engine would start. That was quality time, where we were both present, and I remember it fondly. Even though we needed to get to work or daycare, we laughed and were engrossed in the moment. Looking back, the simplest things in life were the sweetest: the warmth of parental love, a full belly, a way to get from one place to another, and the magic of a writing utensil with something—anything—to scribble on.

By the time I was nine, my mother had remarried, and I was adopted by the man I now proudly call my dad, Ron Gruber, my best friend. But it didn't start that way. At first, I resented the idea of sharing my mom. I wanted it to be just the two of us, as it had always been. As I transitioned to Cassie Marie Gruber, I often found myself in trouble at school for hyphenating my name as Doneza-Gruber—a habit I eventually outgrew.

That changed when we moved into a house with a yard and garage in a nice suburban neighborhood. It felt like a new chapter, full of unfamiliar comforts. My mom and I often clashed like mothers and preteen daughters, but my dad and I grew close. He was passionate about cooking, while my mom preferred the ease of takeout. Slowly, the kitchen became our shared sanctuary. I was drawn to his love for creating meals; he was patient and eager to teach. My dad didn't have patience with everything, a trait I think was shaped by being independent until he was 32. He had never been married before my mom and never had children until he adopted me when I was nine. Those moments in the kitchen weren't just about cooking. They were about immensely connecting and discovering an unconfined, heartfelt space.

Middle school was a challenging chapter in my life. I was often bullied, beaten up, and even jumped by a group of girls who, looking back, were likely grappling with their own insecurities. Instead of confronting their fears, they grouped together, directing their pain toward someone they saw as vulnerable—someone alone. That someone was me.

I learned a concept from Phil Johnson, who I mentioned later, that I've come to understand about people. There are sheep, sheepdogs, and wolves. The sheep, the rarest among us, are the true leaders—calm, confident, and unshaken by chaos. The wolves are like bullies, forming packs not out of love for each other but to amplify their collective energy and prey on the weak. The sheepdogs, representing the majority, stand in the middle, torn between being inspired by the sheep or dragged down by the chaos of the wolves. At that time, I was neither a sheep nor a sheepdog. I was scared, stuck in survival mode, and unsure how to face the wolves.

That all changed the day one of the girls decided to schedule a fight with me. I was terrified. My strength had always come from my mother's, not mine. I tried everything to avoid the confrontation but couldn't escape it. The moment arrived when half the school gathered across the street, forming a tight circle around us. My hands trembled as they made me remove my rings and told me to stand my ground. I was shaking with fear but forced myself to focus on the moment, the now.

The fight began. My hair was pulled, my skin scratched, and I felt the sting of humiliation and pain. But then, something shifted. I threw a punch with all the strength I could muster, and her nose started bleeding. She ran. For the first time, the crowd wasn't mocking me—they were cheering. It felt like a small victory, a glimpse of strength I didn't know I had.

The girl returned for a rematch, but something unexpected happened this time. Almost everyone stood up for me. I didn't have to fight again. That day changed everything. It was a pivotal moment in my youth, a lesson in courage, vigor, and emotional awareness. It's likely why, to this day, I am so sensitive to physical reactions and deeply empathetic toward those who feel powerless. That fight reminded me of my mom; it wasn't just about defending myself, it was about realizing we can overcome our fears.

Bridges Between Worlds: Raw Edges and Bold Strokes

I've always felt the dualities of being a dreamer and a doer, deeply sensitive yet resilient, navigating life with intuition and adaptability. I wasn't an "A" student; math felt like a labyrinth, and reading was a slow and deliberate process. But where I lacked speed, I made up for it with creativity and the joy of working with my hands. In high school, my free-spirited nature drew me to diverse groups of friends, reflecting my need to explore different worlds and personalities. Over time, I gravitated more toward the company of adults with my parents, aunts, and uncles, where conversations carried a depth and wisdom that fascinated me. By senior year, I felt ready to move beyond the chaos and drama of adolescence, eager to step into the next phase of my life.

That same year, I dropped out of high school, entered a relationship with someone much older, and thrived. I felt more mature, and we had a lot of fun going out to nice dinners, seeing live music, spending time in Toronto, Canada, and exploring cooking together. Being around new people in their 30s and older awakened a yearning to grow intellectually and emotionally. I didn't feel unintelligent, yet I recognized a gap in my ability to contribute to the witty conversations around me. This realization drove me to seek wisdom and self-improvement. Despite dropping out of high school, I was determined to continue my education. I earned my GED through a local Catholic college, Villa Maria. I was accepted into their fine arts program, submitting a portfolio reflecting my passion for creativity. Around the same time, I flew across the country to meet my biological father, Byron, and my half-sisters for the first time. It was an emotional whirlwind, equal parts excitement and overwhelm. Still, my goals had to take precedence as classes were set to begin the following week.

Art became my sanctuary and philosophy my compass. One of my greatest moments was giving birth to my first child, my son Tristan, on December 30, 1998. I transferred from Villa Maria to the University at Buffalo (UB) the following year. I spent several years immersed in multimedia art and metaphysical philosophy while bartending to support myself and contribute to my family. Philosophy, like painting, became a medium for self-expression and growth. It taught me to embrace imperfection, to focus on the instance, and to let go of the fear of failure. Each philosophical text I read felt like a bridge between thought and action that helped me navigate life's frustrations.

On the other hand, bartending was where I honed my emotional intelligence. I learned to read people, decode their behaviors, and connect with them on a deeper level. It wasn't just about serving drinks; it was unveiled that we can synchronize in a state of flow and pure connection even in brief moments with almost strangers.

I began to understand the power of presence and the importance of focusing on what I could control. Life, I'd learned, is like a painting. Each stroke represents a moment, and while some strokes can't be undone, you can always layer over them to transform the picture. Not disregarding the previous strokes, as they are part of the journey, I embraced a forward-thinking mindset, focusing on growth and the possibilities ahead rather than basking in the past. Each moment, whether a triumph or a challenge, has been a brushstroke in the broader canvas of my life, adding depth and texture. However, the strokes yet to be painted ignite my imagination and inspire my path forward.

Navigating the Storm: from Canvas to Currency

I always wanted a daughter, and my heart melted on April 8, 2003, when I brought Trinity into this world. By the time Tristan was six, and Trinity was two, life had entered a whirlwind of change. After nearly a decade of balancing art, philosophy, and bartending, I navigated the challenges of divorce and the long, grueling road of family court battles. These experiences shaped my tenacity and deepened my focus on abundance over scarcity, driving me to strive for constant growth. Amidst the upheaval, a printed newspaper ad for an electronics recycling company caught my eye, sparking a new chapter. The job involved refurbishing and dismantling computers and electronics for reuse or recycling, a perfect fit for my geeky and mechanical inclinations. I worked weekends at Electronic Recycling Technologies (ERT) when my children were with their father and quickly excelled, matching or surpassing the output of seasoned employees.

Despite my growing responsibilities, I held onto my artistic roots. My easel stood beside my bed, ready for late nights when sleep eluded me. Painting was still a solace, the dreamy strokes of oil on canvas soothing my restless mind. Eventually, I transitioned to full-time work at ERT and became a managing partner as I expanded sales. My business partner,

Mike Lodick, a brilliant chemist twice my age with a theatrical flair and decades of experience in chemical waste, taught me invaluable lessons. Together, we navigated the challenges of running a small business, often robbing Peter to pay Paul, learning through trial and error what it truly meant to pioneer and persevere.

Mike and I eventually set up shop in Buffalo's historic Wonder Bread factory. This sprawling 180,000-square-foot building once filled the east-side air with the comforting aroma of bread and sweets. The factory held so much promise for our dreams, including creating a top-floor space dedicated to electronic art made from reused materials. Though our business eventually closed its doors in 2010, the lessons learned there propelled me forward in the sustainability, circular economy, and electronics reuse industries. From recovering gold strips from ink cartridges to exploring innovative methods of lead leaching from CRT monitors, each experience shaped my journey at a time when e-waste regulations barely existed. My partner's brilliance and passion left an unforgettable mark, fueling my drive to create and contribute meaningfully to the world. Since Mike's passing, he has always held a special place in my heart and life. I'm forever grateful for him giving me a chance and his trust when I needed someone to believe in me.

Transitioning into corporate America as a single mother with two children was undeniably challenging. However, I approached it with a strategic focus, knowing that my success would be shaped by how I prioritized both my personal life and my work. Thankfully, I started working remotely for a company with whom Mike and I had built trust through prior collaborations, which helped me navigate that transition. While being away from my children was difficult, I focused on making the most impact, beginning with "me," my mindset and dedication.

Working a remote job was a foreign and almost unthinkable concept back then for those around me. Often, my family thought I was doing something mischievous, as I sometimes had evening or weekend meetings. However, it proved invaluable when my grandfather was overcome by Dementia, and my grandmother needed help. My mom and her siblings all worked full time, yet I could bring my work to my grandparents and enjoy lunch with them while keeping an eye out. My grandmother and I cherished our conversations at the kitchen table, where warmth and wisdom flowed alongside the aroma of a simmering pot of soup. I remember how she believed my boyfriend had secured my impressive job, unable to envision a woman achieving success on her own. Both my grandparents passed away in mid to late 2012—I miss them often.

My desire for cultural exposure and international experiences tremendously influenced my decisions in the first few years post-divorce. I traveled whenever possible, often maintaining long-distance relationships since my work was portable. I planned my travels, as best I could, outside my scheduled time with my children. When my children were with me, I worked long, focused days—10 hours of dedication. My parents were instrumental in helping with childcare, allowing me to complete my tasks. When they were with their father, I pushed myself to work 16-hour days, eating at my desk and only taking breaks to exercise. Little did I know, I was building a brand, a trusting network, something priceless, driven mainly by feelings and connections to others.

As my dad at times struggled with inconveniences, he was always there and would do anything to help. My mother was often stubborn and liked to be the center of attention, likely stemming from being the middle child of five. She also felt that others and the world around her should embrace her beliefs. She was obsessed with many fad trends, especially those around body, nutrition, diet, etc. I remember learning a lot from her about the blood type diets, Atkins, Dr. Oz. and so on. My mom was vegetarian, vegan, and this and that, often changing her stance. She despises onions, still doesn't like them to this day and has since eased up. Sometimes, she would cause a scene at a family gathering and storm out if someone accidentally added onions to a dish. I often prepared three meal versions, one that was spicy for myself and others, another that didn't include onions or meat, and a non-spicy version for the children. My genesis built a path at a very young age paved by giving, sharing, and nurturing.

In those early remote working days, I worried about measuring success. I began tracking every minute, even noting bathroom breaks in a small book, as one thing I could measure was time. Evolving from crayons and any surface to scribble, I realized that I could accomplish anything with a mobile phone, laptop, pen, and pad. As I gained confidence in my role, I learned to establish trust over the phone long before video conferencing became a thing. One toolbox essential I had by my nightstand since 2005 was *The Power of Now* by Eckhart Tolle. This book helped me navigate challenging divorce battles and daily obstacles. I could open it at any moment, read a single paragraph, and instantly feel grounded, with a clearer perspective on the now. While I had come far, I knew there was always more to learn, and I remained committed to evolving with each challenge.

Since childhood, I have wanted to be a teacher. I envisioned becoming a professor, teaching an interdisciplinary curriculum that blended art, philosophy, and perhaps even science. I've explored a variety of media throughout my artistic journey, but one of my later projects was particularly memorable. Together with my partner, Paul Visco, a Master of Fine Arts (MFA) student, we designed an interactive clothing line called FiveV, powered by a simple 5-volt battery. The concept was born from energy physics—the idea that all things, even inanimate objects, interact and respond to energy in their environment. We sourced jackets from a thrift store, each with a unique style. The male piece was a classic suit jacket, while the female jacket was a slim, ¾ length pleather with faux fur accents. Our logo, a small circuit board, lit up to showcase the FiveV brand. We programmed the jackets to respond to one another in close proximity: the male jacket held the circuit board and chip, while the female jacket featured vibrating motors in the fur and lights along the lining, connected by a wired earbud headset. The closer the proximity, the more the lights, sound, and vibrations would intensify. When both male and female desired calmness, they naturally distanced themselves. However, they gravitated toward each other when they sought overwhelming intensity, finding a harmonious balance. But if neither was on the same wavelength, it could lead to a constant tug-of-war, with one pulling away while the other pushing, creating a cycle of discord.

I loved the idea of creating environments where people could connect, explore, and bond—much like how I approach life, my career, and relationships. An organization, a family, or any group of people is nothing without the individuals who make it up. While I understand that anyone can be replaced in theory, no one can truly be replicated. Each person is unique, and authenticity is irreplaceable. Looking back, every organization I departed stemmed from a misalignment between what I aspired to achieve for the company and the priorities of the key stakeholders.

My final artwork was an interactive room that I built using raw materials, much of it sourced from second-hand shops or repurposed from things around me. The slim and tall but long structure was predominantly wooden portraying confinement. The floor was made of plexiglass, beneath which I placed old clothing and strands of my first long haircut, pressed underneath to symbolize my sense of oppression. To enter, one had to squeeze through a slit in the middle of a stretched piece of roofing rubber. The structure was twelve feet long, with one side standing ten feet high and the other eight feet high. There was no roof—open to the sky, it symbolized the freedom that lay above and beyond.

Inside, the walls had a flushed television monitor at the back and sound speakers along the sides. I recorded several videos of myself and the natural sounds I often made, capturing my internal dialogue. I placed activity sensors around the plexiglass floor. The video and sound would amplify depending on the movement inside the structure. The more activity, the more intense the response. I never gave the piece a title, but those who experienced it shared different interpretations. Some found it calming, while others felt a sense of anxiety. A few described it as womb-like or likened it to a uterus, representing both a space of confinement and potential.

My desire to travel brought me throughout the U.S., Toronto, Canada, and I finally made my first trip from North America to London, United Kingdom. One of my first serious and impactful relationships was with Michael, who was also much older than me. Michael, an earth sign from the Taurus zodiac, an incredibly dependable and loyal partner, grounded me. Yet, the exposure shaped my sense of self and creative energy. Michael was deeply rooted in classic rock, a gifted musician, and an entertainment lawyer. As a child, he grew up obnoxiously playing his drums surrounded by posters of Ian Gillian from Deep Purple on his walls. Michael dreamed of meeting Ian, and his parents chuckled a sort of "white man can't jump" philosophy. But that never stopped him. He eventually met Ian, became the manager of the Ian Gillian Band, and today is one of his closest friends. Michael's encouragement was one of the first I had experienced that anything is possible. I had the opportunity alongside Michael to meet several famous artists, including Ian Gillan, Judas Priest, and the Scorpions. In fact, in 2005, I had the incredible experience of seeing all three acts perform live at the Royal Albert Hall in London as part of Roger Daltrey's Teenage Cancer Trust. This unforgettable event added another layer of inspiration to my journey. Michael and I eventually went on different paths but always kept in touch, and now we are great friends.

Maturing Tides: Taming the Fire Within

After closing the doors of ERT in 2010, my first job was with a private North American aftermarket imaging supplies company focused on remanufacturing ink and toner cartridges. This was the next stepping stone that launched my career, marking the beginning of a wave of success. The company, Clover Environmental Technologies, was and still is Headquartered outside Chicago, Illinois, with an office in Mississauga, Canada, I often found myself in Toronto. I ventured into a new market within the electronic recycling and IT Asset Disposition (ITAD) industry. I gained a 60% market share in less than two years and grew sales 86% year-over-year. I often found myself swimming between a world of fantasy and reality, especially in my younger years. Having success and the money that came with it inflated my ego, leading me to set unrealistic expectations for those who supported me. With my mind racing ahead, driven by an insatiable desire to progress, my communication often became abrupt and overly direct—rooted in brutal honesty but lacking the tact and consideration to meet others where they were. This was a newly surfaced behavior of mine; born from my relentless drive and the pressure I placed on myself to always move forward. While I achieved much, I eventually realized that I could have communicated with greater compassion and honesty.

Spending time in a pedestrian-friendly international city, I embraced the joy of cycling to meetings and running errands. Exercise became a lifestyle, especially after gaining almost 70 pounds during my first pregnancy. I was always athletic, having played volleyball and track in high school. As my children grew, I turned to running, cycling, and spin classes. The endorphin high I got from exercise became something I craved daily, helping me manage stress and stay focused. Nutrition also became a priority; I focused on fueling my family's bodies with the proper nutrients, minerals, and vitamins. I spent over an hour each day on my scheduled time prepping my children's lunches, ensuring they had balanced, wholesome meals. I became a student of nutrition. I firmly believe how we fuel our bodies and minds shapes who we are and who we become. Thankfully, my lack of a sweet tooth helped me maintain a healthier diet for myself and my family.

During that time, I met Burke through a mutual friend from Buffalo. He happened to live in Toronto, was Canadian, and studied and taught art at UB. We both shared a free-spirited outlook and a passion for creativity. He was empathetic and had very high levels of emotional intelligence, and we were deeply connected. Shared travel desires sparked, and I finally reached New York City (NYC), just a six-hour drive from Buffalo. My friends used to joke that I would be banned if I didn't visit NYC by the time I turned 30. During our trip, Burke and I attended a grand wedding where I had the chance to meet and sit near Michael Kors and Heidi Klum. It's always cool to meet famous people, but it's even more special when you get to spend time with them and connect as equals, as human beings. Though Burke and I ended that side of our relationship, we are forever close friends.

My first trip to Mexico was with Clover in November 2010. We attended a sales summit at a Cancun resort, where we celebrated reaching the billion-dollar milestone. At the start of my career, I was heavily influenced by an "A" student who was highly intellectual. However, this part of my journey was quite different—working for a couple guys who had barely made it out of the University of Illinois, both "C" students. This shift was eye-opening and motivating in ways I hadn't expected. I realized that a brilliant mind and vigorous intellect, like those of an "A" student, can often be held back by the subconscious.

On the other hand, "C" students who combined creativity and forward-thinking had the ability to focus on problem-solving and solutions, propelling them forward. During this time, I witnessed the exceptional leadership of Jim Cerkleski, the CEO (and now Executive Chairman), and Eric Martin, President of Clover Imaging Group and Clover Environmental Technologies. In just eight years, they grew a two-million-dollar company into a billion-dollar powerhouse—"C" students hiring "A" students. That's right, the very same two guys who started out selling imaging supplies from the trunks of their cars. And the same two guys who, years later, landed in their private jet to visit Mike and me at our Buffalo recycling business. The contrast was striking, a testament to how far they had come, yet their entrepreneurial spirit and drive remained unmistakable.

Twenty years ago, the electronics recycling industry—and higher-ranking business roles within it—was predominantly a man's world. Women were few and far between. Early in my career, I was often the only woman in the room. Adapting to my surroundings came naturally, even in environments primarily filled with men. I also discovered ways to enhance that by wearing full suits, minus the tie, during business engagements. That decision made me feel comfortable and confident, embodying an aura that matched the professional world around me. However, finding women's dress shirts that buttoned from top to bottom was incredibly frustrating—most had openings near the chest, which felt impractical and inappropriate.

I frequently traveled alone for work, and while unfamiliar at first, those individual experiences gradually built my confidence, eventually leading me to embrace solo travel—even for leisure, exploring new countries on my own. Something I admired about Michael was that he often traveled internationally. I recall his trip to Kuala Lumpur; I was enamored by the idea of traveling to such a distant, breathtaking place.

Over time, the e-waste and ITAD industry regenerated into a community of great friendships, some of which felt like family. Walking into a room rarely meant exchanging formal handshakes; instead, it brought warm hugs and joyful conversations about family and life. As a young woman traveling unattended each year to the E-Scrap conference, my confidence carried me. Still, my elusive, childlike spirit often ran wild. I was fortunate to build a vast network of industry professionals and companies who looked out for me—a support system I never sought but am deeply grateful for when I reflect on those moments.

Later, some of my customers shared that they thought I was the owner of Clover. No discredit was intended to Jim or any of the other leaders, but the question and impression reflected the unique role I played. The new market I had opened and nurtured was somewhat siloed in the beginning, and I operated as a kind of one-woman show, building and nourishing it from the ground up.

Looking back and reflecting on where I stand today, I projected the early characteristics of a concept called Horizontal Leadership. Ron Ashkenas introduced Horizontal Leadership, *Your Career Needs to Be Horizontal*, Harvard Business Review, March 27, 2012. Titles and traditional career growth had never consumed me; in fact, the pursuit of such things sometimes felt elusive. I focused on what drove purpose and meaning, ensuring I remained connected to my personal definition of success—being and feeling truly fulfilled.

At around 33, I had an epiphany—life felt incredibly sweet. My career was thriving, and I found myself eagerly anticipating the wisdom that would come with turning 40. It wasn't that I was rushing time. Still, I truly believed that my early desire to contribute to conversations had evolved into a drive to make a real impact and be the best version of myself.

During this period, I had the opportunity to travel further across the

United States for conferences in Las Vegas, Nevada; Orlando, Florida; and New Orleans, Louisiana. New Orleans quickly became one of my favorite destinations, mainly because of its vibrant food scene and dynamic atmosphere. However, despite the excitement of these cities, I didn't take the time to personally enjoy them. With my children still young, I was laser-focused on execution and success, always striving to balance my professional ambitions with spending quality time with my family.

A few years later, I was offered an exciting opportunity from a competitor that aligned with my passion—leading sustainability strategy and program management, global business and customer engagement, innovation, and new market development. My career began in 2005, working for a small business where I became a partner. In 2010, I transitioned to corporate America as a Business Development Manager. By 2014, I had advanced to Vice President of Sustainability at a public European company, following my time as Director of Compliance at The Turbon Group. My enthusiasm and relentless motivation have propelled me to strive for excellence and transformation in every career step. Although my career values were not rooted in traditional corporate ladder, the leaders around me recognized the importance of aligning appropriate titles with responsibilities that resonated with my principles. This alignment honored both my contributions and my commitment to purpose-driven work.

At the heart of the philosophy that drives me is a commitment to authenticity, integrity, trust, and equality. I almost always could connect with people, regardless of their role or background, and earned trust quickly. This wasn't a strategy I consciously employed. Still, a tool kit somehow picked up along the way, which helped me communicate openly and equally with everyone. Treating others respectfully and without bias allowed me to break through barriers, recognizing that influence can be found at all levels. These commitments helped pave the way for long-lasting relationships built on mutual respect.

This approach empowered me at Turbon to lead purposefully as the Director of Compliance, overseeing operations, environmental, health, and safety (EHS). Under my leadership, we launched a new division that grew revenue by 50%, and in just a few months, I led the certification against three different standards for a 100,000-square-foot facility. By the beginning of my second year, my efforts tripled our sales and drove significant growth within our U.S. division. This experience reinforced my mantra that anything is possible when you lead with integrity, trust, and authenticity.

The Art of Pesto: A Ritual of Patience and Passion

It was early spring of 2013—the first truly warm day after months of Buffalo's icy grip when the air finally carried the scent of melting snow and damp earth. The kitchen windows, cracked just enough to invite in the crisp breeze, let sunlight dance across my counters, where vibrant greens lay in abundance. Basil leaves, freshly sourced from Guercio's Italian Market in Buffalo, spilled across the surface, their sweet, peppery perfume weaving through the room. Nearby, garlic cloves rested in their papery skins, lemon halves glistened with their bright acidity, and a small pool of golden olive oil reflected the light. Pine nuts waited patiently, ready to release their nutty flavor into the mixture next to a mound of salty shaved Pecorino Romano to bring it all together. As I settled into the rhythmic ritual of chopping and blending, the weight of the day lifted, dissolving into the intoxicating aroma of creation.

This wasn't just about making pesto. Cooking had long been my dad's sacred ritual, where patience was both the method and the reward. "Take your time, Cassie, and let the ingredients teach you," he would say as I accompanied his mastery when I was younger. As I crushed the garlic with the back of my knife, I began leading the kitchen, just as he once guided me. To this day, the kitchen is where he finds peace, a space where time slows, and life's imbalances cannot intrude.

From my preface, you might think pizza is my signature dish—but there is one recipe that holds my soul: my pesto. A six to eight-hour symphony of patience and precision, where pesto is merely the star of an intricate, layered masterpiece. Radiant green swirls painted my bright white square plates, cradling a decadent heap of penne. Above it, raw shrimp, bathed in cast-iron heat, curled into tender perfection after just minutes in a pan infused with hours of slow-simmered garlic, sliced shallots, and fiery Fresno peppers. Cherry tomatoes, bursting with sweetness, nestled between roasted walnuts, their smoky richness lending depth to every bite. Fresh basil, parsley, and cilantro showered over the dish, their vibrance only rivaled by the generous snowfall of aged Parmesan Reggiano and Pecorino Romano, each strand melting softly into the warm layers below. A final touch—Celtic sea salt, scattered with precision, its delicate crunch unlocking the last dimension of flavor.

Later that evening, friends, family, and animals gathered around the table, ravenous from the aromas and sight of the bright, rich, and intoxicatingly layered entrees. Conversation slowed, laughter softened, as each forkful delivered something beyond taste: nostalgia, comfort, connection. It was a dish that did more than satisfy hunger—it wove us together, moment by moment, bite by bite. That night, as the last drop of wine kissed the rims of our glasses and the hum of contentment filled the room, I realized that food is not just sustenance. It is healing. It is love. It is an unspoken language that binds us, reminding us that some of life's most profound connections are revealed in the simplest of moments, at the warmth of the table.

Fragments and Foundations: The Alchemy of Reinvention

In 2015 I decided to tie up loose ends, earning the final few math credits to complete my Bachelor of Fine Arts (BFA) degree. By that point in my career, a degree wasn't required, but there was a sense of completion and commitment to myself, even though it was ten years later. I had spent nearly a decade in college, adoring exploring boundless imaginations, and studying whatever deeply inspired me. Along the way, choices I made, combined with unforeseen circumstances, deprioritized completing my degree in 2005, reflecting a focus on survival and career exploration over finality.

Around this time began an extremely challenging five years with Tristan when he was about 17. I learned hard lessons on effective communication with teenagers. I had previously dived into *The Five Love Languages*, a solid and worthy read by Gary Chapman. So, I purchased *The Five Love Languages for Teenagers*, also by Gary Chapman, which helped ground me and navigate my future conversations based on my son's personality (his love languages) and focused on following through with my words and actions. All the while, I realized I had to change my parenting skills, which was not an easy task, let alone attempting in later parenting years. I had taken a carefree approach to raising my children. I probably spoiled them with very few rules, likely a crutch I built from the guilt of divorce combined with how my mother raised me. As tough as it was at times (for him and me), we reached a healthier relationship built on love, trust and respect without sacrificing rules and accountability.

That summer I also started building a relationship with my biological family and father, embracing the belief that there is no better time than now to explore the other half of my identity and forge a connection. Letting go of everything I had heard growing up about why my father wasn't part of my life allowed me to approach this bond with openness and presence. Whenever I traveled out west or to California, I prioritized making time to see Byron and get to know one another. The early years were a foundation, but it wasn't until the final years of his life that we truly intertwined. Spending time with my aunt and him, particularly cooking together, awakened me to the power of DNA—how deeply ingrained traits and passions can surface. I realized my natural instinct to nurture through food was deeply rooted in this side of my heritage, despite not being raised by them since I was five. Yet, it was my dad, Ron, who truly shaped my love for cooking and exploration in the kitchen. Through my biological father, adoptive father (both Sagittarius fire signs), and mother, I gained a fusion of traits—creativity and sensitivity intertwined with exceptional intuition and empathy, balanced by a fiery directness, boundless energy, unshakable confidence, and an infectious enthusiasm for life.

However, there was still room for more change. In late 2015 Turbon decided to scale back its U.S. operations and focus on Europe, which led to the closure of our division and the layoff of my team and me. This change was entirely out of my control, but I was determined to make the most of it. Having already worked for the two largest aftermarket imaging supplies companies, I saw this as an opportunity to pivot and explore a new industry. Through my network, I discovered an innovative Dallas-based company employing roughly 50 people. They specialized in refurbishing LCDs for iPhones and Samsung devices, with a unique approach to repurposing shaved glass for future LCD manufacturing. Intrigued by their vision, I had a few conversations with their CEO. I later took a position as Vice President of Business Development at Re-LCD.

At first, I spent a few days every other week in Dallas. The transition became significant as I later spent half my time away, developing a second life with its own condo, vehicle, and relationships while maintaining my home base in Buffalo. The common theme at Re-LCD was that we were better together, and the business thrived when I was in the office. That is when I met Kristian, who lived in Plano, TX, where he and I began a long-distance relationship. His Virgo traits complemented mine, with a touch of perfectionism and a logical and systematic approach to life. As my children grew older, I embraced frequent travel, as much as possible during their time with their father and focused on building something meaningful in this new industry. It wasn't an easy start—six months in, I was told things weren't working out. That conversation with the CEO and CFO became a turning point. I shifted my strategy, recognizing that our current market approach and reliance on my existing network weren't yielding results. Starting from scratch, I built new relationships across mobile carriers and their partner networks, focusing on understanding their needs and fostering trust.

I've always tried to turn my setbacks into success. I brought in a game-changing program, tapped into a new market, and was responsible for most of the company's revenue in under three years. Beyond the numbers, I found immense value in the relationships I built—relationships that remain strong today. This experience reinforced the importance of adaptability, relationship-building, and viewing challenges as opportunities for transformation and growth.

Kristian often liked to share small things, but with big rewards and that was one meaningful reason, for me, he and I entered a relationship. It brought me back to my childhood with my mom and the "messy space" with my children (more on the "messy space" later). One was Success Stories on CDs—yes, those were a thing, and vehicles still came equipped with CD players back then. These short, 30-minute interviews, perfect for a drive on route to a customer meeting or appointment, would always end with the question, "How do you define success?" Some of the most memorable responses came from Jocko Willink, Mel Robbins, Gretchen Rubin, Tony Robbins, and Megyn Kelly. Megyn and I had a shared perspective defining success as "being, feeling fulfilled." Fulfillment can mean different things to different people. Still, for me, it's about finding that delicate balance that brings both peace and purpose.

Studies show, the healthiest people who live the longest prioritize eating vegetables, while the happiest cultivate meaningful relationships, not that the two are mutually exclusive. In my observation, the most successful people, don't let failures or lessons learned hold them back. They embrace challenges with resilience and maintain forward-thinking perspectives, often embodying the spirit of "C" students I wrote about earlier—those who break free from conventional molds to innovate and create, much like Thomas Edison, Henry Ford, Walt Disney, Richard Branson, and Steve Jobs. These trailblazers didn't necessarily excel in traditional academic settings, but their unconventional paths led to groundbreaking achievements. Consider figures like Bill Gates and Steve Jobs; their journeys are marked by setbacks, pivots, and relentless perseverance. Success is rarely a straight line—it's about adapting, learning, and continuously striving for improvement, even when the road gets rough. Steve Jobs and Albert Einstein exemplified the depth of visionary thinking, imaginative creativity, and interconnectedness that are hallmarks of Pisces, channeling their dreamy natures into divergent legacies.

In 2017, I finally understood the value of taking time off and fully disconnecting from work, something I had never done before. In the past, I'd work through vacations, answering emails and taking calls. This time, I made a promise to myself to truly step away. In November, I decided to take my dad, who was nearing retirement, anywhere in the world he wanted to go. I expected him to choose a destination in Germany due to his heritage. Still, I was surprised when he chose Italy. We explored Rome, Florence, and Venice, each offering its own charm, but Rome captured my heart. The vibrant energy, the chaos, and the pedestrian-friendly atmosphere reminded me of New York City. This brought me back to times with Burke, and in fact, there was a bicycle nestled in a rack near a café I was enjoying a glass of wine at that looked identical to the one Burke had renovated for me years back that I had put many miles on in Toronto.

Walking through the Colosseum in Rome was an experience beyond imagination—remarkable and humbling as if stepping back in ancient times. St. Peter's Cathedral, illuminated at night, was nothing short of breathtaking, its grandeur leaving an indelible mark on my memory. I was consumed with memories of my grandparents as my senses lured many magnificent Catholic churches. The Sistine Chapel, with its awe-inspiring frescoes, was a masterpiece I could have admired endlessly, captivated by the intricate details adorning its walls and ceiling. Witnessing the statue of David in Florence felt like receiving an extravagant gift from history, while standing before the Mona Lisa was a surreal moment, her enigmatic gaze evoking a quiet reverence for art's timeless allure.

The food alone is reason enough to return to Europe often, where meals are crafted fresh daily, free from the mass production, genetic modification, and pesticides so prevalent in the U.S. Carbohydrates take on a whole new meaning there—nourishing and wholesome, made from fresh grains and flours that are easier to digest. After experiencing the joy of handmade pasta, I could never return to boxed varieties. The incredible difference of fresh pasta was one of the many lessons I took home from that trip—simple to make, yet infinitely more satisfying.

The following year, I set out on a long-awaited trip to Asia with Kristian. After experiencing the organized chaos of Hong Kong and its impressive efficiency, we ventured to Bangkok, Thailand, where the cuisine was a delightful assault on the senses. I also had the opportunity to attend an innovative circular economy roundtable in Singapore, Malaysia, hosted by a major brand. One evening, I stood atop the towering 1-Altitude building, the highest alfresco bar in the world, taking in the stunning panoramic view of Singapore's city and port, lit up and inviting under the night sky. I enjoyed Hong Kong equally with Thailand and would revisit both.

Being a foodie, I'll try just about anything, and my culinary adventures have included goat brains, bull testicles, lamb thymus, cow intestines, liver, heart, frog legs, chicken feet, turtle soup, snails of all sorts, and countless treasures from the sea. However, one experience I dare not repeat is the infamous thousand-year egg. This Asian delicacy, buried raw for months or even years, undergoes a metamorphosis that challenges even the most adventurous palate. The once-clear egg white turns a gelatinous dark green on the outside, transitioning to black, chalky textures in the middle, with the occasional burst of orange ooze from the center. I made the mistake of confusing its unique textures with flavor, only to find my senses overwhelmed and my stomach queasy. Once was enough for that daring experiment!

The Fire and the Phoenix: Rising from the Depths

As I approached the fourth decade of my life, I eagerly anticipated the growth and wisdom I had accumulated. It felt like a significant milestone, one that held the promise of deeper understanding and new opportunities for both personal and professional transformation. I had big plans to celebrate my 40th on a solo journey to Northern Italy for a week-long co-ed cycling trip, where I would embrace adventure and new relationships alongside a private chef and plenty of wine.

At the same time, my mom and I were planning our own 1:1 world trip, much like I had done with my dad. She had chosen Norway, inspired by a large connection to her mother's heritage. But three months before my birthday, life threw us a curveball. My mom and daughter had been enjoying a manicure together, a treat I had given them when I received an urgent call. My mom's blood pressure was dangerously high, and we feared a stroke. At the Buffalo General Hospital cardiac and vascular care center, we learned it wasn't a stroke or heart attack, but a 5mm aneurysm in her brain, with a growth attached. The neurosurgeon laid out two options: monitoring it or surgery. We opted for surgery, which began as a small incision but turned into a much more complex procedure, with nearly half her skull being opened. The weeks that followed were filled with uncertainty as she spent time in ICU.

During that time, I chose to shield her from visitors. I was terrified, yet immensely proud of my mom—the true hero in my life. She was just 65 at the time. That experience brought me closer to the present moment, deepened my strength, and reinforced my commitment to family. It reminded me of how fragile life can be and how my dreams can shift unexpectedly, no matter how well-planned. Following, I took four weeks off work to care for her, knowing that in those moments, nothing mattered more than giving 100% to my mom, as we both navigated through this challenging chapter.

In place of celebrating my birthday cycling through Northern Italy, Kristian surprised me with an unforgettable gift: a journey to Mexico City to see Depeche Mode live in an enormous, historic soccer stadium. The experience was electrifying, with the band's energy perfectly matched by the city's vibrant spirit. Mexico City's architecture and layered history were nothing short of explosive, offering a fascinating blend of ancient and modern influences. And the food—the tacos! Every bite was mouthwatering, complemented perfectly by smooth, rich tequila. It was also where I tried ants for the first time, seasoned with corn and herbs. To my surprise, that crunchy, flavorful dish was absolutely delicious—a culinary adventure I won't soon forget.

In 2018, I was approached by a business unit director running a pioneering division focused on environmental innovation and circular economy at one of the largest public contract manufacturers. Jabil was founded in 1966 by James and Bill. Their story echoed that of Jim and Eric who took Clover from humble beginnings to a formidable force. James and Bill began a printed circuit board assembly (PCBA) business out of their homes in Detroit, Michigan, the company went public in 1993 and in fiscal year 2023, Jabil earned almost $35 billion USD.

After numerous meetings and interviews, I decided to plunge into the global manufacturing world, a new field that I felt aligned with my values and experience. I was inspired by their unique approach to a particular technology, where I saw an opportunity to thrive, leveraging my network, relationships, and the service mindset I carried with me. Had Re-LCD made me a partnership offer, I might not have taken the role at Jabil, but I am glad that didn't happen. Looking back, I do not share the same vision and values as they did.

On April 9, 2018, I took on the Director of Business Development role within Jabil's Environmental Technologies Business Unit. Not long after, a senior leader, who eventually became an officer of Jabil, took me under his wing, helping me navigate Jabil's vast global leadership. Through Roberto Ferri's mentorship, I was connected with a wealth of talent, intellect, and diverse perspectives spanning multiple industries. I learned the art of cross-functional collaboration, which proved invaluable as I later moved on to report directly to Roberto, Chief Sales, Marketing, Communications, and Strategy Officer, in a role developing our Circular Economy initiatives and new business development.

Roberto's influence extended far beyond guidance; it was transposing. He introduced me to a web of cultures, personalities, and industries, embodying a unique charisma that effortlessly connected people. As one of the most skilled negotiators I've encountered, Roberto taught me the art of finding common ground while achieving strategic goals. Under his mentorship, I honed my ability to cooperate effectively and navigate

Jabil's varying and dynamic personalities, profoundly shaping my leadership approach.

Settling in at Jabil, I felt empowered to make an impact centered at the heart of where ideas turn to design, where innovation runs wild, yielding sustainable manufacturing practices with technology that changes lives. A place where both "C" and "A" students thrive amid a chaotic yet, at times, calming world, there was no better place or time to lead circular change.

Another deeply impactful relationship in my career was with Jozsef Kocsis. At the time, he was a Senior Business Unit Director at Jabil, whom I reported to for a brief but altering period. Leading a Business Unit comes with immense pressure—managing business continuity, profit and loss, and customer satisfaction, all while driving growth. Despite these demands, Jozsef excelled, particularly in optimizing existing customer relationships and uncovering tremendous layers of value. Born and raised in Hungary, he brought a pragmatic and results-driven perspective that complemented my own.

Our dynamic was one of learning and growth. As I shared insights from my industry expertise, Jozsef offered me a critical lesson in return—one that stung at first but ultimately reshaped my approach. His feedback illuminated the limits of relying heavily on optimism, positivity, and confidence to drive results. He reminded me of the importance of pairing my vision with data, grounding my ideas in evidence to build stronger, more credible propositions.

Jozsef's critique, though direct, was constructive and transformative. It reminded me of the balance between intuition and analysis, a principle I had known but perhaps lost sight of. By integrating his guidance, I strengthened my professional approach. I gained a deeper appreciation for the value of constructive criticism when delivered effectively. For that, I remain extremely grateful for the exposure and experience he provided.

The Reawakening: Finding Clarity in the Chaos

A daunting, somber cloud floated above me for months. I felt like a foreigner in my own skin, lashing out at the world and those around me while quietly tearing myself apart inside. Almost every ounce of energy was consumed by pain and fear. I had endured some traumatizing experiences in my past—situations others believed would break me—but I had always found a way to conquer them. Yet, here I was, lost in unfamiliar territory.

In March 2020, I had recently embarked on a business venture outside my continuing role at Jabil. Suleman Bhimani and I met at Re-LCD and later founded Mobiletheory. The plan was for me to work in the background, leveraging my relationships and knowledge without becoming involved in daily operations. But things didn't unfold as planned. Instead, I found myself deeply entrenched in nearly every aspect of the business, including the harsh realities of operations. What started as stress quickly turned into burnout. Building something from the ground up requires focus and dedication. While I respected my partner Suleman, a self-made and very successful entrepreneur, I hadn't agreed to take on such a consuming role. To be fair, neither of us could have predicted how things would evolve, and we did our best under the circumstances. Less than a year later, we amicably dissolved the business and remain good friends.

Compounding my stress was a health issue that further strained my state of mind. All while navigating a long-distance relationship with Kristian. We had often talked about making Dallas my new home base once Trinity graduated high school, especially to escape Buffalo's brutal winters. But the combination of personal struggles, professional burnout, and the pressures of maintaining a relationship began to take its toll.

While optimism is second nature to me, even that couldn't shield me from the darkness of 2020. The global pandemic brought uncertainty, isolation, and fear, amplifying the weight I was already carrying. For the first time, I glimpsed what I imagined depression to feel like. The bright days couldn't lift the heavy cloud I carried. This wasn't a string of bad days or something a good night's sleep could fix. It was deeper.

I began questioning every relationship in my life, assigning blame to those closest to me for my pain. I became bitter and resentful, unable to see past the storm. I poured my energy into maintaining composure for my responsibilities at Jabil. Still, at home, I was easily triggered, especially with family.

To cope, I sought escape. I hadn't actively watched television since I was about 20. Suddenly, I was consumed by reality shows and make-believe stories on Netflix. I spent hours each day in front of the screen, obsessed with distractions.

That's when I discovered Phil Johnson and his Master of Business Leadership (MBL) program. His connection to others previously at Jabil piqued my interest. After learning about his approach, I decided to take a leap of faith. Enrolling in the rigorous five-month program was the best investment I've ever made in myself. It wasn't just a course it was a life-changing experience. Through emotional labor, commitment, and a willingness to change, I unearthed a version of myself I hadn't seen in decades. I felt like the free, curious, and hopeful child I once was, but with the wisdom and strength of a woman in her forties.

The MBL program gave me the tools to refine my emotional intelligence and develop sustainable habits. It taught me how to approach life with a clearer mind and a more open heart. I learned how to harness my energy, channel it toward my goals, and create a more balanced, fulfilling life. While business engagements always came more naturally to me, my relationships with family and close friends—those who knew how to push my buttons—required intentional work. Yet, the journey wasn't about perfection but rather consistent growth. Every day brought new challenges. Through journaling discoveries on earning and burning trust and using both sides of my brain to identify how I felt and what I learned, I approached each day with the commitment to being the best version of myself.

Happiness wasn't something external but something I had to create for myself. As I reconnected with the present, I found unexpected peace in the place I longed to retreat—Buffalo. The pandemic forced me to confront my environment, and in doing so, I rediscovered the strength, love, and support of my family, friends, and furry ones. I no longer felt a strong desire to leave, ultimately leading to a shift in Kristian and my relationship. In time, we became terrific friends. His financial advisory business keeps my family and me frequently connected.

Through these challenges, I learned to embrace stillness and rediscover joy in the simple things I knew were some of the most fulfilling. It wasn't an easy journey, but it was one of notable growth, allowing me to emerge stronger, more grounded, and more connected to the life I once knew which had been missing. As I nurtured myself, I again found solace in fostering the life around me. What began as a few resilient plants soon flourished into an ever-growing tropical indoor jungle, creating a peaceful yet thriving environment. Their existence mirrored my evolution, reminding me that growth happens in layers, seasons, and sometimes in ways we don't immediately see.

Lessons in Green: Growth, Stillness, and Being

There's a sacred hour in my home when the world is still asleep. It's when I wander barefoot throughout my sunlit office, a cup of tea in hand, and greet my plants. Each one has its place: the fiddle leaf fig in the corner, stubbornly slow to grow; the pothos spilling over the edge of its shelf, ever wild and abundant; and the succulents, buoyant and steadfast, despite their arid roots.

Tending to them feels like meditation. I mist their leaves, rotate their pots toward the light, and check their soil with the kind of care I often forget to give myself. Some mornings, I talk to them—thanking them for purifying the air, for their beauty and quiet companionship. It's funny, I think, how plants mirror life. The fiddle leaf's struggle reminds me of times when growth felt painfully slow yet steady. The pothos reminds me to embrace abundance when it comes. And the succulents remind me that sometimes, you thrive by needing less.

I return to this ritual when I feel lost and when life feels overwhelming. In the quiet company of my plants, I find clarity. Their gentle and patient growth reminds me that resilience doesn't have to be loud or grand—it can simply be the act of continuing, day by day, reaching for the light. My tropical forest is a testament to one of the pandemic's most unexpected yet beautiful outcomes. What began as a simple way to bring life into my home evolved into a deep, almost meditative connection with nature—one that grounds me daily.

Ripples of Influence: A Legacy of Presence

 2020 not only reshaped my life but inspired me to help others. I've learned that changing your habits changes your perspective, responses, and behaviors. By completing the MBL program, I gained clarity and a renewed sense of purpose. I felt I had gained more time in the same 24 hours we all share, focusing on what truly matters to me—my goals, relationships, and well-being. Most importantly, I stopped absorbing the drama and chaos of others and let my energy flow toward my strategic action, commitments and ultimately my results.

 Have you ever walked into a room full of people and felt drawn to someone without exchanging a word while simultaneously sensing a need to avoid another part of the room? That energy is real. Even plants experience energy physics, though different from how animals and humans communicate subconsciously through energy and pheromones. I encountered Amy Cuddy, a Harvard Psychology Professor, whose book *Presence* and TED talks on body language resonated deeply with me. *Presence* is my second favorite book, just behind Eckhart Tolle's *The Power of Now*. Cuddy shares her journey and emphasizes the importance of choosing when to be fully present, as it's impossible to do so all the time. Without habits to rely on, we would be mentally drained—imagine if we had to relearn how to tie our shoes every morning as a toddler does. Both Cuddy and Johnson emphasize the power of being in the moment in similar ways. However, through his spiritual philosophy, Tolle teaches us to stay rooted in the now. For me, *The Power of Now* remains my all-time favorite read, a resource that can almost instantly ground me.

Simon Sinek has always inspired me, as I would imagine many others. His talks, interviews, and social media—what I like to call "Simon Sinek's Daily Dose of Positivity"—echo deeply with my own optimistic nature. Like Sinek, I believe in the power of perspective. When we see the glass as half empty, we can convince ourselves that life is lacking, even manifesting mental or physical ailments, just as I experienced in 2020. Conversely, optimists tend to extract the most out of life, turning challenges into opportunities for growth and connection. Sprinkling Sinek's daily optimism can elevate the bigger picture of change, shifting perspectives during challenging times. The tools developed by Johnson are invaluable in transforming individuals. Combined, Sinek provides the optimism needed to navigate difficult moments. At the same time, Johnson offers practical strategies for embracing and enduring fundamental change. Together, they motivate people to push forward, find growth, and thrive, even in the face of adversity. Both play crucial roles in empowerment.

This philosophy was at the heart of a team effort I was part of in 2021, where we developed and introduced Jabil's first Mental Wellness and Resiliency program. Over a couple of years, I helped train and educate employees globally, combining my passion for service with a deep commitment to helping others. Mentoring those who are truly ready for change brings me the greatest joy. I've observed that change, whether personal or organizational, typically stems from two sources: pain or passion. Pain could mean an unforeseen challenge, like the one I faced in 2020, or, for an organization, a reaction to save or grow the business. Passion, while powerful, must align with purpose, value creation, and measurable impact to sustain meaningful change.

Cuddy highlights how busy our lives are, balancing work, mortgages, and countless responsibilities, often leaving little room for intentional reconditioning. Yet, choosing moments to be fully present can unlock significant change. Tolle, Cuddy, Sinek, and Johnson's MBL Program amplified my journey of self-awareness and growth, giving me tools and habits that I use daily to transform lives, including my own.

I was so proud of the young adults my children were becoming. The kindness and love they had for themselves mirrored how they treated others. They started to enjoy hanging out with me and looked up to me in a different way than children often do because they need their parents. I will never forget one afternoon I was hosting a remote Mental Wellness and Resiliency workshop with roughly 20 Jabil employees in attendance. Trinity was eating lunch in our kitchen and overheard the entire event. She approached me afterward and told me how proud she was of me. She shared how passionate I was and that my authenticity moved the audience as they were deeply engaged. I hold that special moment near my heart, as I am unsure how often children tell their parents they're proud of them.

Tristan eventually went on to study art at UB. He produces magnificent artwork, but he could also be an engineer, as math and science are natural to him. He chose the creative path. Trinity, organized, exuberated enthusiasm to work hard and follow a passionate medical field. She is wrapping up her biochemistry degree at Canisius University, and after graduating, she will enter a three-year-round program to pursue her doctorate in pharmacy. I cannot imagine the amount of dedication and energy she puts forth every day, and I am utterly proud of her. Tristan's commitment to nurture himself alongside his matured family values is extremely rewarding. I often think of Tristan characterizing the first part of my life and Trinity symbolizing the second part.

My first formal mentee at Jabil was Silvia Martin, a remarkable individual whose journey remains deeply etched in my heart. Silvia had taken on significant responsibilities, managing a large team within one of Jabil's Mezzovico, Switzerland site's work cells. Recognized as a high achiever, she was connected with me through the talent team. Silvia's story was unique because she sought mentorship not out of desperation or failure but out of sheer passion. Her drive to grow, evolve, and improve was palpable from the start, a rarity in my experience.

Silvia's background as an engineer posed challenges, such as embracing mastering human skills, some referred to as soft skills, which required her to step far outside her comfort zone. She came to me with a desire to bridge gaps in communication, cultural understanding, and personalities and develop stronger delegation skills. Drawing from the MBL Program, my approach was straightforward: focus on changing habits. I knew that achieving narrow goals like effective communication or better delegation would naturally unfold over time if Silvia dedicated herself to the process.

Six months into our journey, I'll never forget the moment Silvia shared how enlightening the experience had been. Excited and humbling, she admitted that she was almost afraid to say it aloud—she had gained time. Time to think creatively, time to strategize, and time to lead proactively rather than reactively. Her work cell was thriving, consistently in the green, and for the first time, she allowed herself to take real time off. This shift empowered her team to take ownership in her absence and rejuvenated her personally. Her newfound balance brought out the best in her and her team, creating a ripple effect of positivity and productivity.

When Silvia shared this with me, my eyes welled up with tears of joy. Seeing her hard work, paired with my guidance, yield such exceptional results was a moment of deep fulfillment. It solidified my belief that mentoring was not just a role I enjoyed but a lifelong commitment I wanted to make—to help others achieve their potential and drive extraordinary outcomes for themselves and their organizations.

In early-mid-2022, our mentorship story gained recognition within Jabil's blog, *Jabil Joules*, featuring two articles: *The Power of Being Present: Lessons Learned as a Mentee* and *The Power of Being Present: Lessons from a Mentor*. Shortly after these stories were published, Jabil's CEO, Kenny Wilson, took notice and sponsored the creation of the One Jabil Mentorship Program. This initiative unified all formal mentoring programs across the enterprise, where Silvia and I worked closely with HR and talent teams for months to help shape the program's best practices.

For several years now, since mentoring Silvia, I've formally mentored one or two people annually while informally supporting others. Whether I bring a smile to someone's day or help them achieve fundamental life changes, those moments drive immense purpose and joy for me.

My empathy has run deep since childhood, metabolizing others' experiences—having drawn pictures for every child at daycare, even those mischievous ones, simply because it felt good to include everyone. That innate desire to connect and uplift has been a constant. I've learned that the most impactful leaders blend strong human skills with intellect. While learned intellect is critical for tasks like programming or technical expertise, emotional intelligence is the thread that binds human interactions. Our subconscious drives 97% of our behaviors, shaped by the environments we grew up in and the biases we absorbed early on. We must address these ingrained patterns by changing habits and acquiring new knowledge to create positive, impactful change.

Byron passed away in October of 2021, and while I could wish for more time to explore the world together, as he and I had hoped to visit the Philippines, I chose to focus on abundance rather than scarcity—one of several habits I embrace. The moments we shared in laughter and cooking meals that nurture the soul are treasures I carry forward. Just as I mention in the beginning of my story in The Unscripted Arrival; being in the now taught me that the richness of life isn't measured by how long we have but by how deeply we live and connect in the time we're given.

Having discovered joy from the simplest moments as a child, I carried that spirit into motherhood, raising my two children to find happiness in life's small, meaningful experiences. When my children were young, we didn't have much—no cable, internet, or luxuries. Back then, the company I worked for provided an internet connection solely for my laptop so I could work. But we had a spare room named the "messy space," where creativity flourished. Every day after school, we'd dive into themed projects like building the tallest Harry Potter castles from soup cans, cracker boxes, and recycled materials. The room stayed messy by design, freeing us from cleanup stress and letting creativity flow. These small, simple moments brought immense happiness, a reminder that fulfillment often lies in the unassuming corners of life.

This perspective has guided my choices, priorities, and actions. While none of us can control the world, we can contribute to developing our environments and meaningfully shaping a better future for ourselves and others.

Forged in Trust: A Leaders Evolution

As Jabil evolved, I transitioned to the legal department, working inside the Compliance Office and Corporate Sustainability. I am now reporting to our Chief Compliance Officer, Thomas Cetta. My prior exposure to working with lawyers during my time at Clover made this transition feel seamless. In this new role, I was entrusted with overseeing our Scope 3 and Circular Economy strategy and programs while continuing to support Jabil's customers across 16 industries on their sustainability journeys.

The road wasn't without its challenges. Leading and managing a team I inherited through transformation demanded tenacity and trust. We faced hurdles without a clear view of where we would land. It was highly stressful. Throughout my career, management was not an area of focus, it felt like having more children. It required considerable presence and significant emotional labor to lower my walls, allowing me to connect deeply with others while holding them accountable. It was juggling vulnerability tied to strategic action and the steadfast commitment to making thoughtful, impactful decisions. At times, this brought me back to how Tristan and I navigated those rough years. Combining Roberto's skillful tactics with Jozsef's navigational mind and Thomas's gentle approach, I focused on balancing analysis and intuition while maintaining fairness, all centered around my vision. Yet, over time, I saw growth and a shift in perspective that I had hoped for. Our small but mighty team overcame many obstacles, and in turn, we built a strong foundation I am proud of today.

Roots and Wings: A Life in Full Bloom

For me, life's meaning is found in the people we meet, the meals we share, and the spaces we foster within ourselves and the world around us. It's in the steam rising from a simmering dish, the laughter echoing from evenings spent with loved ones, and the morning light filtering through the leaves of my thriving indoor forest. Every life I've touched, every lesson I've learned, and every path I've walked, each has been a brushstroke in the masterpiece of my journey.

To nurture others is to cultivate the world, from the roots which I've grown. My hands have crushed basil into vibrant pesto and coaxed the perfect char onto Neapolitan pizza, just as they have shaped ideas, raised children into adults, guided mentees, and enriched trust in leadership. I've seen how food dissolves barriers and how a simple dish can revolutionize a moment into something unforgettable. Cooking, like connection, is a universal language that transcends borders and time.

My plants remind me of this cycle, the way a fiddle leaf fig stretches toward the sun, the resilience of succulents that thrive with little, and the wild abundance of pothos cascading my walls, unrestrained by expectations. Each one teaches a lesson in patience, adaptability, and presence—values my children and I have instilled. I've carried this understanding through boardrooms and across oceans, from the cobbled streets of Rome or the golden glow of Barcelona's Gothic Quarter to the dizzying energy of Hong Kong. I have stood in awe beneath the Sistine Chapel, inhaled the intoxicating aroma of fresh spices within the bustling Bangkok night markets, and watched the sun melt into the Indian Ocean from the shores of Bali, where stillness meets the infinite.

For two decades, I have worked toward a more sustainable world and a more connected future, building programs, mentoring leaders, and standing at the intersection of innovation and responsibility. Helping others become the best versions of themselves is not just a calling; it is the most fulfilling legacy I could ever leave.

As I stand now, looking back at the roads I have traveled and the ones still ahead, I know that life's most significant purpose is not in the destination but in the act of becoming. We are all roots and wings, grounded in the relationships that nourish us yet always reaching for something greater. And in this ever-unfolding journey, I will continue to cook, teach, explore, learn, lead with presence, and live the most meaningful life I can.

Cassie Gruber: Circular Economy Thought Leader & Sustainability Strategist

Cassie Gruber is a recognized thought leader in the circular economy, working closely with some of the world's largest brands across 16 industries to drive Jabil's circular economy and Scope 3 emissions reduction strategies. Since joining Jabil in 2018, Cassie has been instrumental in supporting customers across diverse, highly regulated industries to achieve their recycling and circular economy goals through comprehensive reverse supply chain solutions, focusing on product and material reuse and recycling.

Cassie's journey into sustainability began after a decade of studying art and philosophy, when she became a partner in a small e-waste company in Buffalo, NY. Over the next two decades, she built a career centered on environmental sustainability and compliance in the electronics recycling industry. At Jabil, her extensive experience and commitment to sustainability have been pivotal in evolving the company's approach to a data-driven, circular value supply chain. Cassie and her team are key stakeholders in Jabil's enterprise-wide initiatives, prioritizing product carbon footprint (PCF) calculations and lifecycle assessments (LCA) at scale to enhance sustainable design and operational efficiency.

In addition to her sustainability leadership, Cassie is deeply committed to advancing mental health and wellness. She plays an active role in Jabil's Mental Health and Resiliency programs and serves as a mentor within the company's Mentorship Program. Cassie holds a Bachelor of Fine Arts from SUNY University at Buffalo and has completed an intensive Master of Business Leadership (MBL) program, specializing in servant leadership and emotional intelligence.

Cassie's industry involvement is extensive:

- **Conferences:** Active supporter/speaker/attendee at Reverse Logistics Association (RLA), ITAD Summit, NTWK, OpenNex, e-Scrap, eSummit (formerly eReuse), RBA, and Rethink Circularity.

- **SERI:** eSummit newly formed steering committee member and former six-year member of the R2 Technical Advisory Committee, contributing to the development of the R2v3 standard.

- **SGS Advisory Board:** Serving for over 12 years.

- **Circular Electronics Partnership (CEP):** Active member driving circular innovation in electronics.

- **Responsible Business Alliance (RBA) & Responsible Environment Initiative (REI):** Contributor to the Circular Materials and Waste Minimization working group.

- **IPC & iNEMI:** Collaborator on industry standards and initiatives.

- **Global Electronics Council (GEC):** Deeply engaged in EPEAT-related efforts.

Cassie is also a proud member of the Worldwide Women's Association (WWA) and the American Business Women's Association (ABWA), reflecting her commitment to fostering leadership and mentorship among women in business.

Her passion for sustainability, leadership, and collaboration continues to drive meaningful change in both the industry and the communities she serves.

Chapter 4
Never be afraid of being confident

Justus Klüver-Schlotfeldt

When Kristy asked me if I would co-write this book and contribute a section about being a thought leader, sharing how I inspire others to follow their dreams and achieve success—I genuinely thought she was joking.

It wasn't long ago, maybe two or three months, that I discovered my business partner, one of the most influential people in my life, who had been asked to contribute to a similar project, writing a co-chapter in the book, The *Logistics Legends*. My immediate reaction was, *Well, of course! Rudee is a true legend.* He has built businesses, served as a role model to countless people, established an incredible network, and remains one of the most grounded individuals I've ever met. Writing a story for him is meant to be.

But me? A World thought leader? Sure, I've experienced success a few times in my life, and yes, I've occasionally entertained the idea of writing a book. But not now — not when I have young children, a business less than two years old, and possibly the busiest time of my life.

Yet here we are. And, surprisingly, these chapters—the thousands of words you are about to read—only took me a relatively short time. Why? Because they are always in me, and true stories of my life that I've been living and reflecting on for years. It is meant to be shared with you, my friend. As I began writing, I realized most of it was already in my mind, waiting for the right moment to surface.

But it raises the question: Why write a book in the first place?
For me, the answer has multiple layers:

- **Training:** Writing is an incredible exercise in focus, discipline, and creativity. I can only encourage everyone to give it a go — it's rewarding in ways you wouldn't expect.
- **Exposure:** Being an entrepreneur, it's inevitable that everything is connected to your business in some way. Writing a book provides visibility. Not just for yourself but for the ideas and projects you're passionate about.
- **Making Your Relatives Proud:** The opportunity to give my parents and family something tangible—a book with my name on it—fills me with pride. It's a unique opportunity to share a part of my journey with them.
- **Helping Others Grow:** And this, above all, is the most important. If this book, these words, will inspire just one person to step out of their comfort zone, take a leap of faith, or make a positive change in their life, then every minute spent writing it will have been worthwhile.

My hope for my chapter and what it can do for you is simple: I hope my true stories and my leadership lessons can inspire you to share yours and to live your life fully and do what you love.

So, thank you for picking up this book. I hope you find it meaningful, whether it's through a story that resonates, an idea that sparks inspiration, or a reflection that helps you see your own journey in a new light.

Introduction

Before diving into the different chapters of my life, I'd like to take a moment to reflect on the driving forces behind everything I do—the motivations that keep me pushing forward.

People my age, and sometimes those younger, often ask me why I work so hard, why I travel as much as I do, and why I dedicate myself so fully to my career and projects. The answer lies in the goals I want to achieve.

A few years ago, my goals were simple, even vague. I wanted to earn good money and enjoy the process of achieving it. I didn't spend much time considering the deeper meaning behind those goals or asking myself *why* I wanted them. My focus was on the immediate: paying the next invoice or affording a holiday for my family during the rare and precious time I was home.

As the years passed, I attended various training sessions that prompted me to think more about my values and moral compass. Through these reflections, I began to uncover what truly drives me. But even then, it wasn't always clear. I realized I wanted to be successful—but what did that mean? Was it about financial stability? Was it about being good at something? Or was it about outperforming others?

And then there were the ethical challenges. What happens when a great opportunity comes along, but it conflicts with your principles? Do you take the deal? Or what if a business partnership could bring your company to the next level, but the people involved don't share your mindset or values?

I've come to believe that before you can answer these questions, you need to understand what you want to achieve as a life goal. Once you have clarity on your goal, it becomes your guiding star. Every decision, every effort, every sacrifice should bring you closer to that goal and it becomes your no. 1 priority.

For me, this clarity came largely thanks to a meeting with business partners and friends about 2 years ago. I think I'd known my goal for some time, but it only crystallized for me on that weekend in Dubai.

I can't emphasize enough how important it is to listen to yourself—to tune in and identify what drives you. Your goals may evolve as you move through different phases of life, but having a clear purpose allows you to prioritize. And, just as importantly, it teaches you to say **NO**.

One of the biggest lessons I've learned in my career is this: **The more successful you become, the more valuable your time is.** Everything may seem like an opportunity, but not everything aligns with your purpose. Without focus, you risk doing a lot of great things but not growing where it truly matters.

Entrepreneurship as a Child

I had a very pleasant childhood. In stories like these, people often expect a tale of triumph over adversity—a tough beginning, coming from nothing, and then rising to success. But for me, that wasn't the case. I had a good start in life, yet I made my success on my own, thanks to the lessons my parents taught me early on: *your luck is in your own hands, and only you can make yourself successful.*

Growing up in the countryside, by a lakeside and surrounded by three farms, I had everything a little boy could dream of. My bicycle was my primary mode of transport, and I started "working" at one of the farms owned by the Lucht family when I was about 10 years old. Driving tractors and helping with the wheat and corn harvest during school breaks was the best job I could imagine at that age.

I must have been about 12 when I started mowing the grass at the farm with their shiny, new lawnmower tractor. For a kid like me, it was the ultimate dream come true. I earned 10 Deutsche Marks for spending a day driving the little tractor. It didn't feel like work at all.

I wanted to mow grass every chance I could, but there were challenges. Northern Germany isn't exactly known for its dry weather. Other kids wanted their turn at the tractor, and with sports activities after school, I only had Saturdays available. Sunday mowing wasn't an option either, as it was forbidden by law.

Later that summer, I discovered that Mr. Scheel, one of the wealthier residents of our village, had also bought a brand-new John Deere tractor. He had a large property—larger than most of the farms—though it wasn't an actual farm. His children had grown up and his son moved out, so he asked me if I'd like to mow his lawns for 10 Deutsche Marks. Naturally, I said yes.

Mr. Scheel's property became my main project on Saturdays. I was even allowed to use his tractor to mow the grass at my parent's house, saving my dad the trouble of doing it by hand. Driving around the village with the tractor, I noticed other gardens and had an idea: Why not ask the owners of smaller properties if I could mow their lawns too, for a small fee?

I approached Mr. Scheel with the idea, asking if he'd let me use his tractor for this. Not only did he agree, but he also helped by introducing me to the other property owners, many of whom he knew personally. By the end of that week, I had started my first business as a lawn-mowing entrepreneur.

If it didn't rain, I could mow four or five gardens on a Saturday afternoon, earning around 40 Deutsche Marks a week — a significant amount of money for a boy my age. That was when I realized the power of asking for help and networking. Mr. Scheel's connections opened doors for me, and that early lesson stayed with me as I built my career.

A few years later, Mr. Scheel played a role in my next venture: becoming a DJ. By the time I was 16, I had developed a deep love for music, inspired by my parents. My dad's playlists were filled with The Rolling Stones, Otis Redding, and Dire Straits, while my mum preferred artists like Gitte Henning, ABBA and Roxette. Traveling often with my family, I was exposed to a wide variety of music, and I realized that, in my rural community, there was a gap in the market. Every party—birthdays, weddings, anniversaries—was handled by just two DJs. It was the perfect opportunity.

That summer, I earned about 4,000–5,000 Deutsche Marks from DJing. With that money, I upgraded my equipment, modified my motorbike, and funded my first ski trip with friends — all without relying on my parents. The work didn't stop there. At 16, I was also legally allowed to drive large tractors on public roads. One of the pub owners where I'd DJed introduced me to a farm contractor in need of drivers. That summer, I spent four weeks of my school holiday driving tractors and DJing at the weekends. By the time school started, I had earned over 12,000 Deutsche Marks.

That was when I truly understood the value of hard work and self-reliance. Reflecting on that time now, I realize how much I achieved for myself as a teenager. When I received my first official pay cheque at the age of 17 during my apprenticeship as a car mechanic, it was 634 Deutsche Mark for a full month's work. Back then, I was used to earning that amount—or more—in a single night as a DJ.

Those early experiences shaped my understanding of success and entrepreneurship. They taught me two key lessons:

1. **The Importance of Networking:** Knowing the right people can guide you to unexpected opportunities. Your Network is your net worth!
2. **Seizing Opportunities:** If you see a gap in the market, take it.

Take Luck into Your Own Hands

It was early 2013, and my life took an unexpected turn. I had just returned from a week in Norway, where I'd gone to seek solace in the silence of nature after my marriage had ended. Little did I know that my return would bring more upheaval.

At the time, I was working in Hamburg for the largest customs broker in Europe. My primary role was leading Amazon's Central European account, managing the import of their goods into the EU. I was genuinely happy in my job and felt secure—Amazon's business was booming, and we were hiring new people every month.

But when I walked into the office that day, something felt off. The management floor, usually bustling with at least ten people, was eerily empty except for three individuals. My first thought was that I'd missed a company event. The reality, however, was much more shocking: the board in Sweden, following advice from a consultancy firm hired by the company's new owner, had decided to replace the entire European management team. Overnight.

Within the same month, I found myself dealing with not only the loss of my marriage but also my job.

At first, I felt devastated. Even though I received a good severance package, the disappointment lingered. I had loved my work. But in moments like these, you have a choice: let the setback define you or take control of your future.

My best friend, who is now my wife, became my anchor during this time. Her unwavering support helped me focus on the road ahead, and without her, I wouldn't be the person I am today. She gave me the strength to see that this wasn't the end — it was an opportunity to start again.

Determined to rebuild, I applied for four jobs in the logistics and brokerage industry. I was invited to three interviews, and all three companies offered me a position. While the offers felt validating, deep down, I knew I didn't want to take any of them.

Meanwhile, Peter Sunderland, a key figure in my career and someone I deeply admire, reached out to me. Peter was unaware of my dismissal, as my former employer had failed to inform him or his company, Kendall Group, that I was no longer managing the Amazon account on their behalf.

Here it is important to know that the Kendall Group was the overall Account contract owner with Amazon, for all their customs brokerage in the EU and the UK, and the company I worked for, KGH, acted as a sub-contractor on their behalf.

Peter's call sparked an idea. *Why not work for Kendall?* I knew the business, the market, and the key players. It seemed like a perfect fit.

But reaching Peter wasn't straightforward. He was incredibly busy, often travelling for half the year. So, I came up with a plan. I called Paul, the main account manager at Kendall's London office, and asked about Peter's schedule. Paul told me that Peter would return from Dubai on Friday but would leave for the US shortly after.

Armed with this information, I booked a flight to London and sent Peter an email, casually mentioning that I'd be in the city over the weekend and would love to meet for coffee.

The plan worked and Peter gave me a bit of his time.

When I arrived at the office, I pitched my idea to Peter. I was confident, prepared, and hopeful. But his response was not what I'd expected: **No.**

While Peter appreciated my enthusiasm and respected my work, expanding into continental Europe wasn't part of Kendall's growth strategy at the time. It was a blow, but I didn't regret trying. I knew it was the right thing to do, and I also knew it would not be the last time, I would be speaking to him.

A few weeks later, I accepted a position with a multinational company to lead their operations in Hamburg and establish a new office. It was a promising opportunity, but something didn't feel right. My heart wasn't in it as I wanted something else.

Then, just days before I was due to start, I received an unexpected call from Peter. He asked if I'd be home the next morning at 10:00 AM. At exactly 10:00, a courier arrived with an envelope containing a job offer for the global HQ of Kendall in London.

Peter explained his change of heart: While expanding into Europe wasn't Kendall's immediate plan, he didn't want to risk losing the opportunity to work with me. He recognized that if I joined the multinational company, I might never look back. And that was something he didn't want to happen.

The offer wasn't financially the best, but that didn't matter. I immediately said yes. A week later, I was in London, immersing myself in Kendall's operations, learning about their systems, ethics, and history. Never, I felt so welcomed in a company. Everyone had an open ear, was friendly and excited. Years later I also endeavored this with the teams in the US, China, and the Middle East. The company culture and it's people were nothing less than welcoming and supportive.

I returned to Germany, ready to build something extraordinary.

Over the next six years, I opened multiple offices for Kendall from scratch, learned every aspect of international freight forwarding beyond my customs expertise, and developed skills I didn't know I had. I pushed myself, seeking guidance from Peter and other regional managers, partners, and even clients.

The most valuable lesson I learned during this time was this: **The key to success lies in collaboration.** You can't grow alone. You need the right partners to challenge and support you.

One of the best decisions I made during this period was to collaborate with perceived competitors, like my friends at TCI. I met Markus and Johannes at a WCA conference in Qingdao, China, in 2015. Despite being competitors on paper, we immediately clicked. Their focus on LCL and air consolidation complemented my expertise in customs brokerage, creating a win-win partnership. Together, we combined buying power and expanded our offerings.

Funnily enough, as much as that drove my business units forward, most of my colleagues and managers around the globe did not appreciate that approach. For me it was a key lesson learned and one of the reasons I am now running a global network as the key lies in collaboration – I am very convinced of that.

Looking back, flying to London and pitching to Peter—even after his initial refusal—was one of the best decisions of my life. It reinforced a belief I carry to this day: **trust your instincts, take risks, and success will follow.**

Leave Your Comfort Zone and Be Open-Minded

It was 2006, the football world cup in my home country, the "Sommermärchen" as we call it, was just finished and I had one of the best summers of my life.

I had just finished my education at Germany's largest retailer, Karstadt AG. I'd graduated as the best in my class in practical exams, earning the state honors, and was offered a place in their prestigious trainee program. For most people, this was the opportunity of a lifetime—working across different departments nationwide with a clear pathway to management. My parents were super happy, (finally, the boy would do something proper) as were my neighbors, friends, and even my parents' friends. This was it, they thought: A bright and stable future for the young Justus who as a child always did what he wanted, despite the tips and guidance from them.

But I (again) had other plans.

Growing up in a small village in Northern Germany, about 100 kilometers north of Hamburg, life was predictable. It was a close-knit community where everyone knew everyone, and success was often measured by either the academic grade, the car you drove, or the house you built. It was a comfortable and secure environment, it still is but to me, it felt repetitive year after year, month after month, the same routine.

Around this time, my girlfriend received an offer to move to Norway as an expat with her company. They were setting up a customs brokerage entity for their fleet of trucks, and she asked if I would join her. Without hesitation, I said yes.

It was an easy decision. I always loved Norway. My parents bought a cabin in the woods in the early 90"s and I had spent a lot of my school holidays there since I was 7 years old.

The decision shocked everyone around me. I didn't speak Norwegian, I had no job lined up, and I had no financial safety net. To make matters worse, Karstadt's head of HR couldn't believe I was turning down the trainee program, and my parents struggled to understand why I would leave behind such a stable path. But in my heart, I knew I wanted more than the predictable life that lay ahead if I stayed.

The beginning in Norway was tough. At first, it was exciting — everything was new, from the landscape to the culture. But after the initial honeymoon phase, reality set in. I needed a job, and I needed to build a new social circle in an area even less populated than my home village.

Months passed, and despite learning the language and being fluent in English, I couldn't find work.

My profile as a sales professional in retail was not really what they were waiting for in the area and the only shops in and around 80 km were either furniture stores or outlets, mainly for groceries on the other side of the border in Sweden.

After about 3 months in, I got approached by a new brand from Austria, knowing that I was selling Tennis rackets during my education and also knowing that I was a fairly good player for tennis in my youth, asking if I would like to try to sell their stuff in the Nordics. I said yes and thought, great, this is my chance, building up a new brand up here coming from the sport I loved the most. But the reality was that tennis was a dying sport in Norway. Sweden had a strong Tennis community, but they were not really waiting for a new brand, and working fully on commission made it tough for me to travel this massive region by car and survive. So, I failed to build this and the only money I was earning was to help one of my friends who was a truck driver, prepare his cooled tours at night for the supermarkets.

It was a humbling experience—one that tested my patience and resilience. I was about to give up and ask my girlfriend to move elsewhere.

Then, out of nowhere, I received a call from the landlord of the company my girlfriend worked for. He offered me a job in customs.

Wait, customs?

At first, I was confused. I thought customs was a governmental duty, and I wasn't even Norwegian. I didn't know back then that customs declarations are also made by private companies. How could I, if you are not in that industry, you do not know anything about customs, logistics or supply chain management.

As it turned out, he needed someone who could speak German to handle clients and drivers at the border. He just lost his only German-speaking employee.

This marked the beginning of my journey into logistics—a field I would come to specialize in and learn to love over the years.

Working in customs taught me invaluable lessons. Customs is the bottleneck of all cross-border trade, and understanding it is essential for grasping the entire supply chain. It also exposed me to every stakeholder in the logistics process, from cargo owners to transport operators.

Over the next four years, I became a licensed customs broker, learned three languages, became a father, and gained a deep appreciation for Norwegian culture. Even though it shares similarities with Germany, Norway taught me the subtle but important nuances of cultural differences.

Looking back, moving to Norway was one of the best decisions of my life. It wasn't easy, but it pushed me out of my comfort zone and broadened my horizons. It's a lesson I carry with me to this day: **if you want to grow, you need to take risks and embrace the unknown.**

As the Norwegians say: *"The world is like a book, and those who do not travel only read one page."*

Never Be Afraid and Do What You Love

The phrase *"Find what you love, and you'll never work a day in your life"* is often quoted, and it's one I've found to be profoundly true.

It was late 2022, and I found myself in a bar in London on a rainy December evening, meeting Rudee Bertie—a long-time business friend and someone I deeply respected. Rudee and I had crossed paths several times over the years, often sharing speaking stages at logistics events in Asia. Despite never working directly together, I always admired his energy, knowledge, and ability to connect people.

That evening, Rudee introduced me to his latest idea: NeX, a network for e-commerce cross-border logistics companies. He described how it would connect stakeholders, foster collaboration, and address key challenges in the industry. As he spoke, something clicked. This wasn't just a good idea; it was something I wanted to be a part of. Something that I had in my mind for a long time. Funnily enough, Rudee and I were both consulting on this idea about 3 years earlier for a very large network of logistics companies, without knowing that the other one was doing it as well.

Initially, that day, he envisioned me joining as an advisor or as his first member. But as we continued discussing the concept, I realized I wanted more. By the end of our conversation, I told him, "Take me seriously on this NeX idea—I think it has real potential, and I know I can add value."

What followed exceeded my expectations. Rudee and his partners not only asked me to join NeX—they wanted me to run it full-time. Who could they trust more than someone willing to invest into a new idea?!

This was a pivotal moment for me. At 39 years old, with four kids, two mortgages, and responsibilities as a provider, it was a significant risk. Unlike starting a typical VC-funded start-up, this was a real deal: investing my own money, energy, and time. It was daunting, but deep down, I knew it was the right decision. The truth is, I would never done it alone at that stage in my life, but the opportunity was there, so I had to take it.

I took the leap, and it's been one of the most rewarding experiences of my life. NeX has grown into more than just a network—it's an ecosystem with four distinct business units: a network, a SaaS tech platform, an academy, and an event-organizing company.

Of course, the journey wasn't without its challenges. Starting a new venture is never easy, and NeX was no exception. There were moments of doubt, setbacks that felt insurmountable, and days when it seemed like we were taking one step forward and two steps back.

But in those moments, I leaned on the lessons I'd learned throughout my career. I remembered the importance of resilience, the power of collaboration, and the value of trusting my instincts.

I also leaned on the incredible team we had assembled. NeX wouldn't have been possible without the dedication and expertise of the people who believed in the vision and worked tirelessly to bring it to life.

Looking back, I'm proud of the risks I took to help build it. It wasn't an easy decision, but it was the right one. The experience reinforced a belief I've held throughout my life: **Never be afraid to do what you love.**

When you're passionate about something, challenges become opportunities, and the hard work becomes a source of fulfillment. Taking risks isn't about being reckless; it's about having the courage to pursue what matters most to you.

The lesson here is simple: **don't let fear hold you back. If something feels right, trust your instincts and go for it.**

As the Americans say: *"Success is where opportunity meets preparation."* Looking back, I realize that my years of experience had prepared me for this moment. The hard work wasn't easy, but it felt natural because I was/am doing what I love.

Honest Feedback and Growth

One of the hardest lessons I've learned in my career is the importance of honesty —especially when it comes to giving feedback. As a leader, you are often the one people turn to for guidance, mentorship, and validation. But being a leader also means having difficult conversations, even when the truth is uncomfortable or unwelcome.

Looking back, I can see how these moments of honesty helped shape not only the people I worked with but also my own growth as a leader. It's a skill I had to develop, and it didn't come naturally to me.

When I first started taking on leadership roles, I struggled with certain aspects of managing people. I loved motivating teams and driving results, but I wasn't naturally inclined toward the softer side of management — especially when it came to HR. I lacked the patience needed for one-on-one development conversations and often found it difficult to handle sensitive topics.

Over time, I realized that if I was going to grow as a leader, I needed to address this gap. I sought advice from HR professionals and attended courses to improve my communication and coaching skills. But as much as these tools helped, they didn't solve the underlying challenge: I didn't enjoy this part of the job, and I did not have a talent for it.

This realization led me to a critical decision: Instead of forcing myself to excel in areas where I lacked natural aptitude, I focused on hiring the right people to complement my weaknesses. I brought in HR professionals who were skilled at employee development, allowing me to focus on what I did best: driving strategy, building relationships, and delivering results. Still, as the one driving the company, you have at least to deal with the HR person(s).

One of the most pivotal moments in my leadership journey came during my time at the Kendall Group. After several years of managing Amazon's European account, we lost the contract to a competitor. This was a huge blow—not just for the company but also for the employees who had been working tirelessly on the account.

About seventy percent of our team's workload was tied to Amazon, so the news created a wave of uncertainty. Many employees were concerned about their future and began requesting one-on-one meetings to discuss their roles. As a leader, it was my responsibility to navigate this difficult period and provide guidance to the team.

But this wasn't just about finding new opportunities for people. It was also about being honest—sometimes brutally so.

When employees asked for references to apply for roles elsewhere, I found myself in a tough position. Of course, I wanted to support them and help them find new opportunities. But I also felt it was my duty to be truthful about their strengths and areas for improvement.

For some employees, this meant delivering feedback they didn't want to hear. I had to tell them that while they were talented in certain areas, they weren't as strong in others. I believed it was better for them to go into their next role with an honest understanding of their capabilities than to set them up for failure by sugarcoating the truth.

Not everyone appreciated this approach. In fact, two of the employees I spoke to were deeply upset by my feedback and, for a time, harbored resentment toward me. One of them even stopped speaking to me entirely and went to court.

But years later, I've seen how that honest feedback helped them grow. While I never really reconnected with one of them, I keep following their success stories, online.

This experience taught me a valuable lesson about leadership: **Sometimes, the most supportive thing you can do is tell someone the truth.** Growth often comes from facing uncomfortable realities, and as a leader, it's your job to help people see where they have room to improve.

It also reinforced the importance of balancing honesty with empathy. While it's crucial to be truthful, it's equally important to deliver feedback in a way that encourages growth rather than discouragement. This is a skill I continue to refine, and it's one I believe every leader should strive to develop.

As I reflect on my leadership journey, I realize that some of my proudest moments have come from helping others grow—even when it meant having difficult conversations. Being honest doesn't always make you popular in the short term, but it builds trust and respect in the long run.

Today, I approach feedback with a mindset of growth and collaboration. I don't see it as a one-sided conversation but as an opportunity to work together to find solutions and chart a path forward. And while I still lean on HR professionals for support in certain areas, I've learned to embrace the responsibility of being a leader who can inspire and challenge others.

If you're in a position of leadership, I encourage you to embrace the role of honest feedback-giver. It's not always easy, and it won't always make you popular. But it's one of the most important ways you can help others reach their potential.

Remember: **Growth often comes from discomfort. As a leader, your job is to guide people through that discomfort and help them come out stronger on the other side.**

The Role of Mentorship

Throughout my career, I've had the privilege of learning from some truly exceptional individuals. These mentors have not only shaped my professional journey but also had a profound impact on who I am as a person. Each of them brought unique perspectives, lessons, and values that helped guide me through pivotal moments in my life.

When I think about mentorship, I see it as a combination of guidance, inspiration, and sometimes, tough love. The mentors who've influenced me the most didn't just tell me what I wanted to hear — they challenged me, pushed me to grow, and helped me see the world from new perspectives.

This chapter is a tribute to the people who've played that role in my life.

Jan-Erik Hermanseter: Scandinavian Wisdom

During my time at KGH, I had the honor of working closely with Jan-Erik Hermanseter, who was then the deputy CEO and director of global accounts. From Jan-Erik, I learned invaluable lessons about managing multinational accounts and navigating the complexities of working within a hedge fund-driven company.

KGH was a unique environment, one that required not only operational excellence but also the ability to adapt quickly to the pressures and demands of its investors. Jan-Erik was a master at balancing these challenges. He taught me what it takes to survive—and thrive—in such a high-stakes environment.

But beyond the technical aspects of the job, Jan-Erik also introduced me to the core values of Scandinavian leadership: equality, and humility. These principles have stayed with me ever since, influencing not only how I lead teams but also how I approach relationships in both business and life.

Jan-Erik's mentorship was a beacon of clarity during a demanding period in my career, and I will always be grateful for the guidance and wisdom he shared with me.

Peter Sunderland: A Foundation in Leadership

If I had to name the most influential mentor in my career, it would undoubtedly be Peter Sunderland. Peter's impact on my life cannot be overstated. He taught me nearly everything I know about setting up a business, being a smart and strategic manager, and—most importantly—being a good and fair person.

Peter had an extraordinary ability to see potential in people and ideas. He believed in me at a time when I was still finding my footing and gave me the opportunity to build something meaningful. His trust and guidance were instrumental in helping me grow, both professionally and personally.

From Peter, I learned the importance of building a strong foundation in business. He showed me that success isn't just about having a good idea — it's about execution, ethics, and the ability to inspire trust in others.

But what I admire most about Peter is his character. Despite his immense success, he remains one of the most grounded and fair people I've ever met. His mentorship continues to influence how I approach any person I work with.

Jan-Phillip Pohlmeier: The Visionary

Jan-Phillip Pohlmeier, or JP, was another pivotal figure in my journey. JP embodies the phrase, *"Go big or go home."* From JP, I learned the true meaning of believing in growth—not just incremental progress, but bold, ambitious leaps forward.

JP saw potential in my vision and goals, and he didn't just support them with words, he invested significant time, money, and resources to help bring them to life. His belief in me gave me the confidence to dream bigger and push harder.

However, JP wasn't always the easiest person to deal with. His "business always comes first" mindset often led to challenges between us. We had our moments of disagreement and tension, especially when personal priorities clashed with business demands. But in hindsight, those challenges were some of the most valuable lessons I've ever learned and will ever be grateful.

From JP, I discovered what it takes to build a multi-million-euro company from scratch. He showed me the level of commitment, sacrifice, and determination required to achieve extraordinary results.

JP's mentorship taught me that success often requires taking calculated risks and having the courage to aim for something extraordinary—even when it's uncomfortable or challenging.

Rudee Bertie: Defining Goals and Building by Design

When it comes to building a business by design, no one has taught me more than Rudee Bertie. Rudee has been both a mentor and a partner, and his influence on my career has been profound.

From Rudee, I've learned the value of humility—an essential quality for any leader. He's shown me that true success isn't about boasting or seeking recognition; it's about trusting your instincts, building meaningful collaborations, and staying true to your values.

But perhaps Rudee's most significant impact on me has been helping me define my goals. Before meeting him, I had a vague sense of what I wanted to achieve, but Rudee helped me crystallize those ambitions and see the bigger picture. He showed me that business and personal life are deeply intertwined, especially as an entrepreneur. Understanding what I truly want to achieve—both professionally and personally—has transformed how I approach every decision I make.

Rudee has an exceptional ability to bring people together, fostering partnerships that create value for everyone involved. Through his guidance, I've come to understand the power of working with others toward a shared vision.

Rudee has taught me that success isn't something that happens by accident—it's the result of thoughtful planning, smart decisions, and a commitment to excellence.

My Wife: The Quiet Strength

While all the mentors I've mentioned have shaped my professional journey, my wife has been the cornerstone of my personal growth. She and I couldn't be more different in how we see the world. Our opinions often clash, and our approaches to life couldn't be more opposite.

And yet, I am convinced that these differences are what make our marriage a success and with it my career. Her perspective challenges me to see things in different ways, and her unwavering support for my career pushes me to be a better person.

Without her trust and guidance, I wouldn't have achieved half of what I've accomplished. She is my sounding board, my anchor, and my greatest source of strength.

Other Influences Along the Way

Of course, there have been many other people who've played an important role in my life. Colleagues from companies I've worked for, industry leaders I've met at conferences, and even competitors who've challenged me to raise my game—all of them have left a mark on my journey.

But this is just one part of my career story, and it's far from the end. I hope to have more opportunities to reflect on these relationships in future co-writing projects. After all, I need to save some stories for my next book!

After sharing my true story, and thanking all those who influenced me, I want you to understand that without them in my story, there won't be me who is now influencing and leading many others. Being a thought leader is to understand that PEOPLE are important to you, as you cannot do everything all by yourself. Leadership is about acknowledging people along your journey and following your heart and instincts to make every decision and take full ownership!

Justus Klüver-Schlotfeldt is co-founder and CEO of NeX e-Commerce Hub, the leading global eco system for all things cross-border e-Commerce logistics.

He is an award-winning supply chain expert who is an expert in building global networks and strategic partnerships.

Justus is well known for his talent to read people's strengths, his positivity and to build successful businesses in the supply chain industry.

When he isn't running NeX, he loves to spend time, traveling with his family and doing sports like tennis, running and skiing.

Justus lives near Hamburg, Germany with his amazing Wife and three children.

Website: www.nex-network.com LinkedIn: https://www.linkedin.com/in/justus-kl%C3%BCver-schlotfeldt-265a5380/

Chapter 5
A Learner for Life

Victor Hermosa

I was never among the top students in our class. I had very low self-confidence. I struggled with my studies that even my own parents doubted my capacity to learn and keep up.

So, who would have thought that after all, I could go a long way – far beyond what was expected or thought of me? I got a family, a thriving company of my own, and a life that I have wanted.

It all began with a dream.

Since young, I had a secret ambition. Perhaps some kind of redemption for myself. I was someone who felt insecure and less when compared to my peers. So I wanted to keep up and aim higher.

I wanted to become a millionaire. I carved my path towards that goal.

As I grew older and saw more of life, that dream became even bigger. I wanted to become a billionaire. Over the years, I was relentless and searched for more. I wondered if I become a billionaire, then what's next for me? I always think of what's ahead of me. Is that it? Surely money is one thing but not everything.

So I aimed for more. I found God and purpose in my life. This time, I wanted to become a billionaire missionary.

I believe money comes from God. I am just a steward. I am blessed for a reason. I thought about doing missions. Those who are called by God for this work go to far places to share the Good News. But I don't think I was called to leave my family and business behind. Then I realized there are other ways to do mission work.

Missionaries need financial support so they can do their work for God. That's where I can still be a part of mission work. I can support missionaries financially. That is what I mean by billionaire missionary – my ultimate goal in life. It's not just about getting rich but also living with a purpose.

From Coins to Millions

I was an altar boy for four years since I was in third grade. I saw that the priest had lots of coins from the mass offering. I wanted to have money, too, so I thought I should become a priest. So I went to a seminary on my first year in high school.

But a year after that, my ambition changed. A relative came home for vacation. He had lots of money – not just coins, but paper bills! He spent a lot on food, drinks, and gifts for people. I wanted to be like him. So, goodbye priesthood. I left the seminary.

I began my homework. I wanted to know how my relative got so rich. I was told he had his own brokerage. He studied Customs Administration in college. So, I decided I will do exactly what he did. I would take Customs Administration in Manila and have my own brokerage company one day.

I was going to be a millionaire.

All throughout high school, that was my mindset.

I observed my town. The ones I knew were teachers, farmers, government employees, tricycle drivers, among others. None of them were millionaires.

I was determined to be different and to do something that would help me achieve my goal. I did well in my studies in Manila. I was so focused. Didn't get into any serious romantic relationships while in college. I didn't go out with friends to have good times.

Then on my junior year, I had some personal setbacks. For a moment I doubted the path I was taking. Did I hold on to something that was not actually true? I was already almost at the finish line. Should I back out? Never. I decided to pursue my dreams regardless of anything. I stayed on track and kept going.

From Weakness to Strength

My learning capacity was slow or delayed. When I read a book or anything to study, I have to read it three or four times so I could fully understand it.

In fact, in grade school, my parents thought it was best that they send me back to third grade. They were both teachers and worried their son was slow in learning and could not read or comprehend quickly. So I had to repeat third grade.

I was branded as retarded or mongoloid.

My confidence sank. That was when I began to doubt myself. I had to join a different batch of students who were a year younger than I was. What a shame.

Quietly, I struggled with insecurities even as I entered high school. I would compare myself to others. My best friend in class always had medals as he excelled in academics. Why not me? Was I really that bad?

When I left my town and went to college in Manila, I promised myself I would strive to be better; to be like my best friend. I will reach my dream to become a millionaire. I embraced my weakness and found a way to manage it, not ignore it.

If it takes three to four times for me to understand what I read, then so be it. I will read three to four times or as many times as it takes. My weakness propelled me to be better.

In college, I reviewed pretty much in advance for the licensure exam. I collected review materials from my schoolmates. Yes, I had to put in more effort – review as early and as many times as needed.

The result was amazing. I was Top 9! All because I had a goal in mind – I had to pass the exam so I could have my own brokerage one day. I did all I could and it paid off. But I didn't just pass. I was one of the topnotchers.

Three Major Blocks Encountered

First, I had doubts in myself because of my childhood experience. It was ingrained in my brain that I wasn't good enough. I had low self-esteem. For years, I had to wrestle with that and overcome.

Second, I didn't have mentors earlier in my life. I was too shy to ask for anyone to help me. If I already had mentors early in my life, maybe my learning journey would have been faster and easier.

Third, I had some negativity in me because of my low self-esteem. There were things I was too afraid to try because I assumed I could not do them because I was not good enough.

But then again, after all, my vision and goal pushed me up. They were stronger than those blocks I had. They were like fire in my heart that kept burning and melting my fears away through the years.

Turning Point

There was no single turning point that happened in my life. Where I am now is the sum of everything that I've been through and the lessons I learned along the way. All of them built me who I am today.

I am grateful for all the difficulties. I turned them into opportunities and motivation for me to learn and be better.

A cake is made of salt, flour, sugar, water, among others. You mix and bake those ingredients together to make it a delicious piece. If you eat just the salt, or sugar, it won't have the same taste. It's the same with my life – like a cake – the good and bad, the ups and downs, and the strengths and weaknesses are all combined together. I'm a product of my experiences in life; all the pieces being put together, like a tapestry. That's what makes it beautiful and worth the journey.

Learning the Business

I passed the licensure exam in 1998. Usually, topnotchers are privileged to work at multinational companies. However, I chose not to. If I did, I would only be assigned to a specific task or department and therefore limit my opportunity to learn. So I worked in a small-medium company because I wanted to learn everything how to run the business.

I was employed for three years. I had the owner's mindset already. When faced with struggles, or when my employer encountered a challenge, I would ask myself, "If I'm the owner, what would I do?"

Finally, at the age of 24, I put up my own company – Excelsior.

I named it Excelsior, a Latin word which means 'higher'. My company is about offering excellent services and higher level of ethical standards in the industry.

But as I was working my way up – building my business, gaining momentum, making money – I suddenly hesitated. I realized I had this notion that rich people become greedy and corrupted. Rich people lose their values. But I wondered is money really bad? Is having money the root of evil or is it the lack of it? Then I learned that money is neutral. It's the people who handle it that determines whether it is good or bad. If I want to become a millionaire, I need to be cautious how to manage it and how to live with it. I needed to clear my mind. Certainly, I didn't want to be corrupted by it.

So, once I had peace with it, I felt free and unleashed.

Four Major Goals Achieved

Over the years, with consistency, I have achieved four major goals in my life.

First, physical fitness. I have always wanted to be fit. I clock in at least 200 minutes every week in exercise – jogging or running. I join marathons here and overseas. I also keep a balanced diet. At the age of 47, I am healthy.

Second, financial stability. I am proud to say that I have reached a certain amount already and getting close to my ultimate goal of becoming a billionaire missionary.

It takes discipline and financial literacy to be able to manage and run your finances well. In college, my parents supported me. I was good with budgeting – a skill I have kept with me and has been quite useful in my personal life and business until now. No matter how much money you have, if you are not good in managing it and budgeting, you won't succeed. Budgeting is your defense. Having source of income is your offense. Nobody gets rich just by being frugal. You also have to have many sources of income.

Third, good relationships with my family – a great wife and wonderful kids and my team at work.

I'm grateful to have a partner in my wife. I'm very visionary. I get bored with details. But ask me what are my plans for the future, I can tell you the big picture. My wife is the opposite. She helps me with the details and anything that needs to be put in place in the family and company.

Also I'm thankful for my employees, my team, that I actually call my partners. Those that have stayed with Excelsior and have been loyal to us – five years, 10, 15, or 20 years – are my partners. We call each other partners because that's how we truly treat each other. We have gone a long way in our journey working together in the company.

Fourth, finding meaning in my spiritual life. Having faith in God and knowing that all that I have are from Him keep me humble. This is the reason why my goal of becoming just a millionaire or billionaire turned into a billionaire missionary.

My faith in God give more meaning to financial success and it guides my way of running the business. When you have God in your life, how you lead your people is a reflection of your love for God.

Looking back, I won't be able to achieve these goals if not for the help of my mentors or coaches. If the company has a board of directors, I also have my own personal board of directors, like my mentors. I can access them anytime. They help me in different aspects of my life.

Vision: The Future of Excelsior

Excelsior is now over two decades – twenty-four years and counting – with around 100 employees. Our vision is to become a great global company in the industry.

From our main branch in Manila, we now have our own offices in Cebu, Davao, Cagayan de Oro, Subic, and Batangas. We are also going overseas – partnerships in Singapore, Vietnam, Malaysia, Thailand, Turkey, Japan, Korea, Taiwan, China, Germany, India, and USA.

We establish alignment and partnerships with other companies first in different countries. We need to adapt first, build credibility, and exchange business with them. Later on, when we see that we can stand on our own already, then we will launch our own company overseas.

Looking forward, I see Excelsior to thrive more in the future. One key factor that I continue to work on is raising more leaders in the company. I have worked hard for Excelsior to run and I intend to keep it that way by filling it with quality employees and trustworthy leaders.

Getting in the company is not by blood but by invitation and qualification. I love my children, and I believe in their potential but it doesn't mean they can automatically be employed at Excelsior. They will only get in the company when and if they are qualified.

They need to have three to four years experience working outside Excelsior so that when they already have experience from other companies, it would be ideal for them to come onboard. They have to start from the bottom. There's so much value in hard work, learning, and commitment.

I started from scratch. I had to endure my boss's temper when things went bad. He would curse and slam the table. Three glass tables were broken in front of me in the three years I worked there. It didn't matter if it was me who did something wrong or someone else. I just get the blame. But I chose to learn from those experiences. I was not resentful.

Culture and Practices

We provide them a culture of excellence and continued learning. We equip them with seminars and coaches to help hone and improve their skills.

We don't hire our relatives – both from mine and my wife's families. We learned a lesson. I had one relative employed with us before. I fired him because he engaged in fights. Because of that, I could not attend our family reunions or gatherings anymore because he's mad at me, and my aunties were angry, too. I realized we can help our relatives in other ways but not through employment. Sometimes, our personal relationships and work ethics can get complicated. Most of us are very emotional and sensitive. You can't confront them. They will carry grudges all the way to family reunions.

Here in Excelsior, it's not just me who decides, except when it comes to issues of integrity, or about money. When it comes to cutting jobs or other issues with employees, it will go through the Execom. It's dangerous if one person is given all the authority to do anything in the company. I cannot fire someone simply because I personally don't like him. I stay away from that.

Even if I'm their boss, I told them never come to me and carry my bag when I arrive in the office. Nobody should make me a cup of coffee. My Execom follows my example. Everyone's equal. It's just me who has a room in the office. No cubicles. Open door policy. Come to me to talk your issues. Even the delivery boy gets to come in my office. That's my management style.

The Victor In Me

I may have struggled with self-confidence in my younger days but to be able to reach the place where I am now tells me I'm a winner, a victor in my own ways. I have taken the extra mile, given the extra efforts, and held on to a dream that was way beyond me. For that, I am proud of myself and I thank God for shaping my character and building the person in me.

In my quest for success, I went through acute insomnia in 2018 because of stress. I thank God for the wakeup call. I realized I was already killing myself. So I said this can't go on. Something had to change.

It's common sense. You invest big in your business. You definitely should invest and take care of yourself, too. Your health is your asset.

So, in the midst of my busy schedule, I see it to that I have a balanced lifestyle. There is so much at stake. I have to take care of myself so I can run the company and lead my people the best I could.

If I'm not mindful, life can easily carry me away and I would lose sight of my journey. So I spend once a week in solitude. I go to a farm, or anywhere quiet, to read, meditate, and reflect. And my favorite place to do that would be where trees abound. Trees make me happy and calm. They are my stress-relievers. Just let me sit around them and I would feel nourished and refreshed.

In silence, I give myself an opportunity to go backwards and reflect where I am now in my journey. I take the time to reflect and evaluate – am I doing the right thing? Am I still on track? I check my heart and mind.

I also read a lot. Books feed my heart and mind. I started reading voraciously after my wife gave me *The One Minute Manager* book. That was when we put up Excelsior in 2001. The next book I've read was *Who Moved My Cheese* by Spencer Johnson. A classic. Then the list goes on.

Sleep is very important to me as well. I see to it that I get at least seven hours of sleep. When you have enough sleep, you can exercise well the next day. I usually wake up at 5:30 in the morning and jog for thirty minutes to an hour. The more stressed I am, the longer I run. It releases tension. Stress comes from our mind. Maybe what we're worrying about is not a problem at all. Exercise is a good way to destress.

After running, I go back home, take a bath, and have breakfast. Then I go to a coffee shop, usually at a lobby of a five-star hotel, which is not necessarily expensive, and then only after that when I go to the office.

That is my pattern, my daily routine to get myself equipped and ready – physically, mentally, and emotionally to handle whatever awaits me in the office. If there are problems, the Execom discuss them first and would recommend solutions to me. That way I don't do everything in the company. I empower them to do their tasks.

Another thing that I love doing is hanging out with people with the same vibe. Conversations with them stimulate my mind and bring new inspirations.

While I take care of my body, I also need to ground myself spiritually.

You ever wonder why there are many rich people who commit suicide? They go to the top to be rich and when they're up there in the ladder, they are empty and their riches seem useless. So they decide to end their own lives.

Money is definitely one thing. But it is not everything. There are other aspects in our lives that need to be nourished – physical, emotional, and spiritual.

How can your vision create a ripple of effects for the greater good?
I want to make a difference. I start here in my own company and in my own country. I want our company's culture to stand out, to be different compared to other companies in the industry. I don't aim to become number one in terms of riches but to be a great global company in terms of values, culture, practices, financial standing, and services.

I also use my company as a platform to spread the Word of God as a Christian. Every Monday we do worship. Sometimes we invite pastors to preach, sometimes we just listen to a sermon online. We have staff appreciation and department appreciation days. Free lunch and Town Hall every Monday are also something to look forward to.

By creating a good work culture and good relationship among us, we nourish and empower individuals. With that, we are creating communities of people and families that can contribute to the welfare of society and ultimately, the country.

A ripple of effects for the greater good can start where we are.

Signature Stories

Integrity
At the logistics industry, our clients are the importers. Majority of them have their own logistic officers who will look for brokers to serve them. Usually, they will ask the brokers for P500 to P1,000 per shipment so

that they would engage their services. That is something we refuse to do.

Around eight years ago, Excelsior was challenged. We had a long-time client. His staff told us that he would give us all their shipment on the condition that we pay P2,000 per container. He was going to make it exclusive for us. We declined. It is not us. We value integrity above profit.

We don't do that for two reasons. First, it's short term and unreliable. If we give P2,000 to the logistic officer, then another broker offers him P3,000, we will surely lose the deal.

Second, we won't be able to know if our service is good or not. Were we chosen because our service is good or is it only because we gave money to the logistic officer?

We do the right thing because we are answerable to God. I'm the owner of Excelsior. If I tolerate the employees of our clients, what is the message would I be giving to my own? What if one of my staff does the same thing simply because he knows I tolerate corrupt practices like that?

We have to remember that not all opportunities are good. Erase the myth that once opportunity shows up, grab it. It comes only once in a lifetime or once in a blue moon, they might say. But you have to ask first if that opportunity is aligned with your values? If yes, then by all means claim it. If not, never hesitate to let it go.

Som years ago, I told my wife that our tax is already so high it could actually buy us a car already. I said maybe we can declare less of our income. Who would know? Then she said, "I thought our company's vision is to become a great company? Is there a great company that cheats?"

I stood corrected.

Leadership

Fifteen years ago, I asked myself, "If Victor Hermosa goes out for one or more weeks, or if I die, would Excelsior still continue?" Fifteen years ago, my answer was no. So what should I do? I wrestled with it.

I strategized. Five years ago, I created the Executive Committee

(Execom). They are the ones who have been loyal to the company and have worked with us for more than 10 years already. In case I disappear, they will take charge. I also have the Management Committee (Mancom)- those who have been with us for five to ten years; then team leaders – those that have been on their 2nd to 3rd year with us.

With the leaders that I have raised in the company and the loyal employees I have known and worked with over the years, I can confidently say that my business will run even without me.

Building leaders in the company is a process that I am very much involved in. No one becomes a leader overnight. One has to earn it and learn it.

Becoming a leader is a process that would take years. The culture of the company is that of continued learning and mentoring. That's how I have grown in business and in my personal life and I am happy to give my employees those opportunities, too.

The following are non-negotiable traits for one to be considered and developed as a leader at Excelsior: humility, integrity, and responsibility. Those traits are what have kept me all these years as well. They are the foundation of my life and my company.

First, integrity. If you have issues with money, big or small, you can't be a leader. I am very particular with that.

I'm also reminded of Gandhi's story. He was interviewed by a reporter and was asked if he has a message about integrity. "Mr Gandhi do you have any message?" He replied, "My life is a message."

Integrity is not just what you show and say to people but also those that you don't let people see. It is how you live your life. Your life is your message.

In choosing a leader, I aim to see the things that are invisible. The heart of a person. That's integrity.

Second, responsibility. The person who cannot carry his duties – big or small – cannot be a leader. If you don't do your job well, you won't be promoted. That's basic. The reason you get promoted is when you're good at what you do, you are responsible, and you don't need much supervision. You can be trusted.

Third, humility. I believe in the 'mirror and window approach'. Literally, I have a mirror in my office and a window. When my team is doing well and have achieved something good, I should open my window and find someone I can appreciate. Affirm them.

In fact, one of my ways of showing my appreciation to them is to take them for some trips overseas. I do that because I desire that whatever I have or enjoy with my family, I also want them to have it. They deserve it.

But when there's a problem, I should look at the mirror and ask myself what have I done or have not done which probably contributed to the problem? I shouldn't point fingers or blame others. A good leader should have the humility to learn and improve, to look at the mirror and to claim responsibility for shortcomings or to open the window to appreciate and value others.

Intelligence alone can not make you a leader. You may know a lot but without humility, you cannot lead people. Humility is from the heart. It's something not taught in school. It is about acknowledging that you don't know and you can't do everything. It is about knowing your limitations and being open to learn and allow others to help you, team up with you.

How do you make a difference as a Christian in the business world?

Doing what is right is a decision and a choice. As a believer of Christ, I am compelled to do and choose what is right, and not what is convenient and self-serving.

The reason we do the right thing is because we are answerable to God. Yes, we can accomplish many things but who and what have we become in the end?

My eldest daughter just graduated in college. I asked her what company does she want to work for? She gave me an honest answer. She wants to work where she will be paid with a high salary.

Considering her degree and the school where she's from, her wish is valid. But I told her that might be a mistake. Looking for only a high salary will not make you rich. You should look for opportunities where you earn not just salary but good experiences that would enrich you as a person.

Look at the big picture. Think ahead. Ask yourself: "Three years from now, in the company where I'm working, what would I become being an employee here?" The person that you will become, not the things you will accomplish – that should be the goal.

Message to Aspiring Entrepreneurs

For those who are young and just starting in business, ask yourself what is your purpose of going into business? In Excelsior, our purpose is not to make money. Yes, money is necessary to pay salaries, electricity bills, and other operational costs. But it's not the main purpose why the company exists. Our purpose is to fulfill the mission of the company – which is to give our clients peace of mind about their shipment. Once we fulfill our mission and purpose of doing business, profit will follow.

For older aspiring entrepreneurs, it's never too late to dream something big. First, I would advise that they think of what were their orientation before? What were they good at? Start from there, focus, and hone or upgrade your skills. Develop and improve what you already have and know. If you don't know about restaurant business, don't go there. Don't venture into what your friends do just because they make money. It might not be what's for you.

Second, ask if is it marketable? Is it something you can sell? And third, is it profitable? Profit will sustain you. Profit will follow if you fulfill your purpose in business.

Most people just want to know how much they're going to gain? They easily get attracted to gaining fast and big. It can blind you. Or worse, scam you. That's one reason many businesses fail. Wrong formula. Wrong mindset. There's no short cut to success. Like in almost everything in life, there's a process.

Success – What It Is

Success is personal. Having lots of money is the definition of success for some. Others find fulfillment in helping the community. Some find it in having a stable family. There is just no one way of defining it.

My childhood orientation of being successful is to become a millionaire and overtime, I aimed to become a billionaire missionary. Excelsior's vision is to become a great global company in the industry.

Temptations surround us. There are always options to reach our goal faster if it's just about making money. I am proud to say that I have kept and lived by my principles. As a leader, I set the tone and the standard of excellence, integrity and quality service.

Creating this kind of culture can be very challenging but once set, the staff or employees would just follow. For those who can't, they're always free to go somewhere else where their values or standard align.

We are not spared of challenges too. You see, even if we're practicing integrity, we still get lapses. One employee committed a violation. We didn't know for four years he had been doing some shady deals. So there's no guarantee. But that's part of it. Even Jesus was betrayed by a disciple.

The corporate is a dark world. A believer of God should be the light. So if you have light, no matter how small, you can be seen even in the dark. You will shine like stars. You don't have to do grand things. Just be good in what you do. Big or small, it will matter.

This is one story I keep sharing.

One time, I had a new client. Within three months, we shipped around 20 containers a month with him. Then it went up to 50 containers a month.

I asked him why is he giving almost all of his shipment to us? I wanted to know what did we do right.

He told me, "For almost 10 years, my former broker would ask P10,000 per container."

His broker told him he needed to give money to customs. It could be true. I told him we were actually also asked by customs to give money but we fought our way to do it without extra fees because his shipment was straightforward. No need to pay extra. That is why he didn't need to give us more than just the brokerage fee.

So he said, "For P10,000 per container multiplied by 20, that's already P200,000 a month."

Then one time, there was a change of policy regarding the use of trucks. It only allows trucks to operate on the road at night. Excelsior had three trucks. One truck could do five trips in one week. But with the new truck ban being implemented, those five trips were cut down to two. It resulted into backlogs. Many of us in the brokerage industry were affected.

This client called. "What happened? Why can't you release the shipment?" I told him we don't have enough trucks.

Then he asked why not buy more trucks? Told him I just bought my third truck. Costed me around P2M. I couldn't afford to buy more.

He asked me to see him. I was nervous. Would he pull out from our deal? To my surprise, he gave me a cheque of P2M to buy a truck. Was he for real? I was so amazed! He was buying me a truck so I could transport his containers. Once all his containers were released, I can use the truck for my other clients. So I had four trucks already.

I don't know anyone from my industry where their clients buy them a truck and give it to them for free.

The following month, another client helped. He didn't give but loaned me P2M to buy a truck. No interest, just pay when able. Now I have five trucks. Then another client loaned me money to buy a truck. Now I have six.

My problem was no longer about not having enough trucks but not having enough parking lot!

Indeed, if you honor God in your business, he will bless you abundantly!

What makes you a thought leader?

First, I'm a lifetime learner. It keeps me young and hungry for new things. I always find ways to improve myself – physically, mentally, financially, and spiritually. There is so much to learn and enjoy in life.

I regularly meet with my coaches. I never stop learning, upgrading. There's still more to improve. I still strive. I never settle.

Second, I'm never insecure with anybody in the company who might be better than I am. I know that I am upgradable. I continue to grow. It's that simple for me.

As a thought leader, I develop and empower others to become leaders, too. I am not good in everything. What makes Excelsior successful is that I have a well-rounded team – each of us with different skills and strengths. Together, we are more solid, focused, and successful.

In the end, someone said, "Leadership is not primarily getting things done right but getting the right through other people; not to use people but to develop and empower them."

On the Right Track

As I look back on my journey, there's nothing but gratefulness and ever increasing faith in the God that I believe in. I never forget where I come from and where I'm heading.

Once in a while, I make a trip to my province to see my parents. Every time I am there, I always visit this place called Mili-pili. It's where a public well is located and it's just few steps away from our house. I used to fetch water there.

At a young age, I saw so much poverty in my place. I told myself I should aim for a better life. There must be a bigger world out there – out of this small town where opportunities to grow and have a better life were scarce.

Every time I visit Mili-pili, I always evaluate myself. What have I improved of myself? What have I changed since the last time I was here? I visit the well to remind me where I started most of my dreams and where I come from. That well inspired me to strive harder. That is my foundation.

I learned a lot along the way. Every day is a new day for me to learn and grow. I'm not great, nor intelligent. But God has a purpose why he blessed me – and that is for me to bless others as well.

One of my favorite book authors is Robin Sharma. He wrote "The

Monk Who Sold His Ferrari". He also wrote "Who Will Cry When You Die?" He said, "When we were born, we were the ones who cried. When we die, who will cry?"

Most likely, our families will do. But who else would really cry when we die?

In 2019, I asked my staff to do a eulogy for me. People say what they want to say about the person who passed away. But what's the purpose of eulogy when the person whom the messages are for is already dead? I wanted to know it while I'm still alive so I had the eulogy for me. I would like to know if I am doing the right thing. Am I in the right direction? Do I need to make some adjustment? Am I just a leader? Or am I leader that's worth following? While reading it, I was thinking is this really what I wanted to read for myself? Would they think it's a loss when I'm gone? Or would they be relieved?

I was so moved by what I've read in the eulogy for me. I am indeed on the right track. The once very insecure boy and once teased as retarded must have done well to overcome many challenges and must have done some good things in life to have impacted so many to make their lives better as well.

Now I know it's not just my family who is going to cry when I'm gone, and I am confident the company that I have started will thrive for a long time.

A Learner for Life

Victor G. Hermosa is the President and Founder of Excelsior Worldwide Freight Logistics Corporation.

A leader and a global logistics expert, he runs his company with his key team for more than 20 years now. He started with just himself, his wife, and one staff. Now he has around 100 employees with six branches in the Philippines.

He is also the Co-Founder of Thinkerpreneur Philippines – a small group of thriving entrepreneurs aiming to provide a nourishing environment for growth and building a community of leaders and life-long learners in the business sector.

Victor loves to read books and enjoys traveling with his wife and three children. He joins marathons in the country and overseas. He believes success happens not only in finances but also in having a balanced lifestyle – physical, spiritual, and emotional.

Email: president@excelsior.ph
Facebook: https://www.facebook.com/victor.hermosa.370
Website: https://excelsior.ph

Chapter 6
Life Lessons to become a Thought Leader

Simon De Raadt

Part I – THE FOUNDATION (1982 – 2007)
- 01. What if you read this chapter and learn something?
- 02. Lifting my standards
- 03. Finding my sweet spot

Part II – MY CHINA DREAM (2007 – 2020)
- 04. One encounter can change your life's course
- 05. Getting in Proximity
- 06. The Power of Weak Links
- 07. Expecting versus Accepting
- 08. Becoming a Business Dad
- 09. Failing Forward

Part III – A REFINED PURPOSE (2020 – Present)
- 10. Be Visible
- 11. You are a Business
- 12. Paying it Forward
- 13. My Rocking Chair

Part IV – CONCLUSION
- 14. Becoming a Thought Leader
- 15. My Life Lessons

PART I – THE FOUNDATION (1982 – 2007)

01. What If you read this chapter and learn something?

Have you ever felt that there is something more for you? Wondering what it is you can become? A restless feeling that the world has more in store for you. You don't exactly know what that feeling is, but it is always there. If you recognize this restless feeling, this chapter is for you. I had this feeling ever since I was young. Honestly, I still have this feeling. What has changed is, that I have learned to use this feeling to achieve my personal goals. Throughout my life, I have been able to navigate this restless feeling by listening to my instincts. I had to ask myself questions to be able to know what it would mean to me. So far it has never disappointed me. It was a simple question that anyone can ask. The one question that always helped to chase and overcome this restless feeling is: "What if …..?".

The answers to my "What if" questions always give me clarity. I have to feel it in my heart to know I truly want it. If it did not matter, I would not do it. If it would make me feel proud, I would chase it until it is manifested. Most of the things I aimed for took years to achieve. It always came in baby steps and was always much slower than I was hoping for. I ALWAYS had to put in the work and get UNCOMFORTABLE. The old version of me had to die so that a new version would be reborn. These "what if" questions helped me throughout the years. What if I become even more valuable? What if I reach people I am not reaching right now? What if I can be a thought leader that drives progress? What if I build a stronger and meaningful network? What if I share what I have learned over the years and at the same time continue growing?

This is why I said yes to writing this chapter. I always wanted to write a book about my journey and translate this into life lessons. All these years I have been chasing things that always took longer to achieve. Sharing my life lessons would allow more people to become thought leaders themselves. All hard work is paying off. The past few years things have been coming my way without me chasing it. New opportunities are presented regularly. I still have to show up of course.

But it is no longer an uphill battle. I have to say NO more often than YES (which is already a skill in itself). A weird feeling as nothing was ever given to me. So thank you Kristy Guo for asking me to write this chapter. Reading this chapter will allow you as a reader to increase your skillset, gain practical life lessons to use, and become a powerful thought leader in the area you are passionate about.

02. Lifting my standards

Coming from a lower middle-class family I never felt poor, but we didn't have a lot. My parents could only afford the basics with not much room for extras, such as holidays, branded clothes, dining out, or travel. My hometown is a village 20 kilometers outside of Amsterdam, called Hoofddorp. We lived in a lane house with 3 floors. To this day, my parents still live in this house. They have never been able to pay off any of the house mortgage as they could only afford to pay the interest. The remaining money was needed to keep the family running. My brother, two sisters, and myself knew that there was just not much extra to spend. From the age of 11, I started doing some newspaper routes and continued doing this up until the age of 15. After that, I was allowed other types of jobs and did that until I started my first full-time job. I was always working part-time alongside school and sports. My jobs have been diverse, ranging from supermarket manager, order picking in a warehouse, serving drinks in a hotel, working for an event center, working at the finance department of a casino, doing bookkeeping and archiving as well as driving cars for a car rental company. These jobs allowed me to take care of the extra stuff my family could not afford. It allowed me to go out on the weekend, play sports, buy the NBA shirt I always wanted, and go on holiday. In our household growing up, we learned that if you wanted something extra you had to earn this yourself. All of my siblings had part-time jobs up until they got their first job after graduation.

My mother was a former primary school teacher born to be a mother. When she was required to be home with us, she did exactly that thing. With finances running tight, my parents decided that my mom could babysit other kids in our house to make some extra money. It would take some pressure off from my dad, as well as nurture her passion and skills as a caretaker. Although my mom was running the household, my parents had a shared bank account. Regularly there were arguments about how the money was spent. Now being a father myself, I can only imagine how stressful it might have been for them to raise four kids with a limited income. Other than financial limitations, there were some health limitations in the house as well. My mom has been suffering from bipolar depression. As long as I can remember, my mom had good weeks and bad weeks. During the good weeks, she could handle anything and would take up more than she could handle. During her bad weeks, she was on the bed most of the day and we had to come together as a family and help out where we could. It was hard to see our mom this way, but we didn't know what to do either. Three times, my mom was really bad and had to be hospitalized for a longer period to get treatment. The first time I was 11 years old, the second time I was 22 and the last time was last year. I remember celebrating my 11th birthday in the institution my mom was. Even then my parents tried to make the most of it and I still remember that day. I got some gifts and we ate Belgian chocolates.

Our house was always a bit messy when coming home from school, as there was always a child in our house that my mom would babysit. After a cup of tea, we would go to our rooms or play outside with friends. It required us to be more independent and make sure things were handled for our own lives. Homework, sports, and part-time jobs were arranged by ourselves. My dad would always be the one to drive us to the places we needed to go, and my mom would make sure food was prepared and we were listened to. My parents wanted all kids to be playing a team sport. My sisters played handball and volleyball, and my brother and I played basketball. The fact we had to play a team sport has been pivotal in my life for which I am still very grateful until this day.

My dad worked at an accounting firm in the payroll department. His peak times were always towards the end of a month, the end of a quarter, or the end of the year. I remember him working overtime at our house with a calculator next to him. He always checked every amount to the last penny. Unfortunately he never really picked up the technology development and therefore his career development was limited. I remember him coming home with printed emails we sent to him later in our twenties. His loyalty was always there. He stayed over 35 years at his employer until his retirement. In his free time, he volunteered at the church collecting paper from the community for recycling purposes. The proceeds would go to the local church. For years, I helped my dad by bringing all the old newspapers, books, boxes, and so on, from the storage location into a container. These Saturday mornings were great for bonding with my father. Until a couple of years ago he remained active and even ran the whole thing. The majority of his time was working, collecting paper, playing tennis, or driving us to places where we needed to be.

Both my parents were involved in the church and knew the neighborhood very well. As kids, we were always outside playing with other kids. We would just go outside, ring the doorbell, and see who wanted to come play. I still remember that we had to take an official family picture. It wasn't until then that my mom realized I didn't have any pants without a patch on the knees. That picture has been on the wall at my parent's for as long as I can remember. Growing up I was able to get along with all types of kids. I wasn't popular or anything, but nobody disliked me. I did have one strong weakness. I was shy. Very shy. Whenever the teacher would ask me to say something in front of the whole class, my face would turn red. Considering that my hair was white blond it was super visible. I have struggled with this for a long time. It wasn't until my career kicked off in China that I dared to face this fear.

Growing up I have been raised to consider the costs when making decisions. When you don't have much money you focus on costs. Every store I went into I looked at the price and if that was acceptable I would consider it. I have had to retrain my brain to not just look at expenses, but look for ways to increase my income instead. My parents never discussed what they could do to increase the household income nor showed much ambition to get further ahead in life financially. Sustaining the existing was the norm while reducing expenses if possible. All of us have learned habits growing up that we don't even realize until much later in life. You as a reader have that too. I am still looking at prices, but I have learned to accept that if my income is sufficient I should not overthink it. I used to always buy what was cheaper, not what was better. I had to lift my standard to buy what actually would improve my happiness and quality of life.

03. Finding my sweet spot

From the age of 11 up until my late twenties', basketball was the red thread throughout my life. No practice would be skipped. Basketball was a given and the rest had to fit in around that. Most of my friends still today come from the game of basketball. Other friends outside of basketball knew how important it was for me. Often they would show up and watch our games.

My brother had taught me some basic basketball skills on the street. After my failed water polo experiment, I decided to join the local basketball club. Soon the skills paid off. Within two months I was asked to join a team. Normally it would take a year before you can play games, but there was an open spot, and I already had the basics. That year was wonderful. Years later, I found out from one of my teammates that he was jealous as he used to be the best on his team, and now, he had to share that spot with me. I never realized this as I just came to play. After my second season, I was put in a team with very skilled players. We ended up competing for the local, then regional, and even national championship. I couldn't believe it. I was playing with several boys I looked up to. The championship run is still one of my best memories of my basketball career. We won the national title and even repeated that two years later again with almost the same team. I was truly hooked on the sport. Basketball was so ingrained in my personal life. Years later, even after I stopped playing basketball, my two best men at my wedding were two of my former teammates.

After finishing middle school at the age of 18, I decided to continue my studies. I wasn't sure what I wanted to do, but I knew I didn't want to study a language or any of the sciences. I didn't mind the economics classes and wasn't ready to start working somewhere full-time. Although my middle school diploma would allow me to enroll in University, I decided to go for an Applied Science degree in Business Economics in Amsterdam. This would be a more practical approach, and it would allow me to continue playing basketball.

Towards the end of my first year, a friend of my friend told me he was looking for a roommate and was thinking of me moving in with him. I decided to take it. It just felt right and I could afford the rent. It wasn't always easy to mix living in Amsterdam with other things as most of my life was still happening in my hometown. I had no car so always had to take public transportation, and my bike was never at the place where I needed it to be at the end of the day. Although I wanted to explore living in Amsterdam. I still wanted to combine playing basketball as well as dating my first ever serious girlfriend in my hometown. Eventually, basketball stayed in my life, but the relationship ended. I wanted to explore the single life a bit more, and not commit to something that looked like it would turn into a long-term relationship. I asked myself What if we would buy a house together, start a family, and start a career? That part scared the hell out of me. Although I loved her as she was my first true love. I ended the relationship after dating for three years. I just wanted to date more, travel more, and experience more. I wanted to be independent. Settling down didn't feel right just yet.

During my bachelor's degree, I always had a part-time job to support myself going through college. We were required to have an internship and each time this internship resulted in a part-time job afterwards. These internships and part-time jobs have helped me tremendously. I learned that I didn't like to work in finance for the rest of my life. I also got to learn how companies work, what job roles are out there, and how to navigate company cultures. It always surprised me that when you do what is expected you already excel in your job. I also taught myself to be able to level with all walks of life easily.

Besides school, basketball, and part-time jobs, I also volunteered at my basketball club. In 5 years I revived the PR, Sponsor, and Event commission into a group of 10 volunteers. We organized various events for young and old. Raised sponsors for multiple teams. Recreated the monthly club magazine and kickstarted the website with team pages, game reviews, and news updates. I put a lot of my energy into it. To my surprise, many people wanted to join and help me out. In my final year, I also joined as a board member and got to know the club from a whole different angle. That was fascinating as you learn about the difficulties within the organization and the personal stories of club members that normally stay hidden from you as a player. The club had over 400 members so you can imagine a lot was going on. Those years as a volunteer boosted my confidence. I was able to mobilize people to join the cause I was chasing. I received an award as a member of merit just before moving to China. Although we positively changed the club, I always felt I had gained more from the experience than anyone else. I learned that I could create something out of nothing and motivate others to join in. Key skills invaluable for anyone chasing to be a thought leader.[1]

I tried many different things until something stuck. I tried many jobs, competed in basketball at a high level, and volunteered. I learned my sweet pot involved working closely with others towards a goal. I am a consistent team player who is reliable, energetic, and emphatic. I found a strong attraction to different cultures from all over the world. Your sweet spot is not linked to a role. It is linked to a skillset that sets you apart from the rest and puts you in a position to win.

---

[1] Frank Wammes defines mobilization as one of the skills of a thought leader in his Thought Leadership Model book.

PART II – MY CHINA DREAM (2007 – 2020)

04. One encounter can change everything

My first time in Asia happens on 15th January 2005, during a stopover on my way backpacking through Australia and New Zealand for 3.5 months. It's 20 years ago from the time I publish this book (how time flies). In Hong Kong, my eyes open to how differently people can live, behave, and talk. I still remember walking on Nathan Road on the Kowloon side in Hong Kong at 10 PM on a Sunday night, struggling to move through the crowd. It is one of the busiest streets in Hong Kong. I hear the street noises everywhere—cars, taxis, and buses passing by. And people. Lots of people. It's already confusing to walk on the left side of the road, but the sheer number of people outside surprises me even more. It's Sunday at 10 PM! I've never experienced anything like this in any other country. I can safely say this moment marks the beginning of my China dream. I'm intrigued, to say the least.

While sightseeing in Hong Kong, I go on a trip to one of its many islands. One of the spots is the Ngong Ping Big Buddha on Lantau Island. There is a long stairway leading up to the top, towards the Buddha statue. On the stairs, I notice this woman walking there as well. I remember seeing her on the bus earlier on the way to the statue. I decide to walk next to her and start a conversation. While we talk, I learn she is there with her grandparents, walking a bit slower behind us. She tells me that she was born in New Zealand, grew up in Scotland, and lives in the United States. She has also learned some Mandarin. As I love different cultures, I'm intrigued and enjoy her presence. After reaching the top, we say our farewells until we bump into each other again later in the day. I ask her to meet me the next day. We meet up and walk around the Hong Kong Zoological and Botanical Gardens Green House on Hong Kong Island. It's a beautiful day. In the years that follow, we meet multiple times in different cities. We meet in New York, Edinburgh, Amsterdam, and Beijing. The fact that she lives in Beijing in 2007 becomes an important reason for me to do my master's thesis research in China instead of India. I keep telling people it's a coin flip. One side is China, and the other side is India. But actually, this young woman plays an important part in the reason. China suddenly comes onto my radar. To this day, we are still friends. It's so interesting how one encounter can change your life. If I did not have the guts to walk alongside her and talk to her, who knows what my life would look like today.

05. Getting in Proximity

In 2007, I decided to write my master's thesis in China. After doing two internships for my bachelor's degree, I wanted to do independent research. It was an overly ambitious plan, but I felt like I had to give it a try. It would be a good excuse to go visit China. Most of my classmates were doing their research at a company or for a company. I was the only one embarking on this journey. I had to arrange and fund it myself. I had to come up with a topic I wanted to research on. I decided to measure the Chinese culture on how companies measure performance in China. A topic full of challenges that were immediately highlighted by my professor. In my first meeting with him, he laid it out for me. How do you define culture? How will you measure this? How will you collect sufficient data? In what industry will you measure performance? Will you look at Chinese nationals only? In what position and age group are they?

I felt defeated as I had no clue that doing independent scientific research would be that complex. This was a big setback for me. I decided to quit my part-time jobs, live on a student loan, and focus on getting this research done. I booked a flight ticket to stay 6 weeks in China. It created pressure on me and work towards that date. Ideally, by then, I would have all theory written down and only have to collect my data in China. For two months I fell into a hole. Not having the structure of classes and a part-time job made me extremely lazy. I ended up watching all seasons of Prison Break and 24. I wanted to enjoy doing nothing after working all these years to provide for myself. I had to shake this lazy feeling off of me. I needed to get things moving now as my flight date was closing in. I started to go to the university library reading all the articles I could find about culture, performance management, and China. I broke down my thesis into a more defined topic and came up with 5 hypotheses I wanted to test during my research. My thesis was finally defined. The topic was to measure the Influence of the National Culture on Reward Systems in China. I used the cultural dimensions of Geert Hofstede[2] and got his Value Survey Module translated into Mandarin.

I started reaching out to everyone I knew who knew someone in China. I built a list of people to meet. Once in China, I interviewed business leaders and professors located in Beijing and Shanghai. I discussed the theory with them to validate my understanding and put it into context. I also collected more than two hundred hard paper-filled questionnaires that I used to validate my hypothesis. I had not only learned about China. I had deep and meaningful conversations with industry leaders. And most of all, I got a glimpse of what life would be like living in a different country. I got in proximity to a life I wanted to have. It became clear to me that Shanghai was going to be the place for me to live and work one day. I just loved the energy of the city. A similar vibe that I only found in New York before that. Each time I met someone I would ask them if they knew anyone I could talk to as well. Because I got in proximity I was able to tap into people's network, knowledge, and daily life.

06. The Power of Weak Links

After finishing my master's thesis and graduating my master's degree, I decided to work for an international consulting company in the Netherlands. Hoping that they would send me to China as an expat. Ever since my China visit, I started dreaming of a China career. In Shanghai, I saw all those expats and I wanted the same life. I noticed that every foreigner I met was sent by their company with relevant work experience and certain skills. That meant for me that, if I wanted to replicate that I would have to do the same. I wanted to get that great contract,

---

[2] Geert Hofstede developed the Value Survey Module with a set of questions to measure national cultures across multiple dimensions. Geert was a Dutch social psychologist who did a pioneering study of cultures across modern nations (https://geerthofstede.com/).

great housing, great travels, and great pay. After working 3 years for the consulting company, I still wasn't even close to going to China. This was highly frustrating as it held me back from buying a house, starting a relationship, and settling down. All my efforts were leading me nowhere. Looking back at it, I simply chose the wrong job and industry. The job and experience simply did not add enough value to send me as an expat to China. It would have been much smarter to define at the beginning already whether there would be opportunities for me in China in that consulting company. Working for this company in China would require me to have local communication and language skills that I simply didn't have back then. A transfer as an expat was not possible in the field I was in. I falsely assumed that once I got the skills, the company would automatically send me to China.

I started applying for other jobs online with job openings in China. After applying to 30+ positions online I got zero responses. I needed a different approach. I decided to book a flight to China and contact everyone I knew who might know someone. It wasn't my first time doing this as using my relationships had proven to lead to success during my master thesis. I just had to put in the work and fingers crossed it would result in a job. The worst-case scenario was that I would have fun meeting a lot of people I didn't know before. To spread my chances, I booked a week in Beijing followed by a week in Shanghai. Lining up meetings wasn't the hardest thing to do. It turns out that many people know someone who lives in China. You just have to ask. Once I got to China, the hardest part started. I had to pitch myself. During my master's thesis in 2007, I had a competitive edge as I spoke English. The level of English was improving for local Chinese people. I decided to target Dutch companies with a China presence. At least I would have a shot of bridging two countries. My working experience was diverse and I never reached an expert level in anything. I decided to be open to any opportunity provided to me as long as it would allow me to live in China. In the end, I lined up 50 different meetings in two weeks. I met anyone I could for a cup of coffee, lunch, dinner, drink, or job interview. I was going around all over the city to maximize the time I had. If you don't know already,

Beijing and Shanghai are huge cities. Most of these conversations had no tangible outcome. The conversations were great and every person I met applauded the fact that I sacrificed my holiday to find a job. I didn't care about this encouragement. I just needed one person to give me a shot. It had to work. My discipline pushed me forward, but my confidence started to run low. Finally, I got a break. I was introduced to a company in Shanghai that showed interest. Nothing was final yet after returning to the Netherlands, but I followed up aggressively to make it a reality. I still remember how shocked I was to see my phone bill for making all the calls to China to get things moving forward. The job offer finally came and I signed it. It wasn't a family member or a lifetime friend that helped me get the job. It was my classmate's friend whose sister wanted to introduce me to her boss. Talking about the Power of Weak Links.

07. Expecting versus Accepting

I finally made my dream a reality. I was able to start my China career. I started at TNT Post on the 6th of May 2011 in Shanghai. 3 years after my dream began. I finally landed my very first job in China. Not as an expat, but as a flexpat[3]. With a local contract and local terms. A big cut in salary, but at least I could be where I wanted to be. It took me years to find this chance and I would not let this slip away. I felt proud as I made my dream a reality. In the beginning, there were still two other Dutch people in the company, but after a few months, it was just me and 99 Chinese in one office. The excitement for the job quickly faded away. I was bored out of my mind. I joined meetings as the white face of the company. Most meetings were in Mandarin. I wasn't clear what was expected of me. Many times I was working on things nobody ever looked

---

[3] A flexpat is a flexible expat. The concept is created by Francis Kremer and Patrick Frick. It basically means a foreigner hired for a job in a different country based on local terms. A flexpat comes with traits to bridge cultural and language gaps. Check out the www.chinaflexpat.com for more information.

at. Life outside of work kept me going. I made a lot of new friends and I joined a basketball team with a group of other foreigners.

Of course not everything in the job was bad. My colleagues were great. And my highlight of the week was the English corner on Mondays during lunchtime. It was just one hour and one colleague prepared a short presentation about any topic in English, we played some games and did some role play. Without a doubt, it was the most fun hour I had all week. Something that kept me going.

I did learn a lot from this job. Especially about how real cultural differences are. I remember having a company meeting where 40 of us are squeezed into a meeting room. Most of them don't have a seat around the table and have to stand. For one hour, we listen to our Managing Director discuss his plan. The entire presentation happens in Mandarin, as I am the only foreigner in the room. My Mandarin isn't great yet, so I don't dare ask any questions in Mandarin. I do raise one or two questions in English, but I don't understand everything being said and just try to decode the slides. Once the meeting finishes, I leave the room and walk toward my desk. Within a few seconds, a Chinese colleague runs up to me, asking where I am going. I tell her the meeting is over and I'm heading back to my desk. She laughs and tells me, "We all now go into the meeting room next door and discuss what we think the boss meant and what we should be doing." I'm confused but decide to join. We squeeze into an even smaller room, with almost the same number of people. I can hardly remember what is discussed in this meeting. I keep wondering why nobody asks any questions before, as it's obvious none of them are clear about what is expected after the meeting. I was confused and completely out of my expectations.

Another cultural experience I got was from going to a karaoke with our colleagues. If you have been to China yourself, I am sure you have been to a karaoke with colleagues or friends. If not then I highly recommend it. As it was my first job in China, I never experienced that with colleagues. I had some great karaoke nights with foreign friends, but not with a room full of Chinese colleagues. I do enjoy singing, but experiencing this with colleagues was new. It's my first week on the job, and I feel like I am bonding that night. I remember going home feeling proud that I have made so many relationships in the company. I feel connected. The next day, I walk into the office still hyped about last night's experience. I walk in with a smile and greet everyone with a cheerful "Good morning." Most of them hardly look up from their desks. I'm confused. How come no one is smiling? Was it all fake the night before? It turns out that it wasn't fake, and relationships are built outside the office. Inside the office, you focus on the work to be done… apparently. I have to accept a new norm for building relationships.

The worst time at the company came when the big boss flew in from Singapore. When I arrive at the office, I can feel the energy is already low. I've heard stories about him, but I'm not too worried. In the end, he's Dutch as well. I expect it will be fine. I look forward to meeting him, hoping it might cheer me up and make my time in the office a bit more pleasant. That thought quickly leaves my mind once he passes by my desk. He looks at me, turns his back, and without saying anything, walks straight into the Managing Director's office. With the door still open, I hear him loudly say, "What is this white face doing in this office?" while pointing at me. I'm shocked and don't know what to say. I can't believe it. How can someone respond like this? He has no idea how much effort it took for me to get this job. How can he just say that without even talking to me? From that moment on, I decide that I will never treat anyone like that. I will always listen to what someone has to say before commenting. No one should ever feel the way I felt that morning in the office. I still get tears in my eyes writing this down. I felt alone. Useless. Defeated. I hated him for not giving me the respect I deserved.

Five months into the job, it was announced that the company would close my branch office and it would continue in a separate local entity. They would get rid of the company name and continue in a local entity with a registration in Kunshan City just outside of Shanghai. I had to decide whether I wanted to continue working in a local entity or leave the company. It was a hard decision as I wasn't ready to give up on my dream. I was miserable in the job, but I did love the life I had in Shanghai. I knew how hard it was to find a job and I dreaded going through the whole process again. I also didn't want to work for anyone who treated me like trash. I provided no value and it drove me crazy. On top of that, I could hardly pay my bills and my savings were starting to run out. I decided to quit and look for something else. Although the job was a very bad fit for me, it was a very tough decision to make. This decision could mean these will be my last months in China. I had to accept this potential outcome.

I signed my resignation letter, sat out my time in the office, and dove back into my contact list. I informed everyone I knew that I was looking for a new job. Via my China network built over the past years, I had built up some solid connections that I put back to work. I applied for a few jobs and went on interviews. One interview stood out. It was for a Dutch trading company MAiNS International doing sourcing for retail companies in the Netherlands. Coincidentally, they just finished writing a market research for TNT Post. I was planning to go home for Christmas in 2011 knowing I would leave China without a job. It caused a lot of stress as I left the only job I ever had in China and I had no replacement. I did have a good feeling about this trading company and I wasn't ready to give up. During my trip to the Netherlands, I had a meeting lined up with the owners of MAiNS. I also decided to meet the person I was dealing with as well at the TNT Post head office in the Netherlands. Long story short, both meetings went really well and I secured my next job. I was able to fly back to Shanghai with a job in my pocket. I seemed to be the perfect man for the job. They were impressed with my drive, and my ability to work part-time from such a young age and take care of myself. I would double my salary compared to TNT Post and I would start as General Manager at MAiNS doing sourcing and executing the action plan that came out of the market research to develop a small parcel business out of China.

My expectations were continuously challenged during these 8 months. I had to learn to accept that things can be done in a way out of my expectations. Instead of getting frustrated about it, I needed to learn to accept it. Only then you can learn to see things differently. I had to appreciate a different way of doing things.

08. Becoming a Business Dad

At the company MAiNS, I felt as if I achieved my China dream. I was living the life I dreamed of. My plan A had worked out. I was also okay with a plan B and going back to the Netherlands, but I was excited about how it worked out. Although it wasn't an expat package, I started to get comfortable living the life I dreamed of.

On top of that, during my first two months in China, I met an amazing and gorgeous woman and we got along well. I remember it like it was yesterday. There she was. A red dress and a beautiful smile. Immediately I could feel her presence in the room. It was Friday 15th July 2011. My flatmate Scott and I went out for a Friday after-work drink. We did this regularly, where we had a group of people that you would reach out to and check what they were up to that night. My flatmate Scott is American and a real connector. He and his Belgian friend Andries were running an advisory firm so there was always someone new joining. That evening we met around 6 PM at a bar called the Apartment and had some snacks and drinks. There were always people coming and going, so always new energies joining the table. We all felt relaxed after an intense working week. It was our way to disconnect from work and hang out with whoever wanted to come and join. It was around 10 PM that a new person joined the group. She was a friend of a friend. She sat on the other side of a large round table and our eyes met multiple times. It was hard to start a conversation, but every time she looked at me I felt some butterflies already. As you never know how a night would end in Shanghai, I decided to talk to her. I got up and sat next to her. We started talking for a bit. Her English name is Annabella. With an "a" as she worked with a lot of Italians. She is Chinese and has a very positive vibe around her. I liked her immediately. Pretty, ambitious, international, and smart. Our conversation went on until some of the group said it was time to go to another location. It was around 23:30 hours already and we were there for over 5 hours so a new location would make sense. The next place was a bar dancing named Mesa on Julu Road. That place was always a safe bet for a good night out. 80's and 90's music mixed with some recent hits. Soon the whole group was on the dance floor. That is where I normally really thrive. I am not a good dancer, but I am a good freestyle dancer. High energy and uncontrolled movements. When the music is good and the crowd feels safe then I can dance all night long. This didn't go unnoticed and soon I was looking for contact with the girl in that red dress. It felt like time flew by. Before we knew it was 3 AM and the bar was closing. I didn't want this to be the last time I saw her and asked for her number. The next day I reached out and it wasn't until a few days later we managed to go for dinner together. We had a wonderful dinner in Bali Laguna in Jing'an Park and ever since we have been inseparable. That girl on the Friday after-work drink is now my wife and the mother of our two boys. Annabella has been pivotal for my personal development into the person I am today. I am still in love with her every single day. I never felt like settling down with someone, but with her, it is not a problem. She is ambitious, beautiful, caring, and active. There has never been a dull moment in our lives. I believe it was meant to be that our paths crossed. The picture of her as beautiful as she was that night will stick with me for the rest of my life. All these years leading up to me moving to China just felt like it led me to find her.

At the start of our relationship the problem was that her dream was to do an MBA in London and my dream was to be in China. We spent two months together before she left for London. Every day we were video calling on Skype. We had to talk a lot and got to know each other very well. We met every three months somewhere and then discussed if we wanted to continue the same way for another three months. I picked her up in London and brought her to Amsterdam, we met in Egypt for a trip together and then finally she came back to Shanghai to write her thesis. We continued to get along really well. We pretty much moved in together once she came back and I knew I found my soulmate. I knew that she would be the one for me.

After achieving my China dream and finding someone I wanted to spend the rest of my life with, it was time to develop a new dream. A dream to start a family. I always imagined myself being married before having kids, so I had to pop the question. In 2013, I decided to ask her to marry me during our trip to Bali. The rest of that week was just magical. We were both floating in excitement.

Not long after our wedding, during one of our weekend frisbee sessions with friends, my wife felt weak and tired. That was never the case so we were concerned and for fun decided to do a pregnancy test. It turned out she was pregnant. A new stage of life started. It felt unreal. Another dream becoming a reality. It was a stage I was excited for. I wanted to start a family and become a father. I have had small kids around me growing up with my mom babysitting them. I already had family members and friends with kids and it always brought me a lot of energy. I was ready to be a dad.

Our son was born in May 2015. The real challenge for me was being a father. Playing with someone's kid is easy, but being a parent is next level. Our son woke up every night. Not once, but 6-8 times a night. Every single night. It was exhausting. We woke every day feeling like we did not sleep. Both of us had to run a business and manage a team. We repeated this waking up every night cycle again and again. It lasted for over 2 years. We felt like zombies most of these years. I still don't know how we went through this stage of life. We did learn we are capable of much more than we thought. When the nights started to become a bit more manageable, we decided to aim for a second child. We always pictured ourselves with multiple kids. Our second son was born in September 2017. It was still hands-on, but the nights were much more manageable.

Combining work with family became the norm. There was no time for basketball anymore, limited nights out, and no spontaneous activities. Most of our friends were married with kids as well. Besides, we were living a 45-minute drive away from the center of Shanghai where most friends were living. Most days were working on the business and being a dad. I had become a Business Dad. Our circle of movement became smaller and we started to think about what was next.

When both sons were at preschool, we decided that the rat race for grades would not be something we wanted for our kids. We had seen the amount of homework our kids were getting at the age of 4 when they could not even write. The pressure for a parent to help out with homework, be a parent, and have a full-time job just would be something we found unsustainable. Besides, I have seen firsthand that a Chinese graduate doesn't know what to do on an internship. For me, that was a confirmation that you would set your kid up for competition and not self-exploration without gaining any valuable skill set to use in their career. My wife didn't see any rush to make a plan to move to the Netherlands, so I had to come up with something myself. It wasn't until the business at MAiNS hit rock bottom that I decided I needed to change things up for the better of the family.

09. Fail Forward

At MAiNS, we were providing Dutch companies with a local presence in China. It was a mix of sourcing, logistics, and cross-border e-commerce. A role that was made for me. The moment I started working at MAiNS was the first time in my life I felt recognized as a business leader. I felt more than an employee. I felt I belonged. Looking back at it, my switch from TNT to MAiNS was as if everything was falling into place. I started to realize I never enjoyed working in a department of a large company that had a focus on one area of expertise. I wanted to be involved and get an understanding of the complete business. At MAiNS, I was involved in everything. In the Netherlands, there were 3 owners. In China was just me and my Chinese colleague Helen. Her English wasn't great, nor was my Mandarin. But we made it work. Our office was located on the 11th floor at 500 Xiang Yang South Road. We were sitting in a small office. We had two connecting desks facing each other. We had a closet filled with samples of products sourced in the past. And a meeting table close to our desks. From the beginning, the main focus area was sourcing products for international clients. We visited factories for kitchen products, cleaning products, solar panels, elevator parts as well as building materials. It was a chance to see how products were made. We went to remote places that took hours to get to. Had lunch and dinner with factory owners. Inspected goods ready to be shipped to the Netherlands. I loved it. I never realized how much time and effort it took to produce a product before it was on the shelves in retail stores.

During my first year, we started exploring a new business opportunity that came from the market research for TNT Post. The market research had looked promising, and we were asked to execute on finding ways to test the market. This became a turning point in my career. TNT Post changed its global name to PostNL and that simplified our explanation to sell the solution into the market. We were the local representative of the official Dutch postal organization. With PostNL I came in contact with Chinese e-commerce players. I was the foreigner going around visiting all the major players and soon we built a name for ourselves. We started to get calls from new clients as word of mouth spread fast. As most of our clients were in Shenzhen, we decided to open up an office in Shenzhen and I had to look for my first hire ever. We listed the job opening and I flew to Shenzhen to meet several candidates. As we didn't have an office in Shenzhen yet, I invited the candidates to come to the hotel lobby. Later I learned that a hotel lobby is a very strange location to do job interviews, but I had no idea at the time. I found it practical. One candidate stood out. Not because of his work experience, but because of his first impression. He arrived early and I saw him already while I was still interviewing another candidate. He waited patiently until I approached him to join me. Our conversation was good and he showed eagerness to make it work in an industry we did not have much existence yet. I was right about him. Alex was probably one of my best hires ever. At some point, I had to let him go, but we are still in close contact. He is still one of the first people to call if I need help in Shenzhen.

We were now with the three of us in China and the small parcel business continued growing. We needed more help. We decided to hire more people to be able to continue both the sourcing and the small parcel business. We hired another person in Shanghai and one in Shenzhen. Both of them were very unqualified on paper for the initial job, but it felt right. They became an amazing addition to the team that allowed us to grow. Both of them are still working for this company till this date.

With the five of us, we managed to bring, what started as a side project, the PostNL project from 0 to 170 million Euro annual turnover. The service we offered was relatively straightforward. We found that there were two main options in the market to ship your E-commerce orders from China, either with China Post or with Express (UPS, DHL, FedEx). China

Post would take 3-4 weeks, but it was cheap. Express would take 3-4 days but was expensive. We decided to position it in the middle. Delivery in 1-2 weeks, but for a fraction of the costs of Express. We managed tens of thousands of parcels to be shipped out on a daily base. Customers included parties such as AliExpress, Wish, Yun Express, Yanwen, LightintheBox, and many others. We could not believe this was happening to us.

We went very deep into the industry. We started to come up with creative ideas that would serve the industry. Our first project was to help a client to source Chinese-branded phones and sell them in Europe. The online store would show the differences between the global phone brands compared to the Chinese phone brands. We all know these Chinese brands well by now, but in 2014 this was still early. Together with the store owner, we found that there was a need. But, there was a more striking industry problem to solve. At that time all parcels valued above 22 EUR were required to pay import VAT. Each phone fell into that range. The process to do that was very tedious and not digitalized for postal companies. The store owner and I came up with the first concept of what is now a company called ViaEurope. A custom clearance company digitalizing cross-border e-commerce shipments into the EU. My existing network was strong so getting traction in the market was not that hard. This project grew fast. We were continuously adding more clients and solving all issues together with clients. I got a chance to buy a share of the company and did just that. It was the first time to become a shareholder. We built the local presence for ViaEurope in China and then let it run by itself. End of 2024 the company was sold to Swissport. Although the company was able to build it out to what it is today, I still carry pride in seeing the opportunity before it was even there.

Besides the export of parcels leaving China, there was a lot of traction for importing products from 2015 into China. Especially the import of milk powder from the Netherlands to China was thriving due to a local milk powder scandal. Most of these orders were shipped by post, so PostNL had huge volumes going into China. As a company, we got involved in import. This was our third business unit, besides sourcing and logistics. It became too much for me to manage all the stakeholders. We hired another Dutch person in 2017. He helped me manage the relationships and push things forward in China. We got in touch with more and more brands and launched a platform with other SinoDutch companies called DigiDutch. We opened positions for interns to help us out with the various projects that came in. This development led to the opening of a fourth business unit, where we supported businesses to be their local office and hire someone under our management. By then we had 15 people employed. 3 in Shenzhen, 8 in Shanghai and 3 in the Netherlands. We had moved to a larger office and also opened an office in Shenzhen. We were active in many verticals ranging from logistics, film distribution, medical devices, beauty products, milk powder, and much more. It was challenging. But everything we touched seemed to work… until ….. it didn't.

My biggest life lesson came from this period. Everything we worked for started to fall apart. For the small parcel business, it didn't go unnoticed by the head office. Their daughter company in Hong Kong already started to get active in the market independent of us. We were competing against each other and the head office had to make a decision. We were forced to report to them and act as part of their sales organization. Our commission got squeezed, and eventually, we were pushed out. All these years we spent building it up from nothing. Suddenly it was all gone. It was part of the business I was extremely proud of and closely identified myself with this success. My soul was crushed. I felt like a failure. I failed myself, my team, and my ambitions. We tried to replicate what we did by partnering with another European postal company, but the market had changed. There was no place anymore for us to compete. You don't easily build a 100+ million Euro business.

Luckily we had other business units to rely on, but these also started to fall apart. For each project, we hired a person working 100% for a client. For successful projects, our client hired that person directly away from us. These successful projects were taken away one by one. The projects that weren't that successful were canceled. Leaving us with an employee we couldn't use anymore. Something we should have seen coming, but we were just too busy to see it.

We had to make some tough decisions and go for a complete rebuild. We started to focus again on our core business around sourcing consumer products and kept some import business. We went from 12 people to 4. Firing people was hard for me, as I considered all as family. We shut down our Shenzhen office and allowed two team members to work from their hometown. We moved to a smaller office space to reduce our costs. As owners, we went multiple months without paying ourselves any salary. The sourcing business remained stable, but it wasn't big enough to pay for the bills. We still had a beauty brand we represented for import to China, but the cash cow always was the logistics business, and that went back to zero. We tried to revive this, but we simply didn't have the resources to pull it off. Without capital and IT, we could not make it scalable or competitive.

I had to make a decision. I couldn't continue like this. I had invested 60K Euro in this business myself (40K with a personal loan). Had set up a holding company and my compensation had practically stayed the same for 8 years. I was married with two kids by now and I could hardly pay for my living. Living in Shanghai got more and more expensive. It was a challenging time for me. It felt like an impossible choice. Choosing the business I loved or choosing financial stability for the family. I chose the latter. It still moves me thinking back at that time. I had numerous conversations with the owners trying to find new ways to generate income. I went back and forth so many times, but I had to prioritize myself.

I have learned so many lessons during this time. Without this experience, I would not be who I am today. You can easily get stuck in your misery, but there is always a lesson to learn. I just had to fail forward.

PART III – A REFINED PURPOSE (2020 – Present)

10. Be Visible

I needed a plan to move out of China. Our business was losing money and I couldn't take care of my family. Luckily my wife has been there for me all this time. After her MBA in London, she started her own company in 2013. With her support, we were okay as a family, but I felt I was falling short in many ways. I had to scramble to pay for my share of the family expenses. Still leaving me with zero and an empty bank account.

I began planning a move to the Netherlands, but we decided to do a trial run first to see if we would enjoy living there. In the end, we had never lived there as a family for a longer period. That was a very stressful experience as we lived in an apartment just outside of Amsterdam juggling running a household, our businesses, and our family. We repeated this a year later in a lane house in a different city and both of us felt much more at home there. The kids had friends to play with, we had a garden, and we were making it work. One thing was still missing. We had to find a solution to manage our household. Working at China speed is impossible to do without help in the house. Having a helper would be the solution as we have to do fewer light chores in the house ourselves and have someone available for our kids when needed. The only problem left was finding a successor for my role in the business.

Back in Shanghai, we decided to plan to move the year after. I decided to look for a new project or look for a new job that would allow me to live and work in the Netherlands. At the company, we started looking for a replacement for my role. We succeeded in promoting two people to jointly take the General Manager role. That backfired as a few months after their promotion they both decided to quit. One joined a competitor and took away a client, and another one joined a client we helped get set up in our neighboring office. This left the business back in my hands. It was one of the lowest periods in my life, but I could not leave now. I learned that although my intentions are well intended, that doesn't mean that others will have the same intentions. They are on their path. Ideally, you have an open conversation to help each other forward, but not everyone can do so. Instead, they force change without a timely notice. I had to stick around in China longer to navigate the business.

Our search for new revenue projects continued. I tried to be visible, hoping it would result in something new. During a presentation in 2019 about my vision of how to help Dutch online sellers source and ship from China, a headhunter heard my speech. She approached me afterward and asked if I wanted a job at Alibaba in Hangzhou. I kindly refused saying that I was looking to move to the Netherlands. Moving to Hangzhou would not be something I was interested in. A few months later, the headhunter called me again with another offer to work in Belgium, again for Alibaba. I went through all the interview rounds, and just before the last round the headhunter called me and introduced me to another job opportunity. A Chinese start-up based in Shenzhen was looking for a foreigner to represent them in Europe. They had built an online platform to service global online sellers with sourcing and shipping from China, also known as dropshipping. It was a perfect fit. It would combine my knowledge and experience in sourcing, small parcels, and e-commerce. Besides that, I would be a bridge between China and Europe and I would be able to move to the Netherlands. It would also double my salary and create financial stability. I confirmed the job in early January 2020. It was just before, Covid started. Although the job would not start until May 2020, again I would not be able to leave China with my family. We would be "stuck" in China again for a longer period. COVID-19 in China seemed to be under control around the Summer of 2020, but that is when Europe was in full lockdown. It wasn't until May 2021 that we could finally move to the Netherlands and start a new life.

I truly underestimated how impactful a move is after living abroad for 10 years. I moved to China with a backpack and came back with 8 suitcases, a wife and two kids. Although both my kids held a Dutch passport they had no civil service number yet. I always spoke Dutch to them, but most of the time they responded to me in Mandarin. The first few months were making sure all of our paperwork was done, so our kids could get health insurance, attend school, join sports, and settle in. My wife had to apply for an immigration visa which required a lot of calls to figure out what steps to follow. We figured it all out during the first 6 months and started looking for a house for ourselves. We arranged for an au pair to come live with us so that we could get some help in the house. I had found a company that could employ me locally and invoice my Chinese employer so we could get a mortgage. After we picked the house and arranged all the paperwork we hired a designer to help make it ours. We got ourselves a contractor to execute the work and the plan was that within 3 months we would be living there. At least that was the plan. These 3 months turned into 10 months and many things were not even finished after. We had to fire our contractor and ended up finishing the rest by finding people who would help us finish it. It was extremely challenging, and it was the first and only time my wife and I got into a big argument.

Luckily, we managed to go through this stage of one and a half years of turbulence. We finally moved into our home in October 2022. This is eighteen months after we left China. It was not until December 2022 that I remember feeling joy in being where I was. We simply never had the chance to sit down and relax. It seemed like we made it. I could finally reflect a bit. We did make it. Both of us built a career, together we built a family and have a home in China as well as the Netherlands.

Although I liked the job and the company I was working at, I wasn't happy with the target audience we were serving. Every day I would be bombarded with messages on Skype, WhatsApp, WeChat, Telegram, Slack, and Linkedin. I felt stressed. I had to be "ON" 24/7. I didn't want to do this anymore as I could never switch off. I wanted to help young entrepreneurs, but all of them just wanted to get rich. They wanted to win themselves, and I was nothing more than a tool to make them get there. I was hoping this feeling of stress would go away once we settled into our house. But it didn't. Again, I needed to make a choice. Stay in the job or find something else.

During a business trip in Bangkok, I met the owner of EcommOps. When he realized I wasn't the owner, he asked me to have dinner. Many confused me as the owner of the company as I was the face online and offline. Something I was ok with as it would allow me to use it as a platform to show what I am capable of. Without this platform, I would not have been noticed by EcommOps in the first place. You never know who is watching and creating your next opportunity. For 6 months we were discussing what my role, position, and job could look like. I was able to design it the way I wanted as my profile and experience were unique. I am visible online, know everything about the supply chain, and have built a reputation in the space. We were able to work out all the terms I was asking for and I found my dream job. I would be managing the international team, dealing with new and existing clients. These clients were stable, and the China team would handle day-to-day communications. I would have to stay on track but don't have to be online all the time. I was working from home, traveling when needed, managing an international team, being visible online, and continue building on the China supply chain. Without training myself to step on stages, run a podcast, and create content these opportunities would not have come by. Don't underestimate how powerful it is to be visible online. It is not about the likes and comments, but it is all about the view. You never know who is watching.

11. You are a Business

All these years in China I had a passion for self-development. Every business opportunity in China could get big. As you only needed a small percentage of the market to make it big. All Chinese nationals around me were chasing success. Chasing a better future for themselves and their family. It inspired me to look for ways to achieve this for myself. My whole life, I have seen other people succeeding. I always felt I was left behind. It wasn't until I learned to look at things differently. Once I started to look at my life not from me against the rest, but me against myself, my perspective changed. I was able to applaud people for their success without feeling jealous. I was able to see it wasn't all about me, but about the impact you can have. Just like any business, you can only survive if you have value to offer. I realized that I was no longer working for a company. I was working for me. I was the business. Think about it for a minute. You want to increase your income (Sales), you have expenses (Finance), you need to deal with people (HR), you need to go to places and things are coming to you (Logistics), you need to eat and drink (F&B) and you have a social media presence (Marketing). You will need to manage all of these and keep your own business healthy at the same time. All these prior years I was chasing external satisfaction while I should have been looking internally instead.

For the past years, I have been trying to put this into practice. I have given presentations about the topic of "You are a Business". Your company is not your business. You as an individual are the business. I have worked in the E-commerce industry engaging with E-commerce store owners. Many of them think they need to start a business to become successful. Their self-worth is directly correlated to their business success or failure. They are not able to live in the present as they chase this external achievement. It is the same feeling I had. I was devastated by building the postal business from scratch and losing it all. Social media is partly to blame for these e-commerce owners. There are thousands of examples showing so-called overnight successes. It also confused me a lot. I wanted to become more visible to an audience that values what I don't consider to be success. They were chasing financial freedom, location freedom, and time freedom. I am not saying that striving for these goals is bad. I am saying it should not define you. I have learned that money is not evil. Having money is a great tool. It is the love for chasing money that is the biggest evil. You should not be defined by the amount of money you have. Success is a result of being valuable.

For years I was searching how to position myself as I want to stay authentic. I don't care for material success. I care about creating value and building long-term global relationships. I spoke with many of these so-called gurus. Although they claim on their social media that they achieved success, most have no clue who they are as a person. They all face the same issues as the people they are coaching. One Ecom coach is not that different from the next. They want to make money. It is a projection of material success that converts new students. It is mostly built around their ego. It is a vicious circle that I don't want to be part of. It is really hard to grow a business when you refrain from this circle for leads. These coaches can help you find your next clients. Material goals sell, but the outcome of achieving these goals still leaves a huge hole. Once you achieve these goals, you feel lost and jump on something new to chase. You forget to learn who you truly are. What you have to become. Who you want to be. With all that noise out there, I decided to approach it differently. A long-term strategy. Something that would allow me to stay close to who I am. It will be a slow process, but it will allow me to stay authentic. Especially when you become more than a business owner. When you also become a husband and a dad, life becomes more complex. It is no longer about your success alone anymore. How do you define yourself when you always link your well-being to your company's success? It is a serious battle many men are facing, but don't openly talk about. Do not underestimate how big of a thing this is. I went through this process myself and no one was able to help me. My wife was my rock that helped me go through all of this. I had no role model, example, or reference.

This is why I started to develop my mentorship program. I am developing myself to be able to grow this into a valuable service for the long term. It is still in development, but I use a 5-step method that you can use yourself as well. It will help you grow into the person you want to become. Based on my personal experience, these are the key steps:

1. Develop a skill to offer more value (take a course, try things or just put in the work)
2. With more value comes more income (better or new flow of income)
3. That income you should invest and put it to work (create passive income)
4. With extra income, you have more freedom to help others selflessly and do more of what you enjoy doing
5. Go back to step 1 and repeat this with the next skill whenever you feel ready (don't worry you have time)

To be able to build your valuable business, you will have to find out what it is you want your business to be, where your clients are located, and what problems you can solve for them. Once I realized I am not working for an employer and that I am the business, it changed everything for me. I know it will for you as well. All my contracts since 2018 have been an improvement in fixed pay. And dependent on the structure of the business, I always negotiated an upside. This can be a company share, profit share, dividend share, or revenue share. In the case of company shares, you will have to put some money in. In the case of the other three, these are milestone deals where you earn more once time passes by or goals are achieved. My logic is if the company does well my personal business should do well. For them to accept this I need to have skills, network, and value. The angle should either be you help the founder make more money, reduce their costs, or take away some pain from the owner. My time is then translated to equity. I DON'T have a dying need to own a start-up and build a company from the ground up. I don't have to either, as I already developed myself as a business. I DO have a strong need to build something together with others and scale it as far as we can. You can be an intrapreneur and still feel like you are an entrepreneur. You have to see yourself as a business. Then you decide on your terms. That is why I believe every person should consider themselves as a business. Nurture it, grow it, and set it up for long-term value.

12. Paying it Forward

Since I realized that I am a business, I need to become more valuable as a business. I decided to focus on doing things I am good at, knowledgeable about, and have a passion for. Every year I accumulate some new skills. I started to step on stages, joined an existing podcast, invested in businesses, took courses, joined Toastmasters, and negotiated win-win deals with the companies I worked for.

It is hard to find the right platforms that will enable you to grow. You should be very picky. I have stepped onto stages where no one was listening and people were only seated during my speech to take a rest as these were the only chairs at the fair. When you are visible, people will reach out and pitch their services. Decide for yourself if it is worth your time. When people approach you who are eager to learn from you could have a recorded video ready. Send the link to the video and let them send you any questions they might have in a message. This saves you time and also filters out people that are not serious enough. Only a few will reach out and the conversations with them are normally much deeper and worth your time. It took a long time for me to figure out and set boundaries. I still have to improve this myself.

My area of focus lies in leveraging China fulfillment the right way. Shipping parcels out of China has many advantages. I cover these advantages in the EcommOps Podcast so check that out for sure. I want to advise, enable, and scale companies that want to leverage shipping small parcels from China. I was part of this development from the early days and I am convinced it is a game changer overlooked by many global brands.

Besides that, I am launching a mentorship program. It wasn't until recently that I realized whom I wanted to help as a mentor. When you start something new you tend to overthink it. It was right under my nose all these years. I want to help male e-commerce entrepreneurs between 25-35 years old striving for material success but feel lost in life. I also want to give back so I joined a foundation Leergeld as a board member to help kids in the age of 4-17 years old to participate as their parents can't afford this. The foundation pays for their sports clubs, clothing, laptops, bikes, and much more so that the kid can be part of something. Over 200 kids in my town can now afford to belong and participate.

In addition, I will continue to invest in my well-being, my business, and my loved ones. It will allow me to grow and become even more valuable. My wife and I have worked hard to achieve where we are today. Still, we both feel as if we only just touched the tip of our potential. It excites me to know I will help so many more business owners reach their full potential. There is still a lot of work to be done, but now I can decide the direction myself and leverage my experience.

Remember your life is never about you. It is about making sure we as humans progress in life. You will need to pay it forward.

13. My Rocking Chair

Priorities shift during different stages of life. During my twenties, it was all about basketball and travel. During my thirties, I wanted to build a China career. Currently, in my forties, I want to put self-care first, then family, and then business. Before, it was in the reversed order and that completely failed. If I am not feeling well about myself the other areas will fall apart.

Self-care for me means taking care of my body and mind. Being forgiving towards yourself. I screw up many times. I can have ongoing conversations in my head that are energy-draining and unproductive. We all talk to ourselves in our heads. It is more about what are we telling ourselves and who is the voice that is speaking to us. Being able to take care of myself is also setting me up for a longer life. Being able to enjoy the time I have with my wife, my siblings, my kids, and hopefully grandkids one day. Be more present in the moment. Life is just less fun when you don't feel well yourself. You can be much more present when you take care of yourself. It is still hard for me to sit down and not be productive, but I am getting better at it. Your energy can only be spent once and then you have to recharge somehow. We are all wired differently on where we lose energy and where we gain energy. Figuring out what are your triggers is worth exploring. I still haven't figured it all out, but investing in a mentor to help me get more clarity was a great first step.

The concept of the rocking chair is fascinating to me. Picturing myself sitting in a chair in the last stage of my life. It is the "What If" concept, I explained earlier. Where will you look back at proudly and what do you want to be remembered for? I am proud of my journey and I want to be remembered as someone that has helped a lot of people progress in life. That my encounter with them has helped them become better. Inspired them to pay it forward. I want to leave something in a better condition after I walk away. Whether it is a conversation, a project, a company, or life in general. To me, happiness comes from progress. A real legacy is a consequence of you doing the right thing, being authentic and just being you.

This doesn't mean I am helping everyone who approaches me. I have done that in the past and this resulted in hours of meetings with individuals only looking to progress themselves to never hear from again. I believe in creating win-win and long-term relationships. I want to follow your journey not just have a conversation.

Connect with me and let me know how you are progressing and paying it forward. That would mean the world to me. You will understand what I mean if you know me a little by now. Picture me in my rocking chair with a huge smile, knowing that you progressed and paid it forward.

PART IV: CONCLUSION

14. Becoming a thought leader

There are many experts out there and there are many jack of all trades. I always thought I had to choose to become one or the other. I never enjoyed being an expert and always preferred to know a little bit about everything. At university, I learned that most successful entrepreneurs are jack of all trades, so let me become one then as well. I was wrong. To me being a thought leader is to combine these both. You can be very knowledgeable about one thing, but if you can also put this knowledge into a broader context where it can be applied, then you are on your way to becoming a thought leader. **My definition of thought leadership is to have a deep understanding of personal experience presented authentically while still chasing personal excellence and taking courageous steps.** A thought leader is more than a leader. It is someone who can put information in perspective to understand or drive change. You will need to have a point of view, develop your network, be able to sell your information and mobilize the people around you.

The goal for me was never to become a thought leader. It more or less happened to me. Too many people lead their days passively with no intention to improve their situation. They complain about what they don't have. Your behavior is determined by your thoughts. You can influence your behavior. Which means you can lead your thoughts. If you do this convincingly it will have an impact on the people around you. It takes work to achieve this. So you have to put in the work. You have to connect with others. You have to develop a point of view. You have to be willing to be wrong. You have to be willing to grow. You will have to be willing to get uncomfortable. Not everyone needs to become a thought leader. And that is perfectly fine as well. As you picked up this book I want to help you become one.

Hopefully, you will find inspiration in my story and pursue your dreams, take action, and get in proximity. I know you can make it a reality. It will be a bumpy ride for sure. Remember it is meant to be a bumpy one. Your dream is never a straight line upward. It will be full of ups and downs. Your lows will be your fuel to become the next thought leader. I have had my fair share of lows. And look at me now. I am an author now.

15. My Life Lessons

Each paragraph represented a life lesson. Just for you, I have listed them all below in short. Try them, use them, and develop them. These lessons will set you up to become the next Worlds Thought Leader.

I. **What if you try something and succeed?** Or worst case scenario fail and learn something.
II. **Lift your standards.** Your upbringing has impacted your standards, but what would your new standards be? Acknowledge your past and lift your standards.
III. **Find your sweet spot.** Many people spend a lifetime not knowing what their sweet spot is. Spent time testing things to find your sweet spot.
IV. **One encounter can change your life's course.** We often only need one encounter to make us look at life differently. After that, you can never unsee it anymore. Don't be afraid to start a conversation.
V. **Get in Proximity.** Go to places where it is happening where you want to be.
VI. **The Power of Weak Links.** It is normally a weak link that will introduce you to a new opportunity.
VII. **Expecting versus Accepting.** Letting go of expectations will help to accept things. Acceptance will result in appreciation. This skill will help build powerful understanding and connections.
VIII. **Become ALL-IN on Life.** Many of us are defined by the work we do, not by the life we live. Becoming a dad challenged me to not just be ALL-IN on Business, but to become ALL-IN on Life.
IX. **Fail Forward.** I fail on a daily base. But I will be in a

	better position next year simply because I use my failures as learnings.
X.	**Be Visible.** You will not get your break by just working hard, you need to become visible.
XI.	**You are a Business.** Run your life as it is a business. Nurture it. Take care of it. Grow it. You are a unique business that can't be copied. Don't look for comparison. Look for inspiration.
XII.	**Pay it Forward.** We all got help to get where we are today. It would be selfish to think others don't need your help. You don't get poor by giving.
XIII.	**Your Rocking Chair.** When you look back at your life you will cherish impactful moments. Times you were valuable to others. That is what matters most. Create value and let others define your success.

Life Lessons to become a Thought Leader

Simon de Raadt has built a dynamic career centered on his passion for cultural exchange and global commerce. With a deep understanding of the business landscape in China, he has played a key role in building 7, 8, and 9-figure companies in sectors like sourcing, logistics, customs clearance, and supply chain management for global brands. A recognized thought leader in the Cross-border E-commerce space, Simon is a sought-after speaker at international conferences.

In recent years, Simon has focused on helping Chinese E-commerce logistics companies expand globally, connecting them with international online sellers to streamline direct shipping from Chinese warehouses. He currently owns several businesses, invests in real estate with his wife, and leads the international team at EcommOps. Simon is also developing his mentorship program, offering guidance to others seeking balance and living a purposeful life.

Having spent a decade in China, Simon now lives in the Netherlands with his wife and two sons. His commitment to personal growth continues to inspire both his journey and those of others, making him an invaluable advisor for anyone pursuing an international career or exploring cross-border logistics.

Website: www.simonderaadt.com
Linkedin: https://www.linkedin.com/in/simon-de-raadt-56b0048/
Email: simonderaadt@hotmail.com

Chapter 7
The Journey to Entrepreneurship: Lessons, Challenges & Growth

Douglas Gozmao

Where I was growing up & when I stared my career

I grew up in a small town called **Cochin**, which was previously ruled by the **Dutch** and later the **Portuguese**. My initial school days, way back in the **1970s**, were extremely interesting and meaningful. Everyone knew each other, and it meant that irrespective of whether it was a **sporting event** held now and then at a nearby **football field** or a **social gathering** near **YWCA**, people always **partook** and made the event successful. There was recognition for **sporting success** as well as for **educational achievements**.

My family consisted of my **parents** and two other **siblings**. We came from a **middle-class background**, although my **grandfather**, a **doctor by profession**, mostly served people **experiencing poverty** and, therefore, had an **extremely good reputation**. My father worked for one of the **famous tea companies** near the **Port of Cochin**. This also allowed me to work in the **Port area** from a young age and understand what **Stevedoring** meant.

My earlier career

After completing my **studies** in **Cochin**, I moved to **Chennai, India**, to study **Automotive Engineering** and spent **four years** there. My efforts paid off, and I did **very well**, achieving a **first-class** distinction. Although **cars** were my **passion**, my **destiny** was different, and I did various things after returning to **Cochin**. This was a **difficult moment** for me, as I did not find any meaning in pursuing this field. Ultimately, I ended up **starting a freight and removal company** in the **Port and Customs area**, not far from where I lived.

Initially, it was not **easy** as I had to establish contact with many **forwarders** in the **Middle East** to secure their **business**. However, the effort paid off—I started making **a lot of money** and **building a reputation**. Life was **good** until **business** dropped at the beginning of the **nineties**.

My courage & success of entering different career

Although the **business** was still running, my **interest** in the field **waned**. I decided to **move on**, albeit **maintaining the same office space**. This was when I met an **old friend** who was working as a **franchisee** for a **courier company**. He asked me if I would be interested in **running the operation from the CBD**, which I gladly **accepted**. This meant I had to **handle the entire operation alone**, with **no support**. Although this was initially a **challenge**, I overcame the **difficulties** with much **support** from my **friends** in the **shipping and forwarding industry**.

The **one takeaway** from this experience is that if you are **willing** and **committed** to doing a **task**, however **difficult** it may be, you can **succeed**. It's always the **willpower within oneself** that generates the **much-needed confidence** to move forward.

The **days, months, and years** flew by. Since I had a **small office** and a **license** to work in **customs and the port**, I gradually brought back some **forwarding business** and **merged it** with my **courier operations**. The **challenge** was **enormous**, but the **money** was **good**, and I could **do things** and **enjoy life** like the **rich and famous**.

My down path & how I find my purpose

The **months and years** passed quickly until one **fine day**, the **courier company** decided to **sell its business** to another **entity**, meaning we had to **give up the franchise**. This was certainly a **down moment**—**disappointing**, to say the least. However, I had to **make choices**. It was

December 1993, and a **good friend** of mine, who happened to be in the **Middle East**, came calling.

The **months before that** were **wasteful**, and I was in a **position** where I felt like I had **lost it all**. The **community** saw me as a **hopeless personality**, which, at that point, I certainly was.

It's important to note that each of us has **moments and periods** when we feel that **life has no meaning** and we are **at the point of giving up**. Those are **difficult moments**. However, there are **choices** one has to make. Opting for the **best option**—and the **hardest one**, which is a **reset of your personality**—is not a **simple task**. At the same time, one needs to have a **belief system** and **listen to the inner voice**, which is exactly what I did.

My adventure starting from Dubai

I decided to **make the call**—to leave my **hometown** and head to **Dubai** on a **transit visa**, which was then **valid for two weeks**. With **no financial backing** and **nothing to look forward to**, I arrived in **Dubai** one **sunny morning** in December 1993 with just a **briefcase** and a **few clothes in hand**.

The country was still in a **developmental stage**, consisting mostly of **old buildings** and **pristine deserts**. Having **little money**, I had to **shack up** with my **friend** in a **congested** single-bed **apartment**, with a **small kitchen** and a **tiny washroom**. These were **difficult days** as I was used to staying in a **reasonably big house** with **three square meals** all the time.

The **transition** was **difficult**, and **sleepless nights** followed. However, having a **good friend** by my side, who was **employed**, was a **bonus**, and there was some **support** from that end.

I told myself that I could either **make it or break it**—or **return home**. I decided that, **come what may**, I would **rough things out** until I **succeeded**. My **job** with a **local Arab**, who wanted me to support him with his **removal business**, was not exactly going as I thought it would. **Six months** passed, and I was just about **surviving**, until I decided that it was **time to move on…**

A Period of Loss and Reflection

Through a circle of friends from my hometown, I found a **job** with a new forwarding company. Although I worked in **sales** and handled some **operations**, I was uncomfortable taking orders. The **boss** in question was extremely **dominating**, and I soon realized that I was not meant to be sitting down and taking orders—I had it in me to **be the boss**.

The time spent in that organization, which was under **two years**, was an **eye-opener** for me. Not only did I have to deal with the pressures of work, but I also had to endure the most painful loss of my life—the **passing of my father** and my **brother** just a few days later. Due to an **altercation** with my then-boss, I was unable to travel back for the funeral. That was the most **depressing** period of my life, as my mother had to handle all the **formalities** and the overwhelming grief on her own.

A month later, I **quit** my job and travelled back to India. In a way, the time spent there helped **heal** some of the grief. I was able to spend quality time with my mother, helping her through the **immense sorrow** she was suffering. **Three months passed**, and something inside me urged me to return to the UAE and start over. I took some more time off, but **eventually**, I visited the UAE once again.

Starting Over in the UAE

I found a **job** in an **organization** that dealt with **oil tankers**. My role was that of an **assistant to the operations manager**. The job was relatively comfortable. However, after about a year, my **boss** ran into trouble with **management** and had to leave. He was a highly **knowledgeable** man, and I learned a lot from him about **how to run operations**. Unfortunately, things were **short-lived**—I was forced to leave due to an **unpleasant situation**. This made me reflect on something **important**: **Nothing is ever certain**. But it's essential to **move on** and not remain stuck in difficult situations. It's a lesson for all—most people believe that **landing a good job with great perks** means stability forever. **That's rarely the case.**

After quitting that job, I was forced to **return to India** once again, where I spent **three months** with my mother. This time was deeply **sobering**. I used it to resolve many **pending personal matters**, particularly related to **property issues**. Once that was settled, I felt the pull to return to the UAE again—something about the place **kept calling me back**.

A Fresh Perspective & a New Start

This time, **returning was easier**, as I had the **financial stability** to stay and look for opportunities. Then, one day, I came across a **classified ad** seeking someone with **experience in ocean operations** for a **well-established organization**. I got the job. The **boss**, however, reminded me of my first job—**strict, demanding, and dismissive of contributions**. Initially, everything went smoothly, but I soon realized that although I was **generating significant revenue**, my **efforts were never recognized**. This once again **reinforced my desire** to become **my own boss**.

The Birth of a Dream

During this time, I met a **colleague** who would later become my **business partner**. We built a **strong relationship** and saw **potential** in turning our dreams into **reality**.

A year passed, and we were deeply **involved in the industry**, supporting many **shipping lines and co-loaders**. We became **well-known** in the market. Many of my **hometown friends** were also in Dubai, most of them working in the **shipping and forwarding industry**, which gave me a **valuable network**. Given this **solid foundation**, I discussed my plans with my future **business partner**, and we made a decision—**we would launch our own forwarding company within a year**.

This commitment meant **hard work**, as we both still had **full-time jobs**. Our strategy was to **work during the day** and dedicate our **nights** to the new venture. This meant **14-16 hour workdays—10-12 hours in the office** and another **4-5 hours meeting clients** after hours. At the time, I didn't have a **driver's license**, although I had been **driving since a young age**. Determined to make things easier, I quickly obtained a **UAE driving license**.

Owning a **car** became the next priority. After much **searching**, I finally bought a **used car** through a **friend** who worked at a **car showroom**.

This was **1997**—a time when **Dubai was beginning its transformation**. **Skyscrapers** were rising, **construction** was booming, and the **city's future was taking shape**.

Taking the Leap: Becoming My Own Boss

At the **beginning of 1998**, I finally decided to **call it quits** with the company. My **boss at the time** was not happy to see me go, and my **dues, including gratuity, were withheld**. However, I was in **no mood to argue**. Regardless of whether I received what was owed to me, I had already made up my mind to leave. By that time, we had secured **around 10–15 customers** who were willing to **support us**.

Back then, **finding a sponsor** was a **necessary step** to establish a business, as they were required to **own 51% of the shareholding**. Fortunately, our sponsor was an **exceptional person**. He owned a **travel agency**, which was managed by someone he trusted. He suggested **adding Freight Forwarding activities** to the existing licenses, allowing us to **launch our operations**. Initially, we ran both businesses **in parallel**, under two divisions, working **collaboratively**, and things **progressed smoothly**.

It took me **about six months** to set up the business before my **partner joined me**. That was when we decided to **hire our first employee**, as we had been managing **sales, operations, and accounting** entirely on our own. By the time we entered **1999**, our team had grown to **four employees**. Although we still maintained **significant control** over operations, we recognized the **importance of delegation** to facilitate further growth. Despite the **uncertainties we faced**, my **confidence grew each day**, as did our **customer base**, pushing us to take things to the **next level**.

One of our **first major investments** was purchasing our **first truck** and hiring a **driver—who remains with us to this day**. This stands as a **testament** to how we have treated our **employees over the years**, fostering **loyalty through respect and compassion**.

The **lessons I learned** from my previous bosses **helped shape me** into a **better leader**. They enabled me to make **well-informed decisions** that ultimately benefited both my **personal growth** and the **development of our organization**.

During those **early days**, we operated out of a **single-room office** with **barely enough space to move**. Fortunately, our **local sponsor** was **generous enough** to provide us with **a workspace**. In return, I **promised to assist him** with the challenges he faced in managing his **various businesses**. He was a **true gentleman** who held a **high position in immigration**. Unfortunately, many people **took him for granted**, which meant we often had to **handle issues unrelated** to our business. The office had **four large rooms** and a **reception area**. We only **paid for what we used**—a **single room and a small reception space**. At that moment, we simply had to **make do with what we had** and push forward with our **plans**.

A few months later, towards the **end of 1998**, our **local sponsor** asked the occupants of the **other three rooms** to **vacate**. This set the stage for our **expansion**, and we **seized the opportunity**. We decided to **allocate at least one person to each department**, and soon after, we felt a **significant surge in business**.

Around the **same time**, the individual with whom we had **shared the business license** decided to **run his operations independently**. This left us with no choice but to **obtain our own trade license** from the same **local partner**. Preparing for this transition was a **challenge**, particularly as we needed **financial backing**. However, with the support of some of our **loyal customers**, we successfully **registered our names** as **license holders**.

This marked a **pivotal turning point** in our journey. It wasn't just about **running a business anymore**—it was about **building a name, a reputation, and a legacy** that would take us to the **next level**.

During that period, we had the opportunity to meet some **very important people** from the **USA**, who were in the process of bringing together **like-minded individuals** to form what was then an **unknown network**. A **meeting was called** and organized in **Thailand**, where we met with around **20 freight forwarders worldwide**. At that time, we worked with each other but were **not yet part of a formal network**.

Things took a **turn for the better** when it was decided that a **leader was needed**. At that moment, a **gentleman from the USA** stepped up and was **instantly chosen** to head the network—**which still exists today**. It was then decided to hold **annual meetings**, and after **2-3 days of interaction**, everyone returned to their respective countries. **Business started to flow**, and we interacted well with each other. This became one of the **first networks we were part of**, and it was truly a **proud moment**.

The following years presented **many challenges**, and there were days when **even 18-20 hours** of work was **not enough** to complete tasks and fulfill promises. The **key takeaway** was understanding that to **achieve targets and goals**, there is **no better way** than to be **focused, determined, and believe in oneself**. Along the way, we had the privilege of meeting **amazing individuals**—customers, partners, **network heads**, and many **inspiring people**.

2002: A Turning Point

The year **2002** was particularly **eventful**, as we decided to **invest in a warehouse** in **Mainland Dubai**. Having our own warehouse meant we could **better support our clients and partners** in storing their valuable goods. Before long, we were **running a full warehouse**, proving that our **tireless efforts had paid off**. This milestone marked the beginning of our transition toward becoming a **medium-sized freight forwarder with our own assets**.

To **keep up with growth**, we also began **recruiting new employees** to meet **expanding customer support needs**. Looking back, I felt proud of what had been achieved, yet I sensed that I had **not yet realized my full potential**—there was still **more to be done**.

Venturing into the Coir Business

Around this time, by chance, I met a friend interested in trading **coco peat**, a product used as a **soil replacement**—especially valuable since **water was scarce**. This product **quickly became a hit**, and we were **flooded with orders**.

After a few months, I decided it would be **better to start a manufacturing unit** rather than rely on merchant exporters in India. I **traveled to India**, secured **4 acres of land**, fenced it, and returned to Dubai. The next step was to create a **business plan**, finalize a **partnership deed**, and start **manufacturing**.

Meanwhile, we continued selling **coco peat** in **UAE, Australia, and Qatar**. I had to **balance my time** between **Dubai's business demands** and **setting up the operations in India**. Fortunately, all the **hard work paid off**—we launched **production in 2009**, just as our **forwarding business in Dubai** was also taking off.

By then, we had **45 employees**, and our **turnover kept growing year after year**. In our **coir business**, demand continued **rising**, leading us to **operate three shifts** at the factory, employing **over 50 people** from the **small village** where we were based. The impact was **transformational**—we were now providing **livelihoods** to many families, who in turn expressed **immense gratitude** for the opportunities.

Expansion and Investing in Assets

As our operations grew, we realized we **needed a trading license** in the UAE. In **2011**, we invested in a **multi-purpose license**, which allowed us to **import coco peat** and assist our **partners and customers with shipments**.

With growing **support from banks**, we reached our **goals faster than expected**. By **2017**, we decided to **stop outsourcing our warehousing** to the **free zone** and **purchase our own warehouse**, with **bank assistance**.

Although the **initial results were not as expected**, we took up the **challenge—hiring staff**, ensuring **full warehouse utilization**, and gaining a **competitive edge**. While acquiring **assets like trucks, trailers, and warehouses**, we made sure **not to forget** the **smaller forwarders** who had been part of our journey. We **offered them special rates** for storage, **helping them grow** alongside us.

The most **rewarding experience** was seeing **our employees thrive**. Many came to me every few months, **handing me the key to their new home**, saying, **"If not for you, I wouldn't have a roof over my head."** They even invited me to **inaugurate their new homes**. These moments were **incredibly fulfilling**, and to this day, I **take immense pride** in the impact we made on the **poor and downtrodden**.

Lessons Learned: The Power of Resilience

I share my **life stories** because being a **thought leader** means **inspiring others** through real experiences. Here's what I've learned:

Looking back, there were **many moments** when I felt **completely exhausted**, at the brink of **giving up**. I could have chosen to **walk away** and take an **easier path**, disappearing into **oblivion**.

But something **stronger** took over—**resilience**.

The **urge to succeed** overpowered the **negative feelings**, driving me to **stay focused** on a path that not only shaped **my future** but also **brought happiness and security** to those who **depended on me**.

There were times when I felt like I was on a **sinking ship**, with only two choices:

1. **Go down with it**
2. **Swim to shore**

I chose to **swim**.

The key takeaway from this journey is **resilience**—without it, I would **never be where I am today**.

But beyond **resilience**, success is about **taking action**. Many people **think of great ideas**, but **few put them into motion**. The **true mark of an entrepreneur** is the **ability to narrow down** the best ideas and **execute them effectively**.

That, in the end, is what makes the **difference between a dreamer and a doer**.

Success & Resilience

It's also important to note that **not all plans and ideas** become **successful**, so it's crucial to **weigh the pros and cons** and take proper stock of the **situation**, even when **stocks are down**. Again, my **"never give up"** attitude has brought me to where I am.

Thought Leadership & Practical Thinking

The important thing about being a **thought leader** is **thinking for your people** and putting yourself in their **shoes first**. I also believe in **karma** and understand that **things always happen for a reason**. Another **key takeaway** would be to **immerse yourself** in the situation—whether **good or bad**—and then **take the best out of it**.

These **thought processes** do not require you to be a **rocket scientist**. Rather, using **common sense** and taking a **practical approach** is important.

Entrepreneurial Mindset & Communication

My entire focus throughout my **life as an entrepreneur** has always been to **think about my people**, who were **part and parcel of my family**. Many times, I understood the **importance of having committed people** to drive my **ambitions forward**.

Effective communication has been another **key factor** that has **propelled me** and my **vision** to reach **heights that were once unreachable**. A true example was when I was **outsourcing warehouses** to meet **customer demands**, only to realize this was **not helping customers** because we could not provide the **level of service they needed**.

The idea of **buying and owning a warehouse** came to mind, but how was the question? For this to happen, I needed to go the **extra mile**—finding **banks** and securing **financial resources** to achieve my **objective**. Although there were **moments of doubt**, I never **lost faith in my ability**.

It is important to note that, **come what may**, staying **determined and focused** is **vital** during such transactions. Looking back, I believe it was **confidence** and **determination** that helped me achieve this objective.

Networking & Relationship Building

Another **key factor** in my **list of achievements** was the fact that I engaged in **networking**—both **locally and internationally**. Attending **conferences** and meeting **partners** gave me **different perspectives** on issues that would have otherwise been **difficult** to solve.

Other crucial factors in **building long-term relationships** were **remaining authentic** and **creating trustworthiness**. Today, these relationships remain **strong**, serving as the **foundation for genuine growth** in the **organization**.

People Over Profits & Finding Balance

My goal was always to **build a culture** among my **people**, standing by them in their **most difficult situations** and addressing **socioeconomic issues** relevant to their lives. I believed in **caring for people** more than the **profits earned**, and this principle **helped shape my journey**.

I must admit that finding a **balance** between my **family** and my **extended professional family** was never **easy**. However, I had my **priorities set** and was never afraid to **seek advice** when needed.

The ability to **learn from others**, not just **peers**, was another factor that helped my **growth** happen **sooner rather than later**.

Overcoming Challenges & Decision-Making

I always **welcomed challenges**, and although they sometimes **threw me off balance**, it was always about **bouncing back** and **finding solutions**. This is why the **logistics industry** constantly keeps you on edge, with **everyday issues** requiring quick thinking.

The good thing about **experience** is that it allows you to **reflect on past incidents** and then apply **better solutions** in the future.

Another critical factor is **timely decision-making**. Decisions are **instrumental**, and if not made **at the right time**, they could be **costly** and **ineffective**.

Customer Loyalty & Long-Term Commitment

Over the years, we have consistently created **value for our customers**, ensuring **long-term loyalty**. This is why we have been able to **retain clients** for **over 25 years**.

Looking back at where we **started**, it is clear that **hard work and commitment** have helped us reach **where we are today**. The most important thing is **consistency**—we have done this **repeatedly**, year after year.

This does not mean we have **never failed**. However, we have always **overcome challenges** and maintained the **passion and determination** needed for success.

Leadership & Legacy

I have always believed—and still do—that **hard work always pays off**, and it certainly has. Furthermore, when you have **people who share your vision**, life becomes **easier to navigate**.

Being **human first** is another **principle** I have learned. Apart from showing **compassion**, this has created a **sense of fulfillment** in how I have approached things—not just for my **peers**, but also for my **people**, who are the **backbone and foundation** of my growth.

Looking back on my **leadership journey**, I want to give my readers an **insight** into how they should **plan for the future**. It is important to note that being **adaptive in leadership** is crucial to building a **resilient organization**.

Making **employees feel empowered** is another **key factor** that drives growth. Above all, **creating strong values** is essential to establishing a **positive culture** within an **organization**.

The Journey to Entrepreneurship: Lessons, Challenges & Growth

Douglas Bertram Gozmao

Managing Director, GTZ Shipping LLC | Visionary Leader in Global Logistics

With over 30 years of expertise in shipping logistics, freight forwarding, and international trade, Douglas Bertram Gozmao is a seasoned entrepreneur and strategist. As the Managing Director of GTZ Shipping LLC, he has been instrumental in shaping the logistics landscape in the UAE, driving business growth, and forging global partnerships.

Douglas's leadership journey spans from founding and scaling businesses to optimizing supply chain operations across diverse industries. His commitment to quality, operational excellence, and talent development has earned him multiple global awards and the UAE Government's prestigious **10-year Golden Visa** for his significant contributions to the economy.

Beyond logistics, Douglas has successfully expanded into manufacturing and trading, spearheading ventures in coir exports and international trade. His unwavering belief in innovation, resilience, and service excellence continues to redefine industry standards, making logistics simpler and more efficient for businesses worldwide.

Contact Douglas at: dg@gtzshipping.ae

Chapter 8
Thought Leadership: A Journey of Discipline, Influence, and Transformation

Leslie Swamy

Part 1: The Beginning

Let me begin with this word – **Discipline.**

Born in Mumbai, India, in a humble lower-middle-class family, discipline was the core of my upbringing. My father served in the services for a short time, while my mother was a dedicated homemaker. From a young age, I was instilled with values of hard work, perseverance, and humility. These values would later become the foundation of my leadership journey, shaping my decisions and the way I interacted with people throughout my life.

Unlike many children who struggle to adhere to strict routines, I found comfort in discipline. It provided a structure that allowed me to excel in both academics and extracurricular activities. I was an above-average student, consistently performing well in school while also exploring my creative and athletic interests. Though I had not yet envisioned my future as a leader, the seeds of ambition were unknowingly being planted in my heart.

The Business Card That Changed Everything

One afternoon in the early '90s, while walking with a close friend, I stumbled upon a business card lying on the street. Out of curiosity, I picked it up, examined it, and said, **"Someday, I, too, will have a** card with my name on it." My friend smiled and nodded, not thinking much of it. But for me, that seemingly small moment ignited a lifelong aspiration.

That card represented something more than just a name and a designation. It symbolized **identity, accomplishment, and recognition.** It was a tangible marker of one's contribution to the world. Though I was too young to understand the full implications of that realization, I carried that ambition with me through the years.

What I learned from this experience was the power of **vision.** Thought leadership is not just about possessing knowledge—it is about seeing possibilities before they manifest. Leaders must cultivate the ability to dream beyond their current reality and work relentlessly towards bringing those dreams to fruition.

Early Influencers in My Life

As I reflect on my journey, I realize that certain individuals played a pivotal role in shaping my path. These mentors and role models did not just teach me skills; they instilled in me values and perspectives that would later define my leadership style.

My Mother: The First Leader I Knew

My greatest influence was my mother, though I was blessed to spend only nine precious years with her before she left for her heavenly abode. Her humility, patience, and selflessness left an indelible mark on me. She was always willing to help others, no matter how little she had to offer. Even when resources were scarce, she prioritized the needs of those around her.

She taught me that **true leadership is not about power—it is about service.**

Her quiet strength and resilience made me realize that leadership does not always have to be loud or authoritative. Sometimes, the most impactful leaders are those who lead by example, demonstrating kindness, perseverance, and integrity in their everyday actions. To this day, I strive to embody the values she imparted to me.

My Brother-in-Law, Nagesh: A Master in Sales and Persuasion

Nagesh was an outstanding salesman who worked for Alembic before running his own mid-sized pest control business. He played a crucial role in shaping my entrepreneurial vision. He often observed my hard work in logistics and encouraged me to start my own business.

I vividly remember one of his favourite sayings: **"Leslie, if you ask me to sell a stone, I can do it."**

His confidence in sales and unwavering belief in me fuelled my desire to become an entrepreneur. More importantly, he taught me that **selling is not just about transactions—it is about trust, communication, and understanding people's needs.** A thought leader must not only have great ideas but also the ability to communicate those ideas effectively and inspire others to take action.

Mary, My Mentor and Co-founder: The Art of Leadership Through Action

When I joined my first job as a Dispatch Clerk, Mary was already an established leader in company operations. She was multi-talented, highly communicative, and exceptionally efficient. But what stood out most was her willingness to help others without hesitation.

Unlike traditional leaders who focus solely on performance metrics, Mary believed in the power of **collaboration and mentorship.** She was never threatened by others' growth; instead, she actively sought to uplift her colleagues. Working alongside her taught me invaluable lessons about leadership, teamwork, and operational efficiency.

Through her, I learned that a true leader's success is not measured by personal achievements alone, but by how many people they help rise along the way. Thought leadership is about creating a ripple effect—one act of guidance or encouragement can transform someone's entire trajectory.

The Lessons That Shaped My Thought Leadership

Looking back at my early years, I recognize that each experience, no matter how small, contributed to my growth as a thought leader. Here are some of the key lessons that emerged from my journey:

1. **Discipline is the Foundation of Success** – Without discipline, talent and ambition can only take you so far. Consistency in actions, habits, and decision-making is crucial to long-term success.
2. **Vision is Everything** – That business card I found as a teenager may have seemed insignificant, but it gave me a sense of purpose. Leaders must develop the ability to envision their future and create a roadmap to achieve it.
3. **Service is the Highest Form of Leadership** – Whether it was my mother's selflessness, Nagesh's willingness to share his wisdom, or Mary's mentorship, the greatest leaders are those who focus on **empowering others.**
4. **Communication is Key** – Being a thought leader is not just about having great ideas—it is about sharing them effectively. Whether in business, sales, or mentorship, the ability to articulate your thoughts can determine your level of influence.
5. **Resilience Builds Character** – Life is full of setbacks and challenges. But as I learned from my early experiences, resilience is what separates successful leaders from the rest. The ability to bounce back and adapt to changing circumstances is a defining trait of thought leaders.

The Journey Ahead

As I continue this journey, I am constantly reminded that leadership is not a destination—it is a continuous process of learning, growing, and giving back. The principles I absorbed from my mother, my brother-in-law, and my mentor have guided me through every phase of my career and personal life.

Now, as I share my story, I hope it serves as a source of inspiration for those who aspire to lead, influence, and create meaningful change in the world.

If there is one message I want to leave you with, it is this:

Your leadership journey begins with the choices you make today. Lead with authenticity, embrace discipline, and always strive to uplift those around you. The legacy you build will not be measured by titles or accolades, but by the lives you touch and the impact you leave behind.

So, what story will you write? What legacy will you create?

The answer lies in the steps you take from this moment forward.

Part 2: Journey to Thought Leadership

Tools and Experience

The path to leadership is paved with experience, adaptability, and an unwavering commitment to growth. I have always believed that leadership is not about power—it is about service, authenticity, and making a difference. One of the most profound experiences in my journey involved a decision that changed both my life and someone else's.

My Driver's Story: A Lesson in Leadership

During the COVID-19 pandemic, as uncertainty loomed, I received a late-night call from Prashant, my part-time driver. His voice was strained as he informed me that he had decided to quit his job.

"Why now?" I asked, surprised. "People are already struggling with job losses. You're newly married—this isn't the right time."

His response was filled with frustration. Despite my efforts to convince him otherwise, he had already made up his mind. That night, I discussed his decision with my wife. We were both concerned about his well-being and the difficulty of finding a job during the crisis.

A week passed without any word from him, so I decided to reach out. He reiterated his decision, stating that he was looking for a different job. Understanding the challenges of the pandemic, I realized it would be tough for him to find employment.

That evening, my wife and I discussed our options again. My work-related travel was increasing, and with COVID restrictions gradually easing, I needed a reliable driver.

In that moment, I made an immediate decision.

The next day, I called Prashant. "I'm buying a car," I told him. "Would you like to work for me as my full-time driver?"

Without hesitation, he answered, "Yes, sir."

That single decision changed both our lives. For him, it was a stable job and a renewed sense of purpose. For me, it was a reminder that leadership is about creating opportunities, not just for oneself but for others as well.

Lessons in Thought Leadership

Looking back, I realize that this experience encapsulated several key aspects of thought leadership. It was not just about taking responsibility for someone else's well-being; it was about embodying the values of resilience, adaptability, and empowerment. Here are some critical leadership lessons from this story:

1. Leadership is About Empowering Others

A true leader does not just think about their own progress but also considers the growth and stability of those around them. By offering Prashant a stable job, I was able to turn his uncertainty into a source of security. Thought leadership is about influencing others positively, giving them the tools and confidence to move forward.

2. Adaptability and Decision-Making in Crisis

The pandemic was a time of rapid change, forcing individuals and businesses to rethink their strategies. If I had simply accepted Prashant's resignation without question, he might have ended up struggling without employment. Instead, by adapting to the situation and making an immediate decision, I was able to provide a mutually beneficial solution. Leaders must be agile, making tough decisions that consider long-term consequences rather than short-term setbacks.

3. Emotional Intelligence in Leadership

Prashant's decision to quit was driven by fear—fear of instability, of the unknown, of making the wrong choice. As leaders, we must recognize the emotional aspects of decision-making, both in ourselves and in those we lead. Understanding Prashant's concerns and addressing them through meaningful dialogue and a practical solution was a lesson in emotional intelligence.

4. Taking Ownership and Creating Opportunities

Many people assume that leadership is about managing others, but it is just as much about taking ownership of a situation and finding ways to turn challenges into opportunities. Instead of viewing Prashant's resignation as a loss, I reframed it as a chance to create a stable, long-term working relationship. Great leaders do not wait for opportunities—they create them.

5. Leadership Extends Beyond the Workplace

The role of a thought leader does not end within office walls. It is about influencing lives in meaningful ways. Leadership extends into personal choices, interactions, and the impact we have on people's futures. By stepping in when Prashant was at a crossroads, I was able to provide not just financial stability but also reassurance in uncertain times.

Thought Leadership in Action

This experience reinforced my belief that thought leadership is about more than just expertise or business success—it is about influence, responsibility, and the ability to shape the future. It is about lifting people up, showing them possibilities they might not see for themselves, and leading with authenticity.

We all have moments in life where we can choose to lead or let circumstances dictate our path. Thought leadership is about making those choices consciously, with wisdom, empathy, and a commitment to creating positive change.

To those reading this, I leave you with this thought: Leadership is not just about climbing the ladder yourself—it is about extending a hand to help others climb alongside you. How will you use your influence to make a difference today?

Part 3: Becoming a Thought Leader

Authenticity and Humility in Leadership

Thought leadership is not about having all the answers—it's about sharing experiences, being genuine, and inspiring others. The best leaders are those who uplift others, who leave a lasting impact not just through their words but through their actions.

When I reflect on my journey—from a humble beginning in Mumbai to becoming an entrepreneur and mentor—I see a path shaped by discipline, resilience, and a deep commitment to growth. This story is not just about success; it is about overcoming adversity, learning from failures, and embracing the responsibility that comes with leadership.

True thought leaders are not born; they are shaped by experiences, molded by mentors, and defined by their ability to lead with authenticity. And authenticity, I have learned, is not about perfection but about honesty—being open about struggles, embracing vulnerabilities, and using those experiences to inspire others.

The Power of Discipline and Consistency

Discipline has been a cornerstone of my journey. It is not just about following a set routine; it is about making the right choices every single day, even when no one is watching. Throughout my career, I have learned that success does not come from a single breakthrough moment but from the accumulation of small, consistent actions over time.

When I was a student, waking up at 5 AM to study was not easy, but it was necessary. When I started working, making sacrifices to learn and grow felt difficult, but it was essential. When I ventured into entrepreneurship, facing setbacks and persisting through challenges was not comfortable, but it was the only way forward. Every step of the way, discipline shaped my path, giving me the ability to endure hardships and continue striving for excellence.

The compounding effect of discipline is remarkable. What starts as small, intentional efforts eventually leads to exponential growth. Many people give up when they don't see immediate results, but true leaders understand that consistency is the secret ingredient to long-term success. Whether in business, personal growth, or leadership, those who stay the course are the ones who reap the rewards.

Leading with Empathy and Vision

Leadership is not just about managing people or making decisions—it is about understanding, inspiring, and empowering others.

Early in my career, I observed that the most effective leaders were not necessarily the ones with the highest intelligence or the most impressive resumes. They were the ones who listened, who recognized the efforts of their teams, and who created an environment where people felt valued. I made it a personal mission to lead with empathy—to truly understand the struggles, dreams, and aspirations of those I work with.

Empathy, however, must be paired with vision. A vision without execution is merely a dream. I believe that thought leadership requires both the ability to see the bigger picture and the discipline to bring that vision to life. It requires the courage to take risks, the humility to acknowledge mistakes, and the determination to keep moving forward.

Many businesses fail, not because of a lack of ideas, but because of a lack of execution. Many individuals remain stuck in mediocrity, not because they don't have dreams, but because they never take the necessary steps to pursue them. The difference between a dreamer and a leader is action. Leaders do not just talk about possibilities—they create them.

Mentorship: The Gift That Keeps Giving

Throughout my journey, I have been fortunate to have mentors who guided me, challenged me, and believed in me even when I doubted myself. Today, as a thought leader, I consider it my duty to do the same for others.

One of the greatest joys of leadership is seeing others succeed. I take immense pride in mentoring aspiring leaders, helping them navigate challenges, and guiding them toward success. Leadership is not about standing alone at the top—it is about bringing others along with you. It is about sharing knowledge, opening doors, and creating opportunities for those who are willing to learn and grow.

One of my mentors once told me, "True success is measured by how many people you lift along the way." That lesson stayed with me. I firmly believe that the impact we have on others is the true measure of our leadership. Whether in business or personal life, mentorship is the most valuable gift we can offer.

The Resilience to Overcome Setbacks

No journey is without obstacles. I have faced my share of failures, setbacks, and moments of doubt. But I have also learned that resilience is what separates the ordinary from the extraordinary.

There were times when I questioned my decisions. There were moments when things did not go as planned. But every challenge taught me something invaluable. Failure is not the opposite of success—it is a part of success. Every great leader, entrepreneur, and innovator has faced setbacks. What makes them different is their ability to rise again, stronger and wiser.

One of the biggest misconceptions about leadership is that it is about never making mistakes. In reality, leadership is about how you respond to those mistakes. Do you let them define you, or do you learn from them and keep moving forward?

I have always chosen the latter. And that choice has made all the difference.

Final Thoughts: The Legacy We Leave Behind

Some people lead by words, but others lead by example. Uncle Leslie has been in my life since the day I was born—not just as my parents' friend but as my Uncle, a figure of strength, discipline, and unwavering integrity. His journey is a testament to the fact that success is not just about ambition but about resilience, hard work, and staying true to one's principles.

As I grew older, I saw Uncle Leslie and my mother (Mary Manu) form a professional collaboration that was not just a business but a vision—one that was built on trust, persistence, and hard work. He never sought the easiest path, nor did he let challenges deter him. Instead, he believed in doing things the right way, brick by brick, ensuring that every decision was grounded in hard work and honesty.

His belief in persistence over quick wins has been a lesson I carry with me every day. Now that I am entering the workforce, I get to implement the lessons I have learned from watching him as a beacon. Challenges are inevitable, but the way Uncle Leslie handles them is what sets him apart.

Beyond his professional achievements, what truly defines him is his unwavering commitment to his family. He has always been there for them, ensuring their well-being no matter how busy life gets. He isn't just someone who takes care of his own; he has also been a rock for those around him.

His life is proof that dedication, honesty, and simplicity are not just ideals but powerful forces that shape lasting achievements. He has taught me that success is not measured by what you gain but by how you stand in the face of challenges, how you hold on to your principles, and how you uplift those around you.

To me, he is more than just a businessman. He is a mentor, a guiding presence, and a reminder that the right path is not always the easiest, but it is always the most fulfilling. His journey has left an imprint on mine, and for that, I will always be grateful.

Mallika Manu

What people in Leslie's life say about LESLIE:

"We have known Leslie since our early college days. Initially, he came across as a reserved and somewhat introverted person, but as we spent more time together, we quickly became best buddies.

Leslie comes from a very humble background. He is the youngest of three siblings. Having lost both his parents at an early age, he was raised by his sister and brother. This early loss instilled in him a strong sense of responsibility. To support home financially, Leslie made the difficult decision to quit his studies and take up a job. This demonstrated his strong character and compassion.

Leslie embodies the true meaning of friendship. He is selfless in his relationships, always putting others above himself, much like the unseen foundation of a building that supports the entire structure. He is there for you through thick and thin, offering support, love, and understanding. He respects your personal space and honors your individuality, He is a good listener and listens without judgment and always offers unbiased opinions, making him the perfect go-to friend. Trust, loyalty, and consistency i.e. Reliable is his key quality.

His first job, while still in his late teens, was in the freight forwarding Industry. Being a hardworking individual, he often takes pride in his work and is committed to producing quality results. He shows discipline and resilience, even when things get tough. With confidence, and perseverance, he quickly rose to a senior position and became a recognizable name in the industry. His determination to succeed led him to significantly contribute to the company's revenues and earn the respect of his peers and customers alike.

Leslie's self-confidence and risk-taking abilities eventually led him to partner his mentor and venture to form a company in an already crowded industry. His industry knowledge, customer relationships, and eagerness to learn allowed him to carve out a niche for himself. As a people person, he earned the respect of his team, inspiring them to give their best. His networking skills and collaborative nature lead him to be part of various industry networks, that is helping him further expand his business.

While sharp and astute in business, Leslie is also an extremely dedicated family man. He is not just a provider but brings unconditional love, care, and happiness to his family, regardless of external circumstances. His beautiful wife, Carol, and daughter, Sarah, are equally his support pillars.

Finally, to sum up, we will break down a couple of traits in Leslie which we have observed in him over the years. This encapsulates his approach towards his family, friends and profession.

They are:

AMBITIOUS, CONFIDENT AND HARDWORKING
CONSCIENTIOUS
COMPASSIONATE
COURAGEOUS
HONESTY
HUMBLE
LOYAL & HONORABLE
PATIENT AND PERSISTENT
DISCIPLINE

Leslie is our brother, a leading example to the future generation. We are proud and grateful to have him in our lives."

Three Musketeers

Thought Leadership

Leslie Swamy-Director & Co-Founder of Worldline Logistics Pvt Ltd – Mumbai

Leslie ventured into the logistics industry in June 1998, bringing over 27 years of experience in operations management, pricing, freight forwarding (inbound & outbound), and business development.

He has a strong track record of building and managing high-performance teams to coordinate logistics for organizations.

Starting his career as a dispatch clerk, he steadily climbed the ranks to head the Ocean Freight Department. His self-confidence and willingness to take risks eventually led him to partner with his mentor to establish their own venture in an already competitive industry.

With a clear vision, he is committed to providing a comprehensive range of high-quality, integrated logistics services with a global reach. He played a key role in developing a highly skilled and motivated team focused on "Service Excellence," which has been instrumental in the organization's success.

He strongly believes in the saying, "A soldier never quits until the mission is complete."

Beyond his professional endeavors, he is passionate about art, including painting, crafts, cooking, and singing.

Today, he leads the company's operations and sales, driving toward his ultimate goal of "Making Logistics Simple," which remains the organization's slogan.

Contact Leslie: leslie@worldlinelogistics.in

Let's Connect

If you are interested to be the next co-author in the next book, register and apply here:
The World Thought Leader Book (Form) | Kristy Guo Coaching
Or go to www.kristyguo.com -> Program
https://bm7.19e.myftpupload.com/the-world-thought-leader-book/

Join the World's Thought Leaders Movement!

Have you ever considered sharing your **leadership story** with the world? Do you believe your insights and experiences could inspire others to lead with greater impact?
📢 *The World's Thought Leaders* isn't just a book—it's a **global movement** of visionary leaders who are shaping the future through their stories, wisdom, and influence.

Are You Ready to:

✅ Be recognized as a global thought leader?
✅ Share your leadership journey in an upcoming volume?
✅ Connect with an exclusive community of high-impact leaders?
💡 **Your Voice Matters. Your Story Deserves to Be Heard.**
📩 Join the World's Thought Leader Global Community Today!
Email **cuilanguo@outlook.com** with the subject **"Join WTL"** and take the first step toward inspiring the world with your leadership journey.

🚀 *Your leadership legacy starts here!*

Connect with Kristy by scanning the code above

Connect with SGN by scanning the code above

Powered by

www.ingramcontent.com/pod-product-compliance
Lightning Source LLC
Chambersburg PA
CBHW052136070526
44585CB00017B/1849